~~67 1999

The Maximum

The Maximum Surveillance Society

The Rise of CCTV

Clive Norris and Gary Armstrong

BERG

Oxford • New York

First published in 1999 by
Berg
Editorial offices:
150 Cowley Road, Oxford, OX4 1JJ, UK
70 Washington Square South, New York, NY 10012, USA

Berg is the imprint of Oxford International Publishers Ltd.

Library of Congress Cataloging in Publication Data

A catalogue record for this book is available from the Library of Congress.

British Library Cataloguing in Publication Data

A catalogue record for this book is available from the British Library.

ISBN 1 85973 221 6 (Cloth)
1 85973 226 7 (Paper)

Typeset by JS Typesetting, Wellingborough, Northants.
Printed in the United Kingdom by Biddles Ltd, King's Lynn.

Contents

Acknowledgements

There are many people and institutions to whom we owe thanks in bringing this book to fruition. Gratitude is due to those who granted us access to their CCTV control rooms and allowed us to observe the reality of CCTV surveillance. We are also extremely grateful to the dozens of CCTV operatives who tolerated our presence over long shifts whilst allowing us to watch them at work. Thanks are also due to the system managers and industry representatives throughout the country who gave up their time to be interviewed.

The primary funding for the project came from the Economic and Social Research Council under its Crime and Social Order Programme (Grant no. L210252023). This was given a further boost by the University of Hull's Research Support Fund which financed a project entitled 'Developments in Algorithmic Surveillance'. We are grateful to both institutions.

We are grateful to Macmillan who allowed us to draw freely on an earlier article of ours entitled 'The Rise of the Mass Surveillance Society' which was published in *Crime Unlimited: Questions for the 21st Century* edited by Pat Carlen and Rod Morgan (Macmillan, Basingstoke and London: 1999). We are also grateful to Petards International Limited, 10 Windmill Business Village, Brooklands Close, Sunbury on Thames, Middlesex TW16 7DY for permission to reproduce their 'skinhead' advertisement which appears on our front cover.

Our colleagues at the Centre for Criminology and Criminal Justice at the University of Hull, especially Keith Bottomley, Clive Coleman and Norman Davidson deserve thanks for providing an interesting and supportive environment in which research can be conducted. Christine Kirman and Diana Grey provided the most exceptional administrative support which as well as being supremely efficient, was unfailingly helpful and good-humoured, we thank them both. Thanks are also due to Karen Kinnaird who so efficiently transformed the field notes from a scrawl to immaculate typescript.

Numerous friends and colleagues helped throughout by offering encouragement and providing a sounding board for our ideas. In particular we would like to thank Jon Bannister, Marjorie Bulos, Madeline Colvin, Simon Davis, Jason Ditton, Ian Drury, Nigel Fielding, Nicholas Fyfe, Richard Giulianotti, Stephen Graham, Jenny Hockey, Mike McCahill, Mike Maguire, Richard Nicholls, Peter Noorlander, Alan Reeve, Julie Seymour, David Skinns, Peter Squires, Ian Taylor, Nick Tilley and Malcolm Young. Nigel Norris deserves a special thank you for providing fraternal support and agreeing to read the entire manuscript in an effort to weed out its more obvious failings. The responsibility for those that remain is ours – but they are far fewer in number!

A special thank you is also reserved for Jade Moran, who in her role as research assistant expertly compiled, collated, summarised and indexed the wealth of articles, newspaper clippings and trade reports on which much of this book is based, but also so professionally conducted a series of interviews with representatives from the CCTV industry. We are forever in her debt.

At Berg, our publishers, we thank our commissioning editor Kathryn Earl for her faith and patience, Bobby Gainher who diligently copy-edited the manuscript and Sara Everett for so efficiently transforming our typescript into this book.

And finally to our partners, Laurie Nicholls and Hani Armstrong who supported this project in countless ways but, more importantly, reminded us both that there is more to life than research.

Part I
Images of Social Control

Introduction: Visions of Surveillance

This is a book about watching people. It examines the rise of camera-based surveillance that is embodied in the proliferation of closed circuit television cameras (CCTV). In Britain it is now virtually impossible to move through public (and increasingly private) space without being photographed and recorded. Whatever our role as we pass through the urban landscape we are subject to the presence of the cameras. As consumers we are monitored by the routine use of cameras in retail outlets; whether in the supermarket, department store or corner shop. When we leave the store our image, in all probability, will be captured by high street, town centre and shopping mall camera systems. On our journey home, traffic cameras will monitor our compliance with speed and red light restrictions and, if we travel by rail, cameras at stations and along platforms will ensure a record of our presence. In other roles, whether it be as workers on the factory floor or at the office, as students, from kindergarten to university, as hospital patients, football fans or even customers at a local restaurant, cameras are probably watching over us. Put simply, in urban Britain, at the cusp of the millennium, in almost every area to which the public have access we are under surveillance from CCTV.

The book has three aims: to provided a critical account of the recent exponential growth of camera-based surveillance in Britain; to document the actual practice of CCTV surveillance as it is carried out in the high streets and town centres of British cities; and to anticipate the future direction of this technology of social control. Before outlining the organisation of this book in more detail this introduction will briefly explore how surveillance has been conceptualised in both popular and academic discourse.

Throughout the twentieth century the idea of surveillance has become inscribed in mass consciousness, not primarily through the learned tomes of academics, but through its artistic treatment in popular culture. In the English-speaking world, at least, the most enduring, and often haunting images are to be found in films such as Hitchcock's *Rear Window*, Francis Ford Cappola's *The Conversation* (1974) or Michael Powell's *Peeping Tom* (1960). Popular song has also taken up the theme of surveillance (see Marx 1995) the most memorable being the Police's 'Every Breath You Take' (1983). In literature, George Orwell's *Nineteen Eighty-Four* (1949) and Huxley's *Brave New World* (1932) still feature as essential reading on many school curricula.

What unites these classics of popular culture is their tragic and dystopian portrayal of the personal and political impact of surveillance. In *The Conversation* which is about aural rather than visual surveillance, the main character played by Gene Hackman is 'a painfully lonely, cynical, paranoid and alienated man whose work has driven him to guard his own privacy zealously, although there is precious little to protect' (Monaco, Pallot and Baseline 1993: 159). In *Peeping Tom* it is the pathological voyeurism of a photographer which provides the film's dominant motif but which simultaneously 'accuses the audience of sharing the central character's sickness . . . [and produces] . . . one of the most disturbing films ever made' (ibid.: 662). So disturbing that Powell, until then a highly regarded film-maker, was vilified by the British press who labelled it as a completely repugnant film, and effectively ended his career. The pathological nature of surveillance is also reflected in the Police's hit 'Every Breath You Take', with its central refrain of:

> every breath you take
> every move you make
> every bond you break
> every single day
> I'll be watching you.

The song is, according to its writer Sting, about 'the obsessiveness of ex-lovers, their manical possessiveness' (cited in Marx 1995: 113) and while it does not mention technological supports such as cameras 'for this omnipresent and omni-potent surveillance, it is easy to connect it with contemporary tools' (ibid.: 114) such as the motion detector and video recorder.

In literature, the most enduring image of surveillance is to be found in Orwell's futuristic vision of Britain in nineteen-eighty-four, where the totalitarian rule of the Party is maintained by permanent and omnipresent televisual monitoring. The inhabitants are constantly reminded of the power of the state to monitor them by posters declaring 'Big Brother is Watching You'. And for Huxley, the *Brave New World* of the future is one dominated by a scientific totalitarianism where the socialisation of genetically engineered human clones is managed through permanent surveillance in the Neo-Pavlovian Conditioning Rooms and the continued happiness and compliance of the workers is preserved by the administration of psychotropic drugs.

This brief and selective glimpse of the portrayal of surveillance in popular culture reflects a profound unease with the practice and technology of surveillance. However, as Marx points out in both religious hymns and popular song there is another refrain to be heard: surveillance not as threatening but as offering the promise of the protection and care of a benevolent guardian. Thus, while we would argue that the dominant cultural theme is tragic, either for those engaged in surveillance or subject to its gaze, there is also an ambivalence which recognises that 'Surveillance has two faces.' (Lyon 1994: 201). This ambivalence is reflected in the academic literature on surveillance. It is seen not only as both protective and enabling but also as deeply implicated in the structure of totalitarian rule.

Surveillance is recognised as an elementary building block of all human societies since the act of socialisation would be unthinkable without the surveillance of adults. How else could children be fabricated into cultural competent members of a society? At the more complex level surveillance is also recognised as one of the central mechanisms through which the modern state achieves the routine administrative functions of providing welfare, health, education and security for its population (Rule 1973; Dandeker 1990). This bureaucratic surveillance has largely been achieved through the creation and maintenance of paper and, more recently, electronic records on individuals and the development of systems of storage and retrieval. The modern state would be inconceivable without such systems. How else would taxes be collected, entitlement to welfare benefits be adjudicated, the spread of infectious diseases controlled, law enforced and punishment delivered?

The tragic dystopian concerns of popular culture are also reflected in academic discourse. It has recognised surveillance as essentially a form of power, one which has been dramatically enhanced by the development of sophisticated technology, and whose reach therefore seems to extend further and further across the entire social fabric. In particular, academic discourse on surveillance and especially CCTV surveillance, has been dominated by the extent to which it represents an extension of the Panopticon.

The Panopticon was a revolutionary design for a prison developed by the British philosopher Bentham in the nineteenth century. As Smart has noted, Bentham's design:

> constituted a programme for the efficient exercise of power through the spatial arrangement of subjects according to a diagram of visibility so as to ensure that at each moment any subject might be exposed to 'invisible' observation. The Panopticon was to function as an apparatus of power by virtue of the field of visibility in which individuals were located each in their respective places . . . for a centralized observer. In this schema subjects were to be individualised in their own spaces, to be visible and conscious of their potentially constant visibility. Given that those illuminated by power were unable to see their observer(s) the consciousness of being . . . watched effectively ensured an automatic functioning of power. (1985: 88)

For 150 years interest in Bentham's designs remained limited to prison administrators and penal reformers. However, in 1975 the French philosopher Michael Foucault published *Surveiller et punir: Naissance de la prison* in which he drew heavily on Bentham's idea of the Panopticon to argue that the crystallisation of the power of vision embodied in this architectural form had spread from the prison to a host of other social institutions: hospitals, schools, military barracks and factories all came to resemble the prison.

For Foucault, panoptic surveillance represents a new mode of power: one that is not based on punishing the body through the infliction of pain or deprivation but through training and correction. Panopticonisation facilitates the power of the watchers over the watched not only by enabling swift intervention to displays of non-conformity but also through the promotion of habituated anticipatory conformity. It is hardly surprising, then, given the parallels that can be drawn with CCTV, that many theorists have been drawn to both Foucault's concept of the Panopticon and his analysis of its disciplinary potential (cf. Bannister et al. 1998; Reeve 1998).

While we would not dispute the importance of Foucault in signalling the emergence of a new form of power and the centrality of surveillance to that power, we sound a note of caution about the automatic applicability of these concepts to the rise of CCTV. The disciplinary potential of Foucault's Panopticon or Orwell's 'Big Brother' is only maximised when surveillance is coupled with techniques of behaviour modification, indoctrination and socialisation. While Giddens has argued that 'Totalitarianism is, first of all, an extreme focusing on surveillance' (1985: 303), the crucial observation is 'first of all', because it relies on coupling surveillance to other disciplinary mechanisms. Therefore, while it is not inappropriate to signal the panoptic potential of surveillance gaze, it is an empirical matter as to the extent to which it is linked with other disciplinary techniques to effect complete panoptic power. We need to be cautious about merely equating the power to watch with the disciplinary power implied in Foucault's concept of panoptic surveillance. Similarly, the spread of cameras should not automatically be assumed to herald the arrival of a totalitarian 'Big Brother' state. It is useful here to draw on the work of James Rule who, in his book *Private Lives Public Surveillance*, outlined the essential features of a 'total surveillance' society:

> There would be but a single system of surveillance and control, and its clientele would consist of everyone. The system would work to enforce compliance with a uniform set of norms governing every aspect of everyone's behaviour. Every action of every client would be scrutinised, recorded, evaluated both at the moment of occurrence and for ever afterwards. The system would collate all information at a single point, making it impossible for anyone to evade responsibility for his past by fleeing from the scene of earlier behaviour. Nor would the single master agency compartmentalise information which it collected, keeping data for use only in certain kinds of decision. Instead it would bring the whole fund of its information to bear on every decision it made about everyone. Any sign of disobedience – present or anticipated – would result in corrective action. The fact that the system kept everyone under constant monitoring would mean that in the event of misbehaviour, apprehension and sanctioning would occur immediately. By making detection and retaliation inevitable such a system would make disobedience unthinkable. (Rule 1973: 37)

Dandeker identifies four components contained within this description which provide a reference point for determining the extent to which a total surveillance system is approximated (Dandeker 1990: 40–1):

The size and scope of the files in relation to the subjected population. This relates to the extent to which the records are held on the entire population or only a subsection of them and the level of detail contained within those files. Thus; for the cameras to be truly integrated as part of a total surveillance system, the images of individuals they record must be linked not only to one another but to a named dossier which contains all other relevant biographical information.

The centralisation of those files. Where files are centrally collected and managed, there is the potential for information gathered at one point of the system to be available for reference at another point. The system becomes totalising in that it is impossible to escape ones own biographical record merely by moving to a different point in space, such as another town.

The speed of information flow. While the totalising vision is enhanced by centralisation, its utility for the purposes of control is determined by the speed at which information is collected and disseminated across the system, for instance where pictures can be disseminated electronically via the Internet, rather than physically in the form of a photograph or on videotape.

The number of points of contact between the system and its subject population. In the case of CCTV, this relates not only to the coverage of the cameras in terms of their pervasiveness and their technological capacity to 'zoom in' on the minutiae of everyday life but also to the extent to which this camera surveillance triggers an authoritative reaction to non-conformity.

The extent to which the reality of CCTV surveillance approximates the ideal type outlined in Rule's schema is essentially an empirical matter and one that is the heart of this book. However there is one central qualification: CCTV has been implemented not as one pervasive system but as a series of discrete, localised schemes run by a myriad of different organisations rather than a single state monolith. There is no single 'Big Brother' who is watching over us but lots of little brothers each with their own agendas. This is where Foucault's conception of the dispersal of discipline is especially apposite.

For Foucault, the power of disciplinary social control lay not with its centralisation in a totalitarian state regime but in its dispersal from its idealised form in the prison throughout the myriad of public and private institutions that make up the social fabric. Thus, the deployment of CCTV is not to enable the enforcement of some singular disciplinary norms, but the situational norms relevant to particular sectional interests. As Armstrong and Giulianotti (1998) note, in football stadia, CCTV surveillance is directed not just at the more obvious manifestations of disorder but at even slight gestures or lip movements which are considered out of place and can be subject to disciplinary power. In contrast, in the workplace, McCahill and Norris (1999) have described how CCTV is used in part to ensure compliance with health and safety regulations and restrictions on smoking. And more often than not the deployment of CCTV in city centres is driven by commercial concerns of business wanting to create an environment conducive to attracting the right sort of consumer (Reeve 1998). There is clearly a tension between the panoptic and totalitarian conception of surveillance. For us, one key difference between the maximum surveillance society and Rule's model of a total surveillance system is that the former does not imply a single omniscient repository of power. However, nor does it rule it out for, as we shall see, in the age of the digital superhighway and software developments allowing the integration of discrete databases, it is possible to have both existing simultaneously.

So far we have considered the key elements of surveillance and located its wider significance in debates over the nature and extent of social control. Therefore we want to conclude this introduction with a brief consideration of how recent writers, particularly social geographers, have seen CCTV as implicated in major structural transformations occurring across the urban landscape.

Two American writers, Flusty (1994) and Davis (1990), have, through their case studies of Los Angeles, provided a frightening glimpse of the dystopian potential of surveillance. For both, the city has historically been conceived as an arena which provides spaces for interactions and exchanges between individuals and different social groups. They are democratic spaces in the sense that access to them is not dependent on status, but guaranteed by virtue of being a citizen. These democratic spaces, the streets, parks and squares facilitate interactions which 'synthesise new cultures, alternative ways of living and popular forces occasionally strong enough to upset entrenched status quos' (Flusty 1994: 12). Increasingly, however, this public space is being reconstituted, not as an arena for democratic interaction, but as the site of mass consumption. Individuals are recast as consumers rather than citizens, as potential harbingers of profit, rather than bearers of rights. It is this domination of urban space by business rather than civic concerns and the way that CCTV is used to promote those concerns though the exclusion of 'flawed consumers' and other undesirables which has been highlighted by various commentators (Graham 1998b; Coleman and Sim 1998; Reeve 1998; McCahill 1998).

This privatisation of the democratic sphere and the exclusionary impulses that it has instilled has found its concrete expression in the dramatic rise of walled and gated residential communities where physical barriers are erected to exclude a marginalised and ghettoised underclass from the enclaves of the more affluent elite

(Graham and Marvin 1996; Davis 1992). In these 'fortress cities', CCTV is used to police the boundaries of segregated space and ensure swift response to unauthorised entry. And in the spaces between these fortified zones of affluence, the residual population is subject to a panoply of prohibitions. For example, Davis describes how the Los Angeles Police Department: 'continue relentlessly to restrict the space of public assemblage and the freedom of movement of the young . . . operating extensive juvenile curfews in non-Anglo areas and barricading popular boulevards to prevent "cruising" . . . sealing off entire neighborhoods and housing projects under our local variant of "pass law"' (1990: 258).

And for Flusty it is surveillance which potentially underscores the complete demise of democratic public space:

> Los Angeles is undergoing the intervention and installation, component by component of a physical infrastructure engendering electronically linked islands of privilege embedded in a police state matrix. If left unchecked, this trend may be linearly extrapolated into a worst case composite of hard boundaries, checkpoints and omnipresent surveillance. Los Angeles will become a city consisting of numerous fortified cores of private space, each augmented by more permeable outer perimeters of contorted paths, lights, motion detectors and video cameras projecting in the public realm of the side walk and the street. The public streets will become little more than the interstitial space to these fortified private cores. They will themselves be fragmented by erecting barricading and monitoring by cameras overlapping each private space's permeable outer perimeter. Finally, overseeing it all will be helicopter patrols. (1994: 37)

The extent to which the trends emerging in that most unusual of American cities, Los Angeles, are mirrored in other American cities and, more specifically, British cities is questionable. However, it does illustrate one possible future and a future that we believe should be resisted, but the vision is also too fatalistic. The 'reality of technological innovation is a great deal less deterministic and a great deal more "messy", difficult and open to contested interpretations and applications' (Graham 1998b: 500). But for those who promote CCTV as the panacea to the crime and disorder on our city streets and those who warn of the spectre of the dystopian surveillance state, there is a common assumption: CCTV actually produces the effects claimed for it. They see CCTV surveillance as not only omniscient but omnipotent. In this way, both share a tendency towards technological determinism: an unquestioning belief in the power of technology, whether benign or malevolent. However, we would argue, following Graham and Marvin, that it is necessary to take a social constructionist approach toward the rise of CCTV technology. This approach:

> aims to identify, and analyse and explain causal relationships between social, institutional and political factors and the development and applications of technologies . . . The

purpose of research in the SCOT [social construction of technology] tradition is, therefore, to understand how technology and its uses are socially and politically constructed through complex processes of institutional and personal interaction, whereby many different actors and agencies interplay over periods of time. (Graham and Marvin 1996: 105)

It is this approach that informs our analysis and moves beyond the narrow concerns of the criminologists with their almost exclusive focus on its crime reduction potential, to raise a series of different questions about the nature of CCTV.

First, while it is appropriate to ask whether CCTV reduces crime, a limited focus on outcomes and aggregate crime data tells us little about how it is producing these effects. For instance, is it through the increased detection and incapacitation of prolific offenders or through inducing anticipatory conformity? But CCTV is more than just about crime prevention. It enables a vast amount of visual data, in the form of images on the screen, to be processed and interpreted. What interpretive schemes guide operator judgments? What forms of behaviour or people trigger suspicion and at what point does this result in a deployment? Is this deployment confined to explicitly criminal concerns or is intervention directed at regulating matters of decorum and demeanour in public space and aimed at excluding certain types of people?

Second, while the powerful always have a tendency to promote *their* interests as the *general* interest, we need to ask whose interests are promoted in the deployment of CCTV systems. For instance, are the interests of the business community prioritised above those of other citizens in claims to the appropriate use of public space?

Third, as the rise of CCTV surveillance easily evokes Orwellian concerns of 'Big Brother', we may ask why there has been so little public resistance or challenge to CCTV systems and the extent to which consent has been 'manufactured'.

Fourth, the mediated gaze of the camera fundamentally disrupts the microsociological interactions between the watcher and the watched embodied in face-to-face interactions. What are the implications of this for citizens' subjective experience of public space? If individuals or groups believe they are targets of the camera's gaze, do they adopt avoidance strategies? If one social group feels itself to be disproportionately targeted by such systems, will this lead to a challenge as to the legitimacy of such systems and will such feelings promote more vocal and forceful resistance?

Fifth, by viewing surveillance as a form of power, it is necessary to consider how that power is held to account and what limits are placed on its operation. While such an analysis must take as its necessary starting point the formal law and rules, embodied by codes of conduct, it needs to move beyond this 'law in books' to consider the 'law in action' and examine the extent to which these rules are adhered to and followed in practice.

Finally, we need to consider the impact of new computing and database technologies in growing the scope of power. This is especially pertinent given the growing tendency of CCTV systems to use digital technologies, enabling the rapid retrieval, transfer and matching of images. CCTV systems are now frequently used to automatically identify and log the movements of vehicles in public space, and facial recognition packages are rapidly being developed. Digital technologies enable information gathered from CCTV systems to be easily passed to other systems and extensive dossiers can be produced which document a person's movement through public space.

In addressing these issues this book is divided into three parts. Part I seeks to document and account for the growth of CCTV surveillance in contemporary Britain. The second chapter in this section maps the rise of photographic surveillance for crime control from the birth of photography in the early nineteenth century until the present day. In particular, it seeks to locate the rapid increase in the number of CCTV cameras, not just in terms of its criminological significance but in the wider technological, social, economic and political contexts which have facilitated its growth. In Chapter 3 we present a 'snapshot' of the scale and scope of CCTV surveillance in public and semi-public space in late 1990s Britain and document its use in a range of institutional settings. We conclude by considering the variations that exist between CCTV systems and how this makes it difficult to talk about CCTV as a unitary phenomenon. In the final chapter of Part I we explore the role the media has played in legitimising the expansion of surveillance.

In Part II, we move to consider the actual practice of CCTV surveillance and we draw on our two-year study of the operation of three CCTV control rooms, funded by the Economic and Social Research Council. The study involved nearly 600 hours of observation and the collection of quantitative and qualitative data covering 888 incidents of targeted surveillance. Chapter 5 outlines our theoretical and methodological premises. In Chapter 6 we explore who and what gets surveilled after considering the legal and organisational constraints on CCTV surveillance. In Chapter 7, we extend this analysis to consider why the practice of surveillance produces this particular configuration of targets. Drawing on the work of Harvey Sacks in his seminal article entitled 'Notes on Police Assessment of Moral Character' (1978), we present and document a set of seven working rules which inform operators' choices as to whom, from a myriad of possibilities, should be subject to extended targeting and surveillance. The next two chapters are concerned with the relationship between CCTV operatives, security guards and the police who may be deployed as a result of their observations. This relationship, we argue, is mediated by the technology of the communications system and the formal and informal practices which facilitate 'system integration', leading to major differences in deployment practices between the three sites.

Part III takes us beyond the concerns of the present to consider, on the basis of existing trends, the future of mass visual surveillance. We argue that, with the integration of existing systems and the increasing automation of surveillance through the linking of cameras, computers and databases, the architecture of the maximum surveillance society is now in place.

A History of Photographic
Surveillance and the Rise of CCTV

A Brief History of Crime Control and the Photograph

The use of photography for the purposes of crime control is nearly as old as the camera itself. By the 1840s, less than a decade after the photograph became a practical reality, the 'potential for a new juridical photographic realism, was widely recognised' (Sekula 1992: 344). By 1854, for instance, the governor of Bristol Gaol, James Gardner, was photographing prisoners sentenced to his custody in order to identify habitual criminals, and recommended the practice be introduced 'upon a broad and national scale' (Gardner 1854). Indeed it would appear that his message quickly reached an even wider audience as in 1855 the French writer Ernest Lacan pointed out the 'advantages of using photography in prisons to take each prisoner's portrait with a view to checking escapes and recidivism' and noted that the 'system is already employed in certain institutions in England' (Rouillé 1987: 51).

However, although Gardner's advice was heeded in the following decade and the routine photographing of prisoners by prison officials became more commonplace, it was still localised and piecemeal. Therefore, in the absence of any standardised criminal record system, the problem of how to identify the habitual criminal remained. In effect, at this time, identification rested on being recognised by police, court or prison officers and, therefore, if they were arrested in a different police district, appeared before different courts, or were incarcerated in different prisons the chances of his or her antecedents coming to light were remote.

By the late 1860s this became a more pressing problem with the demise of the transportation system as Crofton reported in 1868:

> During 20 years – from 1827 to 1846 'No less than 64,375 male and female convicts were transported from the from the United Kingdom. In 1853 there was but one colony left, Western Australia, which would any longer receive our convict population, and from that period male convicts have been sent until the last two week, since which transportation has ceased. (Crofton 1868: 3)

The effect of this demise was to deny the penal authorities of their most effective measure for dealing with habitual criminals: banishment and total exclusion. True transportation could be replaced by indefinite incarceration or more draconionally the death penalty, but there were serious financial and practical limits to these responses given that annual prison receptions stood in excess of one hundred thousand and any increase in the length of time served in prison would increase the strain on an already over-burdened system (Crofton 1868: 4). The official response to managing the size of the prison population was an increasing use of the 'ticket to leave' system, whereby convicts were given an 'order of licence' which granted them their liberty, under certain restrictions, before their sentence had expired. However in the absence of a centralised record system it was almost impossible to enforce the conditions of the licence.

It is the spectre of the 'Habitual Criminal' which dominates the official and public discourse of the time and this was reflected in the emergent discipline of criminology, with its Lombrosian concern for identifying the characteristics which 'marked off criminals as in some way different from the law abiding' (Garland 1994: 40). The early criminologists also found the photograph an ideal tool for the recording and documentation of the criminal type. In 1846 Eliza Farnham, the matron of Sing Sing Women's prison in America, was instrumental in reissuing a previously unillustrated English work entitled the *Rationale of Crime*. The new edition was illustrated with engravings made from photographs (there was no means yet of printing photographs directly onto the printed page) of the 'morally insane' in an effort to illustrate the principles of phrenology. This emerging science held there was a relationship between the topology of the skull and various mental attributes including the propensity to criminal behaviour. These ideas found their most influential expression in Cesare Lombroso's *Criminal Man* first published in 1876, whose photographic archive of the criminal type was used to illustrate later editions in an effort to substantiate the 'physiognomic law governing the essence of the origin of crime' (Didi-Huberman 1987: 74). In 1883, Galton published the results of fifteen years of study in his *Inquiries into Human Faculty* which, through statistically based photographic syntheses, produced composite portraits of the diseased, the healthy and the criminal (Sekula 1992: 348–9, 367).

These ideas were received eagerly by social reformers and those responsible for the administration of justice alike, primarily because it served as a means of differentiating the criminal classes into the 'habitual' and the 'casual'. Thus, while criminality was widespread among the urban poor, the vast majority of petty thievery could be assigned to the category of 'casual' offenders who, having no genetic predisposition to crime, would respond to the deterrence offered by a period of 'short and sharp imprisonment' (Hastings 1875: 10). But alternatively, 'given a class who are thus by physical confirmation and hereditary tendency, predetermined to prey upon the industrious portion of society, the question arises by what means are we meant to crush this evil?' (ibid.: 3).

And this question had taken on an urgent public significance. The end of transportation had led, according to the title of one pamphlet published in 1861, to the almost complete 'Immunity of the Habitual Criminals'. These sentiments, in turn led to an increasing moral panic about the growth in crime and fuelled vociferous calls for harsher means of repression from the national press (Crofton 1868: 9). For example, *The Times* of 9 July 1868 catalogued a recent spate of crime in the capital's streets arguing that they were, 'simply the highway robbery of former times practised under different circumstances [and that] the criminal classes seemed to have discovered the power of audacity and rapidity and to be everywhere trying the effect of their invention.' (Cited in Crofton 1868: 3)

The official response to the heightened anxiety was to propose a greater use of police surveillance and supervision of convicted criminals once they were released from prison. This would enable repeat offenders to be identified, to become candidates for the status of 'habitual' criminal and subjected to both harsher punishment and lengthy periods of incarceration. To achieve this, it would be necessary to set up a central registration system 'of all convicts on licence . . . made complete for the purposes of identification by photographic portraits' (Cartwright 1865). This proposal was duly implemented in 1869, administered by the Metropolitan Police, and by 1875 there were 117,586 names on the register (Hastings 1875). By the mid-1870s in England, then, the photographic record was seen as a central part of the apparatus of the State to identify, classify and differentiate the 'habitual criminal'.

Across the Channel in France, this problem of the identification of habitual criminals was also exercising Alphonse Bertillion who in 1872 introduced the routine photographing of prisoners held in Parisian police stations (Didi-Huberman 1987: 74). However, as Bertillion soon found, the creation of a photographic archive was not in itself a sufficient condition for securing identification: first there was a need to standardise the archival and comparative image; for the purpose of comparison it was simply no use to have portraits if they were taken in different positions from different distances and with variable lighting. Therefore, as Sekula explains:

> Bertillion insisted on a standard focal length, even and consistent lighting and a fixed distance between the camera and the unwilling sitter. The profile view served to cancel the contingency of expression, the contour of the head remained consistent with time. The frontal view provided a face that was more likely to be recognisable within other, less systematised departments of police work. These latter photographs served better in the search for suspects who had not yet been arrested, whose faces were to be recognised by detectives on the street. (1992: 361)

The second problem was one of volume as Bertillion himself explained:

> The collection of criminal portraits has already attained a size so considerable that it has become physically impossible to discover among them the likeness of an individual who has assumed a false name. It goes for nothing that in the past ten years the Paris police have collected more than 100,000 photographs. Does the reader believe it practicable to compare successively each of these with each one of the 100 individuals who are arrested each day in Paris? When this was attempted in the case of a criminal particularly easy to identify, the search demanded more than a week of application, not to speak of the errors and oversights which a task so fatiguing to the eye could not fail to occasion. (Cited in Sekula 1992: 356)

This same problem also appeared to be affecting the register of habitual criminals established by the English Metropolitan Police. As the Police Commissioner reported in 1874:

> The registration of 'habitual criminals' has been continued as heretofore, but the numbers on the register have increased so rapidly that there are now 117,568 names on the register, and they increase at an average of 30,000 per annum. Very few inquires have been received from any but the Metropolitan Police: and identifications have been very few . . . . The number of identifications has only been 890 out of 3957 inquiries; and as regards the Metropolitan police a large proportion could be identified without the registry at all. (Cited in Hastings 1875: 13)

In short, as Hastings noted, the register was 'unmanageable' due to its size, there appeared to be no systematic procedure for the matching of records and, according to Hastings, the implication of the commissioner's words was that 'registration is of no use, and might as well be got rid of at once' (ibid.: 13).

The promise of the photograph as a means of enabling police supervision of known offenders and identifying habitual criminals thus seemed to be doomed before it had properly started. Without a means of indexing which was not dependent upon a person's name and without a means of classification by which the archive or register could be organised so as to facilitate efficient matching, the system was crumbling under its own weight.

It fell to Bertillion to solve this problem and create the first effective modern system of criminal identification. He did so by combining the photograph with anthropometrical measurement and a classification system based on the statistical concept of an 'average man' developed by the nineteenth-century French statistician Queletet. The resulting criminal record consisted of two portrait photographs: one full face, one profile; a set of eleven standard measurements, which included height, head circumference, left foot, right ear, and forearm size; and included space for a textual description of a range of other distinguishing features. Bertillion had calculated that the chance of two individuals sharing the same series of anthropo-metric measurements was 1 in 4 million and therefore if one could arrange the classification system so that a candidate for identification was only compared with those most like themselves, the chances of finding an exact match, if it existed in the archive, were high. To do so he utilised the binomial distribution curve of each anthropometric feature in the general population and classified each of the eleven features on a nine-point scale ranging from, for example, extremely small, through to medium and extremely large. This enabled him to locate the exact place in the archive (a grid of filing draws), to position the record where it would be grouped with a subset of around twelve other identification cards (Sekula 1992: 358–9). The process of comparison which had previously taken a week could now be completed in a matter of minutes with the final identification resting on a visual comparison of the photographs.

The importance of Bertillion's system can be judged from its rapid adoption by police forces around the world. By 1893 it was being used in 'The United States, Belgium, Switzerland, Russia, much of South America, Tunisia, the British West Indies and Rumania' (Sekula 1992: 384 fn 54). In Britain in 1893 the Home Secretary, Lord Asquith, still haunted by the spectacle of recidivism, set up a committee 'to enquire into the best means available for identifying the habitual criminal'. The committee recommended the introduction of the Bertillion system with the addition of a fingerprint record, which had been pioneered as a means of criminal identification by Francis Galton, and in 1896 a national system of records was introduced which allowed for the photographing, fingerprinting and anthro-metric measurement of prisoners (Critchley 1978: 162). However the measurements were abandoned in 1901 as the fingerprint was seen as more efficient; it could be collected more quickly than the eleven measurements required by Bertillion and, as Sekula notes, was thus 'more promising in a Taylorist sense, since it could be properly executed by less skilled clerks' (1992: 362).

Bertillion's endeavour was very different from that undertaken by Lombroso and Galton where criminogenic classification was based on the believed statistical correlation between body type and forms of 'degeneracy'. For Bertillion 'the criminal body expressed nothing. No characterlogical secrets were hidden beneath the surface' (Sekula 1992: 360) and provided no clues as to the propensity to crime. The moral enterprise of Bertillon was concerned with perfecting the bureaucratic apparatus for identifying the habitual criminal, rather than with identifying the hereditary basis of criminality. However, for Francis Galton the two aspects were intrinsically linked. Galton not only championed the introduction of the finger-printing of criminals and pioneered the use of photography for the classification of hereditary criminals but was also the founder of the Eugenics movement. And it is here that the link between bureaucratic identification and the 'discovery' of a hereditary base of criminality finds its full expression. At the Presidential address in honour of Galton, given to the Eugenics Education Society in London in 1914, Major Leonard Darwin explained: 'our object is to prevent these innate qualities from reappearing in future generations' by preventing 'those who have committed many crimes from becoming parents' through the prolonged incarceration and 'segregation of these criminals during their period of fertility' (Darwin 1914: 8–10).

These early accounts of photography prioritise its use as a means of identification for the purposes of crime control. However, its potential as a deterrent to criminal activities was yet to emerge; but not because the power of surveillance in instilling conformity had failed to be recognised. As Foucault has argued, throughout the eighteenth and nineteenth centuries, surveillance had become the primary means of controlling and disciplining the institutionalised populations. But this architecture of power, typified by Bentham's panoptic design of the new model prison, relied on the direct unmediated, human monitoring of the supervisors. While the camera could take single 'snapshots' of subjects, these had to be captured onto a chemically coated film and then processed and developed. The power of the camera to offer a deterrent to criminal activity was severely limited since it could not be used for routine monitoring. This would have to wait for the invention of the television, which became commercially viable in the 1930s, and potentially allowed for the surveillance of remote sites by cameras. Such surveillance was limited though, since the film would still have to be developed before it could be viewed – an expensive and time-consuming process.

It was only with the advent of videotape and the Video Cassette Recorder (VCR) in the 1960s, that the images from a camera could be captured on film without the need for chemical processing, allowing a cheap and simple method of recording and the prospect of instant playback. Thus, around 130 years after the birth of photography, its true panoptic potential was about to be realised. It was now possible to have cameras linked to centralised control rooms where the images could be monitored, remotely, by a single person and a permanent record kept of everything that was seen. As Virilio (1994: 44) points out, this marks a significant extension of panoptic principles. Human visual capability has difficulty competing with the high surveillance capabilities of the camera: the camera does not blink, sleep or get bored and, unlike images captured on videotape, the results of human visual surveillance cannot be rewound or replayed in a court of law. The significance of these technological developments was not lost on those who wished to suppress crime and, in 1967, Photoscan launched CCTV into the retail sector primarily as a means of deterring and apprehending shoplifters. And as we will see from Chapter 3 the next thirty years, and particularly the 1990s, have witnessed an explosion of the growth of CCTV and the wholesale expansion of surveillance in public space.

Ironically the same problems that faced the pioneers of the photograph as an adjunct to crime control have re-emerged 150 years later to challenge the new pioneers of CCTV. The early attempts foundered because of the sheer volume of data and the problems this created in comparing new 'mugshots' with those held in the archive. However, with the use of statistical classification and the bureaucratic organisation afforded by the filing cabinet, Bertillion managed to solve the problem. Similarly, the advent of CCTV has posed problems of both volume and identification. Videotape, for all its advantages as a recording medium, is a poor archive medium for the purposes of classification, comparison and identification. Put simply, if you want know whether Johnny Smith was in town last night between the hours of 6 p.m. and midnight, the existence of CCTV is of limited use. True, if the system is permanently monitored by human operators they may have seen him, although even this requires an existing photograph for purposes of comparison. Moreover, even if they had been looking out for him, faced with images from literally dozens of cameras, the chances of him being there and still being missed are relatively high. This is further compounded by the difficultly in remaining alert in the face of a massive volume of information. Without a positive identification from the operative it is necessary to rely on the tapes. This leaves only one course of action: each tape from each camera must be examined, frame by frame. In the case of a twenty-camera system, if the job is done thoroughly, this will take one person, working twelve hours a day, ten days to complete.

The prospect of digitalisation is starting to make inroads into this problem. The digitalisation of images allows them to be processed automatically by computer, and this is increasingly happening with car licence number plates. In this case Bertillion's anthropomorphic statistical classification system has been replaced by the advanced statistical routines contained in the algorithms for number recognition systems, and the filing cabinet by the computer database. The principles are, however, the same: measurement, classification, indexing and comparison. What has changed is the speed at which individual routines can be performed. Thus, the City of London Police's automatic licence plate system is capable of performing 5,000 matches per minute. In the case of facial recognition the problem of statistical classification is much harder. However, by utilising the same anthropomorphic techniques pioneered by Bertillion for classifying the body, but this time confining them to the face, a number of statisticians and software designers are pioneering attempts to come up with automated facial recognition systems. If these are perfected, images taken from closed circuit television can be automatically checked against a database of facial pictures.

This brief history of the technology of photography and its relationship to crime control should not be read as implying a form of technological determinism. The growth of mass visual surveillance, particularly its exponential growth in Britain, has to be understood in a much wider context. Surveillance is, after all, a form of power, exercised for the purposes of control and CCTV is only one example of the application of new technologies to extend the surveillance gaze. Like all forms of power, surveillance is embodied in a set of social practices and its contours shaped by its institutional forms, but also by the levels of contestation that surround it. Thus, while changes in technology were our starting point, the rise of the maximum surveillance society can only be understood in the light of broader social, economic and political trends.

Social Trends and Ideological Transformations

While CCTV has become one of the most visible symbols of the emergence of a surveillance society it should not divert us from the recognition that the growth of surveillance, more generally, is intrinsically bound up with the rise of modernity (Dandecker 1990). Moreover, late modernity has seen an intensification of surveillance in almost all spheres of life, exploiting a whole range of new technologies.

For governments, the cross-checking of computerised files held by government departments in an effort to prevent fraud has become routine. The British Police have now established a DNA database of criminals which after two years of operation has details on over 250,000 individuals. The mandatory drug testing of athletes and prisoners is now commonplace and is increasingly being required by employers. The growth of a computerised workforce has not only enabled the monitoring of its electronic communications but also of workplace activity. For businesses consumer surveillance is essential both to determine creditworthiness and effectively target specialist markets. Increasingly consumers are subjected to what Gandy terms the 'panoptic sort' where more and more electronically held information is processed for the purposes of niche marketing. The growth of CCTV surveillance can therefore be seen as merely one element in a sophisticated array of technologies aimed at classification, uncovering deviance and inducing conformity. CCTV therefore, we argue, cannot be seen in isolation from these wider developments and the pressures which give rise to them.

The Rise of the Stranger Society

> Throughout a major part of human history (and prehistory), in most times and most places, men and women have lived out their lives ... in small isolated worlds – in bands or tribes or villages or towns. However varied the human condition in these little worlds – and it varied enormously – they shared one crucial characteristic: the absence of anonymity. Their peoples were born and reared, they reached adulthood and married, propagated, grew old and died, surrounded always and almost exclusively by persons who knew them and who were known to them. (Lofland 1973: 5)

Industrialisation, land reform, population growth and the consequent growth of cities have radically transformed the intimacy of the pre-industrial age. In the city,

Figure 1. Street sign displayed in a car park in Driffield, East Yorkshire as part of a child safety campaign.

as Simmel argues, the dominance of the money economy gives rise to a transformation of exchange relationships. No longer are producers and purchasers directly acquainted:

> The modern metropolis, however is supplied almost entirely by production for the market, that is, for entirely unknown purchasers who never personally enter the producers' actual field of vision. Through this anonymity the interests of each party acquire an unmerciful matter of factness; and the intellectually calculating economic egoisms of both parties need not fear any deflection because of the imponderables of personal relationships. (Simmel 1950: 411–12)

By fostering anonymity, the city facilitates the growth of individualism, autonomy and personal freedom and this has given rise to what Lofland calls the 'world of strangers'. The city becomes a place where persons find themselves to be 'strangers in the midst of strangers' (Lofland 1973: 19). The growth of the stranger society has intensified in the twentieth century; social and geographic mobility has meant that people no longer spend their lives in the communities into which they were born and brought up. The growth of mass transportation systems, and particularly the private ownership of the motor car has enabled the distancing of home and work. Thus, for example, in 1923 there were only around 1 million private vehicles registered in Great Britain, in 1951, 2.5 million, in 1961, 6 million and in 1981 15 million. The growth in commuting that this facilitated meant that while in 1921 only 14.2 per cent of the economically active rural population travelled to urban areas to work, by 1966 this had increased to 37.4 per cent (*Social Trends* 1971: 134). This rise in mobility associated with private motor cars is also illustrated by the growth in the total distances of journeys made by cars in Great Britain. In the post-war decades it rose from 57 billion in 1951, to 384 billion in 1981 and the average 'number of miles travelled per person per day has quadrupled to 25' (*Guardian*,7 September 1994, Features p. 17).

Lash and Urry (1996) have argued that we have moved from a modernist to a post-modernist political economy which is one of 'the ever more rapid circulation of subjects and objects' with the consequence that 'time and space "empty out", become more abstract; and in which things and people become "disembedded" from concrete space and time' (1996: 13). This disembedding means that people are increasingly removed from the traditional constraints of familial obligations and dislocated from traditional community networks. Witness for instance the growth of single-person households, not just among the old but among the young. Increasingly the young are no longer moving from the parental home immediately into their own family units. As the average age of motherhood has consistently increased in the post-war period so too has the incidence of the young living on their own or with their peers before setting up their own family homes.

For Nock, the effect of the social structural changes is to produce a society with an unprecedented amount of privacy, but the consequence is that an individual's reputation can no longer be vouched for by direct personal knowledge, as he argues: 'When someone has no reputation, that person is a stranger. We don't trust strangers as much as people whose reputations are known. Strangers are suspect and must demonstrate that they can be trusted . . . they must earn other peoples' trust. To do so they must somehow earn a good reputation' (Nock 1993: 2). This, as Nock has argued, has created one of the central problems of late modernity: 'How in an anonymous society of strangers is trust produced?'

Ironically, then, while we normally see surveillance as a diminution of privacy, Nock argues it is actually a consequence of that very privacy. However it is not so much the growth of surveillance to which Nock is alluding but a change in its form: from the local and intimate, based on personal knowledge and mutuality of associations, towards the impersonal and portable, the standardised and the bureaucratic. In a society of strangers there are two primary means to establishing reputations: either through the use of credentials or by ordeals. Credentials may include educational certificates, credit cards or drivers' licences and these not only establish one's competencies, but verify that a person is who they say they are. Where else but in a society of strangers could one have an advert that declares: 'American Express says more about you than cash ever can'?

While credentials establish claims to competence, ordeals resolve disputes about truth. Ordeals allow people to validate their reputations by undergoing a test such as a drug test or lie detector test and mandatory drug testing in prisons and by employers is becoming a central part of American life, obsessed as it is by the War on Drugs (Gilliom 1994).

The collapse of personal knowledge as the basis for establishing reputations is most profoundly illustrated by the case of Ken Payne. In October 1997 California passed an emergency law after a teenage girl was allegedly murdered by a school caretaker with a criminal record. In response it was made mandatory that all those involved with the teaching or supervision of children should have to submit to fingerprinting to establish that they had no criminal histories. Mr Payne, who had taught part-time before the new ruling, applied for a full-time job and was duly appointed, however his inability to submit a set of fingerprints has meant he has never been allowed to take up his post. Mr Payne suffers from atopic dermatitis, a skin complaint which has left him with no recognisable fingerprints. Even though he has no criminal record, a fact verified by the FBI, and a police captain who has known him since childhood has vouched for his good character, these have been to no avail. Mr Payne has been told that unless the law is amended he will not be able to take up his post as a teacher (*Guardian*, 22 April 1998, p. 12).

In the context of CCTV these themes have been taken up by Fyfe and Bannister (1998). They argue that another consequence of the rise of the 'stranger society' is the 'fear of difference'. Historically, this fear was double-edged because, while fear may be considered undesirable, the urban form of the cities gave rise to an arena in which difference could be both managed and celebrated. Following Simmel (1971) they see the appeal of the city as providing the public space in which individuals, no longer constrained by tradition and familial ties, could expand their horizons through their encounters with others from different classes, cultures and backgrounds. While these spaces could excite fear, it was a fear tinged with the frisson of discovery. If crime should occur, they argue that order on the streets was maintained not through the formal intervention of police but from the routine, natural surveillance and intervention of the inhabitants and proprietors of the street (Bannister, Fyfe and Kearns 1998). The process of city planning with its emphasis on zoning into segregated residential, retail and business areas, and the privatisation and commodification of space epitomised by the development of the shopping mall, have seen these traditional forms decay. As space becomes subservient to the interests of business and defined by an 'ecology of fear' difference is not something to be celebrated but to be managed, segregated, and excluded (Davis 1990; Davis 1992).

The Risk Society

For some writers these trends are indicative of a broader structural transformation from an industrial society towards a risk society (Beck 1992). In an industrial society, the 'central conflicts and cleavages were defined by the logic of the distribution of goods', in risk society however, 'these cleavages are increasingly defined by the distribution of "bads", that is, of hazards and risks' (Lash and Urry 1994: 33). For Beck, these risk were ones that flowed from the consequence of the development of the global 'military industrial complex', particularly environmental pollution and the threat of nuclear war or accidents. However, more recently other writers such as Ericson and Haggerty (1997) and Feeley and Simon (1994) have argued that we are also witnessing a transformation of legal forms and policing strategies which reflect the transition to a risk society. As Ericson and Haggerty argue:

> Risk society is fuelled by surveillance, by the routine production of knowledge of populations useful for their administration. Surveillance provides biopower, the power to make biographical profiles of human populations to determine what is probable and possible for them. Surveillance fabricates people around institutionally established norms – risk is always somewhere on the continuum of imprecise normality. (1997: 450).

Under these conditions policing becomes orientated to the future rather than the past. It becomes increasingly proactive rather than reactive. Even where it is reactive, it demands that information be gathered for the purpose of future risk assessment. And, given that risk assessment is probabilistic rather than determinist, it requires the assignment of individuals and events to classificatory schemes which provide differentiated assessment of risk and calls for management strategies. Echoing the concerns of the nineteenth-century positivists, offenders become classified as 'prolific' as opposed to opportunistic. Once designated as prolific, an individual becomes a candidate for targeting by more intensive forms of covert technical or human surveillance (Audit Commission: 1992). Similarly, automated surveillance systems become equipped with 'intelligent scene monitoring' capabilities which classify particular events as 'risky': a stationary car in an area of free-flowing traffic, becomes a potential terrorist threat. Football supporters become differentiated into 'respectable fans' and 'hooligans', the latter's status inscribed in the National Crime Intelligence Unit's databases. What is important here is that the emphasis on risk makes everyone a legitimate target of surveillance: 'Everyone is assumed guilty until the risk profile assumes otherwise.'

In the context of crime control, Cohen portently argued in 1985 that for many:

visionary ideologues and observers, however, the day is ending for individual inter-vention. The real master shift about to take place is towards the control of whole groups, populations and environments – not community control, but the control of communities . . . In this movement technology and resources, particularly at the hard end, are to be directed to surveillance, prevention and control, not 'tracking' the individual adjudicated offender, but preventative surveillance (through closed circuit television, for example) of people and spaces. (1985: 127)

Echoing Cohen's analysis, Feeley and Simon (1994) have argued that during the 1990s we are witnessing a paradigm shift in the discourse of criminal justice policy from an Old Penology to the New Penology. The Old Penology was con-cerned with the identification of the individual criminal for the purpose of ascribing guilt and blame, and the imposition of punishment and treatment. The New Penology, on the other hand, is 'concerned with techniques for identifying, classifying and managing groups assorted by levels of dangerousness' (1994: 180) based not on individualised suspicion, but on the probability that an individual may be an offender. For Feeley and Simon, justice is becoming 'actuarial', and its interventions increasingly based on risk assessment, rather than on the identification of specific criminal behaviour. As a consequence, we are witnessing an increase in, and legal sanction of, such actuarial practices as preventative detention, offender profiling and mass surveillance (Feeley and Simon 1994: 180–5).

Historically, British legal discourse had attempted to limit police surveillance, both technological and personal, on the basis of reasonable and individualised suspicion. Thus, the rules governing stop and search, originally codified under the Police and Criminal Evidence Act (1984), required individualised suspicion. However, under the 1994 Criminal Justice and Public Order Act, the police were given the power to stop and search any person or vehicle within a specified locality where an officer of the rank of Superintendent believes that incidents 'involving serious violence may take place in a locality in his area' (CJPOA 1994 IV, 60, 1). The power to stop and search, then, no longer requires individualised suspicion and may be based on mere presence in an area. The legal safeguard to prevent police stop and search operations (a form of surveillance in their own right) merely on the basis, for example, of subcultural affiliation or the colour of a person's skin has been removed.

The 1994 Act also gave prison authorities the right to demand from any prisoner a urine sample for the purposes of 'ascertaining whether he has any drug in his body' (CJPOA 1994 XII, 151, 1). The provision of such samples is not based on any individualised suspicion that a particular person has been taking drugs, and prisoners are now routinely subject to random testing. In more subtle ways the law has tried to identify and define specific classes of people as the subjects of mass and routine surveillance. The 1985 Sporting Events Act, in effect, gave the police the general right to stop and search coaches, minibuses and fans going to football matches. While maintaining the illusion of reasonable suspicion, the legislation was so permissively framed that the police would almost always be justified in stopping a vehicle and searching it and its occupants, since an officer merely had to have reasonable grounds for believing that somewhere on the coach or in the possession of one of its occupants was alcohol or that an act of drunkenness was being or had been permitted (English and Card, 1991). It is important to note that while the notion of 'equality before the law' was an assumption of the Old Penology, the New Penology had no such qualms and, therefore, the legislation did not apply to those travelling to rugby or cricket matches, only football. Similarly, the CJPOA 1994 goes to great lengths to legally define and single out people associated with 'raves', so they may be subject to increased police powers of stop, search and arrest (CJPOA 1994 V, 63, 1). Most recently, the new Labour government has published plans to extend the use of curfew orders from individual juvenile offenders, to all children under the age of ten. The plans will make it an offence for any unaccompanied child to be out on the street after 9 p.m.

Finally, in serious cases, especially murder and rape, where conventional policing has revealed few leads as to the identity of the culprit, the police are increasingly resorting to the blanket DNA testing of entire communities. Although testing is voluntary, if a person fails to provide a sample, this could be treated as indicating possible involvement and grounds for further investigation (*Hull Daily Mail*, 13 October 1996). In the case of Caroline Dickenson, an English schoolgirl who was murdered in a French youth hostel while on a school trip, five schoolboys who accompanied her were, on their return to England, asked to give samples of DNA to rule themselves out of police enquiries. Since then the entire male population of the village in which the crime occurred has submitted, 'voluntarily', to DNA testing (*Daily Telegraph, and Guardian*, 17 March 1997). Similarly, in the town of Pudsey in Yorkshire, after the rape of a teenage girl, the police requested that 200 local men voluntarily gave saliva swabs, so that DNA matching could eliminate them from their enquiries. Within two days 192 men had come forward and the officers were said 'to be concentrating on the remaining eight men and have warned that the net is now closing in on the rapist' (*Yorkshire Evening Post*, 20 April 1998).

The rise of mass CCTV surveillance can be seen as part of a broader transformation, to a new form of penology based on 'actuarial justice', which is legal abandonment of individualised suspicion. However, in Britain at least, the proliferation of cameras in public space has not been facilitated by the passing of new legislation but by the absence of legislation to regulate or check their installation. There is no legal regulation of the right to take photographs in public space or of those who wish to set up systems for the purpose of taking photographs. This is unlike many other European Countries where video surveillance is regulated by statute, and involves the registration and licensing of surveillance systems, including legally enforceable rules on how the products can be used (Maguire 1998). Furthermore, there is no general right of privacy in British law and those seeking to challenge the right of a local authority or police to photograph them on the grounds of infringement to privacy would have to do so on the basis of trespass and nuisance, defamation, breach of confidence or breach of copyright. According to Sharpe (1989, Ch 5) none of these would succeed in relation to a CCTV system operating in public space. As the High Court recently ruled, even where a local council released video footage of a man who had been filmed after attempting to commit suicide, in the absence of a privacy law, the court was unable to hold that the council was wrong in law or acting irrationally, in releasing the film to BBC1's 'Crime Beat' and other programmes, (*Guardian*, 26 November 26 1997, p. 8). Finally, while the Data Protection Act may afford some limitations on the use and exchange of information about individuals whose identities are known and recorded, there are wide-ranging exemptions for law enforcement agencies (Liberty 1997).

The Political Context of Mass Surveillance

While it would be possible to write a history of the rise of mass surveillance in Britain in terms of domestic politics of crime control, it would in our view be misleading as global and European politics also played a part in influencing the general ideological climate which allowed CCTV to be introduced with hardly a murmur of opposition.

Global Politics and the End of the Cold War

It may at first sight seem strange to suggest the massive expansion of cameras on the streets of British cities in the 1990s is linked to the geopolitics of the Cold War. However, we would argue that it is no coincidence that it occurred in the immediate aftermath of the end of the Cold War, signalled most dramatically with the dismantling of the Berlin Wall in November 1989. The Cold War began with the realignment of the world map at the end of the Second World War, and the division of the world into spheres of influence of the two great, ideologically opposed superpowers, Capitalist America and the Communist Soviet Union, both fearing the threat of colonisation from the other. As Hobsbawm has written:

> In short, while the USA was worried about the danger of a possible Soviet world supremacy some time in the future, Moscow was worried about the actual hegemony of the USA now, over all the parts of the globe not occupied by the red army. It would not take much to turn an exhausted and impoverished USSR into yet another client region of the US. (1995: 234)

Initially the effect of this mutual distrust threatened open warfare especially after the declaration of the Truman Doctrine where the President stated: 'I believe that it must be the policy of the United States to support free peoples who are resisting attempted subjugation by armed minorities or by outside pressure.' However in 1949 the USSR also obtained the atomic bomb and 'both superpowers plainly abandoned war as an instrument of policy against one another, since it was the equivalence of a suicide pact' (Hobsbawn 1994: 229). The logic of the Cold War was to substitute an arms race for an armed struggle: the threat of war for its actuality. For the threat to be credible in the context of mutual distrust, neither side could afford for their destructive capacity to be technologically inferior or numerically smaller than the other's, since this would threaten the stability of what the strategists termed a policy of Mutually Assured Destruction (Krass and Smith 1982: 5). As a result, the economies of NATO countries, particularly Britain and America were increasingly skewed towards sustaining massive investments in armaments technology and maintaining a military capability in readiness for a Soviet attack. Thus, for instance in 1988, at the very end of the Cold War, Britain alone was spending nearly £20 billion on defence, 15 per cent of total government expenditure and greater than the combined budgets for education and science. Moreover, the citizenry was forced to live under the permanent threat of global nuclear war, a threat which was given terrifying substance during the Cuban Missile Crisis of 1961.

For governments to sustain a policy which was predicated on the total destruction of the planet, requiring high and increased levels of taxation and the massive diversion of funds from socially useful expenditure, there was a central need to constantly legitimate their actions. Thus the ideology of the Cold War rested on the leaders of the West reminding the public what was at stake and the consequences of failure. As President Kennedy declared in 1960:

> The enemy is the communist system itself – implacable, insatiable, unceasing in its drive for world domination . . . this is not a struggle for supremacy of arms alone. It is also a struggle for supremacy between two conflicting ideologies: freedom under God versus ruthless, Godless tyranny. (Cited in Hobsbawm 1995: 231)

Mrs Thatcher in her self-described mantle as a 'Cold War warrior' argued it was for the 'defence of values and freedoms fundamental to our way of life' (Augarde 1991: 213). For Reagan, like Kennedy before him, the Cold War could not be reduced to an arms race but had to be seen as the 'struggle between right and wrong, good and evil' (Augarde 1991: 178). The impact of such rhetorics meant that Kennedy could enrol mass political support and win the 1960s Presidential election on a largely anti-communist platform. Indeed the country was 'defined in exclusively ideological terms ("Americanism") which could be virtually defined as the polar opposition of communism' (Hobsbawm 1995: 235).

However, to be effective such ideological messages needed content: what was the difference between societies based on 'freedom' rather than 'tyranny', that embodied 'good' not 'evil'? And one of the most enduring symbols of the difference between the 'Evil Empire' and the Free West was the existence of the Secret Police. The invocation of the Stasi (East Germany), of the KGB (USSR) or any other of the State security police which were central to the political organisation of the communist states in Eastern Europe provided one such powerful political symbol. The secret police were the very embodiment of the totalitarian state. The rhetoric was not without substance: as Fullbrook has so well documented, the Stasi were the means by which the party attempted to 'achieve the total ideological subordin-ation of the population, to be achieved by total party control of all aspects of social and individual life, reaching even into the sphere of the family and parenting as an instrument of political indoctrination and subordination to the higher collective purposes of the state' (Fulbrook 1995: 3).

By 1989, just before the end of the Cold War, the East German Stasi had built up records on an estimated 6 million of its 16 million inhabitants. To maintain this level of surveillance required around 100,000 full-time employees, and an estimated 180,000 paid informers who utilised the range of 'technical prerequisites of the Big Brother state: telephone tapping, bugging devices, postal controls, personal and video surveillance' (Fulbrook 1995: 49). The result was a system that encou-raged children to inform on their parents, churchgoers on their congregations, and pupils on their teachers, and at the heart was the file which documented and recorded the minutiae of potential dissents in everyday life.

While the Stasi relied on the conventional means of surveillance, the Rumanian dictator Ceausescu was envisaging establishing an electronic monitoring system so complex that every family in the land would be subject to periodic, and if necessary, constant, surveillance. Ceausescu told the scientists involved in the project:

> It is too bad that we cannot tell our working people how the communist party is looking out for (sic) them, comrades. Wouldn't the miners go out and dig more coal, if they could just be sure that the party knew exactly what their wives were doing every single instant? They would comrades but we cannot talk about our system today. The western press might accuse us of being a police state. (Cited in Crampton 1994: 248)

The ideology of the Cold War required that the 'free world' was safely distanced from the Eastern Bloc by 'invoking an essential difference between the West guided by humanist principles, and an 'Oriental Other' based on totalitarianism (Sibley 1995: 111). The totalising surveillance activities of the state security police provided one of the most powerful symbols of the difference. This in turn limited the ability of Western governments to sanction activities which could be interpreted as a drift towards the structures and technologies of totalitarianism. As Sibley has argued, totalitarian practices in the West 'had to be explained away in order to sustain this division of "the world" into good or bad. For those in the West with an interest in continuing the cold war, this was a necessary purification of global space, one which required an "other".' (1995: 111)

True, the 'free' nations also had the security services such as the FBI and CIA in the US and Special Branch and the Security Services in Britain. However, their scope, scale and function were altogether on a different scale to those of the Communist states of Russia and Eastern Europe and, in any event, they could be ideologically justified by insisting they were necessary to counter the Communist 'threat from within' or international terrorism.

It could be argued that the anti-communist witch-hunts of Senator McCarthy and the House Un-American Activities Committee (HUAC) in the early 1950s, embodied precisely the structures and practices of the 'enemy'. They did, and, in fact, served as a palpable warning to those responsible for the need to maintain a distinction between 'us and them' in the ideology of the Cold War. As Brogan argues in his majestic *History of the United States*, McCarthyism gave those Europeans who resented and distrusted American power a:

> respectable excuse for expressing their hostility. Less cynically or dishonest elements found their doubts confirmed. They disliked the Cold War, did not blame Russia for it exclusively and disliked some of its consequences: the building up of Germany again . . . and the manufacture of the hydrogen bomb. They began to doubt that the country of McCarthy was a safe guardian of nuclear weapons. (Brogan 1985: 619)

At home, while McCarthyism undoubtedly provided an impetus for the anti-communist hysteria in America of the early 1950s, it also left a nasty taste in the mouth of the American public. By its very techniques McCarthyism raised the possibility that there were few differences between the land of the 'free' and the land of the 'enslaved' and it is no coincidence that it was discredited after the public witnessed his interrogation techniques in the HUAC hearings on television in 1955.

In Britain at least, since the end of the Cold War there has been an unprecedented growth in the whole panoply of the structures of surveillance which have a remarkable similarity with the methods of the State security apparatus of the former Eastern Bloc. In 1989 'Crime Stoppers' was launched, encouraging people to give anonymous tip-offs to the police; in 1996 they received 37,703 calls resulting in over 18,000 arrests. In the wake of this, other 'hotlines' have been set up by a whole range of agencies to encourage anonymous informing: the Department of Social Security launched its benefit fraud hotline in 1996 which received more than 400,000 calls in its first six months of operation; the Environment Agency has established a hotline to report poachers and polluters; under the leadership of Reading Council, sixty local authorities have joined together to set up a Fraud Watch scheme also relying on anonymous calls from the public and so far have received 8,000 calls bearing useful information; Camelot, who run the national lottery, have set up an anonymous phone line for the public to report vendors suspected of selling to those under sixteen years of age. In total, the *Independent on Sunday* estimated that there were now '100 ways you can secretly inform on your neighbours' and suggested that we were now becoming a 'nation of snoopers' (*Independent on Sunday*, 29 December 1996).

In 1993, the Audit Commission recommended an expansion of 'intelligence-led policing' resting on a wholesale increase in the police use of informers (Audit Commission 1993, Dunnighan and Norris 1999) and this has been extended to include the use of juvenile informers, whose parents will not necessarily be informed of their activities (*Express on Sunday*, 5 October 1997). The police have also been instrumental in pushing for increased powers of surveillance. In the Police Bill which came before Parliament in 1997, proposals were put forward which as the *Guardian* rightly reported 'would give the police sweeping new powers to bug and burgle private property greater to those conceded to the forces of law and order in any other modern democracy' (*Guardian*, 13 January 1997). Specifically it would grant the police the right to covertly enter private property to plant bugging devices, with no independent oversight. Nor were there exemptions to protect either journalist-source relationships or lawyer-client relationships. These proposals had multi-party support and it was only a sustained campaign in the press and the opposition of the House of Lords which led the Labour Party to accept the need for independent oversight and authorisation which were eventually included in the act. For the five Chief Constables who wrote to the *Independent* newspaper on 15 January 1997, those critical of the Bill were guilty of employing 'emotive red herrings' which 'should not be allowed to reduce police effectiveness in acting against those involved in organised crime'. Under the terms of the proposed Act, those planning political demonstrations which *might* result in violence would also come under its scope. Given that any demonstration might result in potential violence, it appears that the police and the political supporters of the bill were prepared to countenance a massive increase in police powers against *any* form of organised public protest.

Other techniques to facilitate the mass surveillance of the population have found their way onto the political agenda of the 1990s: the reintroduction of identity cards has been seriously considered by the Home Office and the Police Chief Superintendents Association has called for the establishment of a national DNA database covering the entire population (*Guardian*, 6 May 1998). And, of course, there has been the exponential increase in the number of cameras surveilling public space.

As Sibley has argued, the end of the Cold War 'has rendered a particularly powerful rhetoric which supported a boundary between "good" and "evil" redundant' (1995: 183). Thus, ideas that would have previously been held in check, found that they could now enter mainstream political discourse. There was no need to maintain the symbols of difference: the West had won and, with victory, utilitarian rhetorics of crime control could assert themselves. The fears surrounding the increased use of surveillance could be dismissed by the simple sloganising of the then Prime Minister John Major: 'If you've got nothing to hide you've got nothing to fear'.

Finally we should add that the end of the Cold War not only signalled an ideological shift, but also heralded the need for economic transformation. The so-called 'peace dividend' promised the massive transfer of resources away from military spending towards socially useful projects such as education and health. For the companies which had profited handsomely from military expenditure, the peace dividend represented more of a threat than an opportunity, since it is simply not possible to switch overnight from producing missiles to medicines (Markusen and Yudken 1992). One response was to seek to expand their operations into civil rather than military markets and criminal justice and policing applications were an obvious starting point.

As Lilly and Knepper argue, the immediate impact of this 'technology transfer' saw defence contractors rapidly move in to the 'corrections' market to develop electronic tagging and tracking systems for convicted offenders:

> The new electronics markets not only illustrates some of the international financial and commercial dimensions of contemporary corrections, it also points to connections with the military industrial complex. Two international defence contractors Racal Chubb and GEC Plessey via its Marconi Electronic Devices Ltd neither of which . . . had prior involvement with criminal justice, contracted in 1989 with the Home Office respectively to the Tower Bridge tagging site, and for the Nottingham and North Tyneside. (1992: 184)

As GEC-Marconi made clear, the threat of reduced military expenditure was driving its push into new markets and its Chairman, Lord Prior announced:

> GEC-Marconi will continue to seek opportunities in civil markets to exploit technologies in which it is expert. This process of 'conversion' has been underway for sometime, and already more than 20% of the group's sales are to non military customers. The successful demonstrations of flexibility in adapting defence orientated technologies and management techniques to different imperatives of civil products provides GEC-Marconi with the necessary confidence to tackle a wide variety of projects (cited in Lilly and Knepper 1992: 184).

As Wright points out this transfer was explicitly encouraged by government:

This trend was fuelled in the U.S. in the 1990's by accelerated government funding at the end of the Cold War, with defence and intelligence agencies being refocussed with new missions to justify their budgets, transferring their technologies to certain law enforcement applications such as anti-drug and anti-terror co-operations. In 1993, the US Department of Defence and Justice Department signed a memorandum of under- standing for 'Operations Other Than War and Law enforcement' to facilitate joint development and sharing of technology. (Wright 1998: 16)

And for both Racal-Chubb, GEC-Marconi, and other high-tec companies with their origins as defence contractors, this has also meant expansion into the civilian CCTV market, either as system providers, or more usually providing advanced technological enhancements. As a result, applications originally developed for the military such as intelligent scene monitoring, automated navigation and recognition systems, thermal imaging systems, and integrated database management are being targeted at the civilian market to be used in conjuction with CCTV. For instance, Memex who supply computer software which enables the integration of all police intelligence records and is capable of handling photographic as well as textual information, have found a ready market in over a dozen British police forces. Their origins however are in the defence sectors as one of the advertisements make clear:

In addition to the many users in the UK the Memex solution is utilised by numerous intelligence and defence organisations in the United States such as the Joint Chiefs of Staff at the Pentagon, the United States Secret Service, the Defence Intelligence Agency and the CIA. (Memex product brochure: no date)

European Politics

If the geopolitics of the end of the Cold War facilitated an ideological climate favourable to the introduction of CCTV, it was the divisions within the Conservative Party over European integration, which created the political climate positively conducive to the creation of the mass surveillance society. In early 1993, the Conservative government was in crisis, it was trailing Labour by an average of 16 percentage points in the opinion polls, the party had been trounced in the local elections and a MORI opinion poll found that only 17 per cent of voters thought the Prime Minister, John Major, to be a capable leader (Seldon 1994: 294; Seldon 1997: 373). Moreover the Prime Minister had staked his personal reputation and the continuation of the government on the successful ratification of the Maastrict Treaty which would pave the way to tighter European integration and the formation of a single European currency. This was an anathema to a group of about 30–50 hardline Euro-sceptics, mainly of the Tory Right, who threatened to vote against the government on any measures leading to closer European links. With a majority hovering around twenty, this group not only threatened to bring down the government but also to permanently split the Conservative Party (Seldon 1997: chs 17–25).

In the end Major won the day, but only after turning the issue into a vote of confidence in the government. The cost was to permanently alter the political landscape. Although the Euro-sceptics had been defeated, the process had increased the power of the Tory Right, whose support was central to the government's survival. Until that point, the Right had been kept at arm's length by Major; now however, within the party there was a growing recognition that, to quote one back-bencher although 'the right had the majority of the parliamentary party, the government was being run from the centre left' (cited in Seldon 1997: 340). To reward the loyalty shown on Maastrict and placate a still fractious party, Major in his May 1993 reshuffle appointed the prominent right-winger John Redwood to the Cabinet. Michael Howard, both a Euro-sceptic and right-winger, was rewarded for his loyalty to Major during the Maastrict crisis and was promoted from the political backwater of the Department of the Environment to the centre stage as Home Secretary. The Right of the party could now boast four major players in Cabinet, with Lilley at Social Security, Portillo as Chief Secretary at the Treasury, Redwood as Secretary of State for Wales and Howard at the Home Office. And it was on Law and Order that the Right was truly to make its mark.

Even though Thatcher had won the 1979 election on an ideological crusade resounding with the rhetoric of a tough law and order programme, the reality of her eleven years of office, and the first three of John Major's, was actually a high degree of continuation of the post-war consensus about matters to do with criminal justice.

With the exception of Leon Brittan, the former Tory Home Secretaries Whitelaw, Hurd, Waddington, Baker, and Clarke, were pragmatists rather than ideologists. On matters of policy they had tended to listen to the advice of their civil servants: they were reformists rather than revolutionaries. As David Downes has argued:

> One of the most remarkable developments of the 1980's was the contrast between the fire-and-brimstone rhetoric on law and order of the incoming conservative Government of 1979 and its gradual acceptance during the next decade of the case against high level of imprisonment. The conversion of successive Home Secretaries to a liberal penal reform programme was largely due to the determined efforts of a senior official at the Home Office who . . . was given the scope to assemble a small network of civil servants to pursue that objective. They were greatly aided by timely reports from the Home Office Research and Planning Unit that showed among other things the severe limitation of increasing policing and penal incapacitation. (Downes 1997: 8).

With the arrival of Michael Howard at the Home Office, all this was to change. Flying in the face of the consensus, Howard announced at the 1993 party conference

'Prison works' and launched a 27-point policy for Criminal Justice which he encapsulated in a robust outpouring of rhetoric. 'Let's take the handcuffs off the police and put them on the criminals where they belong,' he declared to an enthralled party. Over the coming year the potential of CCTV was to become an integral part of the new Law and Order campaign and in October 1994 Howard announced the first tranche of government money. This measure which, a decade earlier, would have prompted a vigorous reaction from the Labour 'Left' as to the encroaching police state, received all-party support and hardly a murmur of opposition from any quarter. However to understand this we need to consider the changes in the politics of law and order from the 1970s.

The Domestic Politics of Law and Order: Local and National

While the technology of mass video surveillance became available from the early 1970s, the political climate retarded its introduction. The 1970s and early 1980s saw a fierce political confrontation between elements of the local state, particularly Labour controlled local authorities, and the police regarding accountability (Bundred 1982; Simey 1982). This confrontation was encapsulated in a flurry of books published at the time which highlighted the growing technological sophistication of policing, how it was deployed against trade unionists, peace campaigners and animal rights activists, and how there was little or no democratic control over these practices (Bunyan 1977; Bunyan 1978; Hain 1979; Aubrey 1981; Mainwaring-White 1983). Moreover for many, the inner city riots of the early 1980s were a response to the hostile, aggressive and essentially racist policing of ethnic minorities (Scraton 1982). And these arguments, while not necessarily wholly endorsed, undoubtedly found some resonance with a population which had routinely been exposed as schoolchildren to the dystopian vision of the total surveillance society in George Orwell's classic dystopian text *Nineteen Eighty-Four*.

For those not convinced by the radicals' rhetoric of the drift towards totalitarianism there were, however, more pragmatic reasons for the slow uptake of CCTV – money. The early 1980s, saw local authorities under the financial cosh of a Conservative administration committed to reducing public expenditure and curbing, what it saw as, the excesses of predominantly Labour controlled local councils. Faced with having to cut back on its most basic services, even if a local authority wanted to install a CCTV system, the cost, involving several hundred thousands pounds of capital expenditure and tens of thousands of pounds in annual running costs, could not be justified in the context of cuts in other areas.

But while many local authorities were either ideologically or financially opposed to the introduction of CCTV, the Conservative government was dismayed by its inability to stem the seemingly unstoppable rise of recorded crime. They had increased police pay, increased staffing levels and, between 1982 and 1991, increased capital and revenue spending by 43 per cent (Audit Commission 1993). Despite this, between 1979 and 1992, recorded crime doubled from just under three million offences per annum to over six million and, in 1991 and 1992, there were two massive rises of 17 and 16 per cent respectively.

In the wake of this huge rise in recorded crime, in 1992 the Audit Commission turned its attention to the efficiency of the Criminal Investigations Departments. The Audit Commission had been set up by a previous Conservative administration to promote, within government departments, a 'well-defined responsibility for making the best use of their resources, including a critical scrutiny of output and value for money' (HMSO 1982). The report published in the following year was scathing about the inability of the police to stem rising crime rates or catch those responsible. It stated, 'given current trends in crime figures and clear-ups, by 2002 the number of recorded crimes will have exceeded 9 million and the overall clear up rate could drop to 18%. Society is thus in danger of losing the "battle against crime"' (Audit Commission 1993: 8–9). The Commission called for a massive expansion of proactive, intelligence-led policing, and singled out CCTV as having a major role to play in crime prevention. Its report stated that the introduction of CCTV to Airdrie Town centre led to a 75 per cent reduction in recorded crime and an increase in the clear-up rate to 71 per cent. This authoritative endorsement by the Audit Commission would appear to give substance to the claims from other sites of massive reductions in crime. For a government desperate to reassert its authority on law and order, such figures must have appeared like manna from heaven. CCTV really was the magic bullet which could win the battle against crime and it, perhaps, comes as no surprise that in October 1994, Michael Howard announced that two million pounds of Home Office money would be provided by the Home Office to fund CCTV by means of a City Challenge Competition (*Guardian*, 19 October 1994: 4).

In the event, the Home Office was overwhelmed by applications, receiving 480 bids and, despite increasing the amount dispersed by the competition to £5 million, could only fund 106 of the applications (*CCTV Today* Nov 1995: 5). In response to this demand, two further competitions were staged in 1995/6 and 1996/7 with £15 million allocated to each.

The competitive nature of the funding was important in a number of ways. First, the government would only grant money to fund the capital costs of the schemes and only if partnership funding was also found, particularly from business. Thus, for an outlay of £37 million, around £100 million of investment in CCTV was generated with the government, of course, claiming the credit. Also, the government took no responsibility for meeting the running costs associated with the schemes, these would have to be met locally – predominately by local councils. Of course, such a process had the effect, whether intended or not, of stimulating demand for CCTV way and above that which was funded. Those who had put considerable effort into making the bid, by writing a proposal, garnering local support, and enlisting the media in the appeal to attract private funding, did not suddenly relinquish their aspirations for CCTV systems. Instead they sought other ways to fund them, whether it be increased car parking charges, applying for European Council regeneration money, or by introducing a special 'earmarked' tax as in the case of Cottingham in East Yorkshire. The competition had other advantages: of the 106 grants dispersed in the first wave of funding, seventy-six went to Tory constituencies, thirty-two of them considered marginal. The fact that high crime areas such as London's Elephant and Castle in a Labour constituency were turned down for funding, while affluent Tory suburbs and market towns such as Richmond in London and Harrogate in Yorkshire, were successful, led some commentators to accuse the Home Secretary of gerry-mandering (*Daily Mirror*, 10 April 1995).

CCTV was attractive to the government in other ways. It dovetailed neatly with their ideological demands for privatisation of the public sector. The private sector would be fully involved in building, equipping and maintaining the systems. In many cases, private security firms were responsible for monitoring the screens in the control rooms and, as business had contributed to the setting up of the systems, it would have a say in the shape of the systems and how they were run. Moreover, given that local councils were rate-capped and unable to pay for increased expenditure through increased taxation, this silver bullet could be financed with few implications for the public sector borrowing requirement.

There is one further element in this story: there was by 1994 almost no political resistance to CCTV. The tragic murder of the toddler Jamie Bulger, in Bootle, Merseyside by two ten-year-old schoolboys, in February 1993, had served to crystallise fears about public safety and the nature of childhood. It had also dramatically launched CCTV into the public debate surrounding the control of crime as the fuzzy pictures of the little boy being led from the shopping centre were replayed night after night on television. Even if CCTV had not saved the toddler, at least it contributed to the identification of the killers (Smith 1995). The public mood in the wake of the killing, as evidenced by the newspapers of the time, made those who tried to raise objections to CCTV seem either callous or too concerned with the rights of criminals.

Finally, the Labour Party had been transformed by the process of modernisation, started by Neil Kinnock in the early 1980s and concluding with the launch of New Labour, by Tony Blair in the 1990s. New Labour was no longer in ideological battle with the police over accountability, and its shadow Home Secretary, Jack Straw, was determined that Labour would not be accused of being soft on crime or anti-police as they had been in the 1970s and 1980s (Reiner 1992: 261–6). Like the criminologist Jock Young, the Labour Party had undergone a conversion from Left Idealism to New Left Realism, with its stress on the victim, the impact of crime on the working classes, and lived realities of crime (Young 1991). Indeed,

CCTV was eagerly embraced by the Labour leadership. The former Labour leader, John Smith, publicly officiated at the opening of the Airdrie System and Tony Blair opened the Chester-le-Street system, declaring that CCTV was having a 'tremendous impact' (*CCTV Today*, July 1996). This was reflected at a local level with councils such as Lewisham in South London which, in the early 1980s had followed a policy of non-cooperation with the police (Reiner 1992: 239), actively forging a partnership with the police for the purposes of setting up CCTV systems. Even the civil liberty pressure group, Liberty, was not opposed to the introduction of mass surveillance, but merely argued for statutory regulation of the CCTV industry. It would appear they had no answer to the populist rhetoric of the Prime Minister, John Major, who declared: 'I have no doubt we will hear some protest about a threat to civil liberties. Well I have no sympathy what so ever for so-called liberties of that kind.' (*Independent*, 27 February, 1994)

Shopping and the Economics of the Market Place

So far we have focussed on CCTV in the context of the political response to crime and its control but this is only half the story. The recessions of the early 1980s and 1990s not only resulted in lengthening dole queues, but also put tremendous pressure on high street retailers who witnessed a dramatic fall in consumer spending. Simultaneously, high streets and traditional town centres were being squeezed by the emergence of the out-of-town shopping centres, such as the Metro Centre in Gateshead, and Meadow Hall in Sheffield.

These cathedrals of consumerism, with their ease of parking, cheaper goods, and gleaming, purpose-built environments, were diverting consumers away from the high street. As the major national chains, such as Dixons and Tescos, relocated into the out-of-town sites, leaving empty premises in their wake, the smaller retailers who relied on their magnet effect also found their margins squeezed to the point of bankruptcy as they experienced the full impact of a 40 per cent decline in high street spending (Cahill 1994: Ch 5; Reeve 1998).

This economic decline also exacerbated the feeling that town centres, as opposed to shopping malls, were dirty, threatening places to shop and that the solution would be to fund new-style safe shopping strategies, including CCTV, in order to attract the consumer back from the out-of-town mall (Beck and Willis 1995; Reeve 1998). Those retailers who were left and were committed to high street operations, such as Boots, Marks and Spencers and W.H. Smiths were also acutely aware that, unless the 'environmental competitiveness of the out of town retail centres and in town malls' could be challenged their 'continued investment in' high street 'locations would no longer be profitable' (Reeve 1996: 9).

Out of these fears the concept of Town Centre Management was developed by

Peter Spindal of Marks and Spencer 'in order to give coherence to the principle of managing any urban centre with a retail focus as a single entity' (Reeve 1996: 7). In essence, the principle of town centre management is to coordinate the activities of various parties with an interest in the city centre, (both public and private sector) in order to promote competitive advantage. As the town centre managers in Reeve's study revealed, they wanted to discourage certain people and activities within the city centre which were seen as non-conducive to their consumer-led vision of the desirable: a quarter wanted to discourage political gatherings, half wanted to discourage youths from 'hanging out', and half to prohibit begging in the streets (1996: 22). Importantly, the number of towns operating town centre management schemes has risen from under six in 1986 to over a hundred in 1995 (Reeve 1996: 13).

The TCM movement has provided an impetus for CCTV and created a platform for joint, public-private funding of CCTV schemes which prioritise commercial concerns in the management of city centre space. And it was the argument that CCTV would promote the 'feel-good factor' and revitalise the high street and city centre that provided the sales pitch to attract business funding. Thus, the Glasgow Development Association (GDA) who required funding from business to set up their CCTV scheme stressed the financial benefits under the slogan 'CCTV doesn't just make sense – it makes business sense'. The GDA backed up this claim by calculating that introducing CCTV would encourage 22,500 more visits to the city a year, create 1,500 jobs and produce an extra £40 million of income to city centre business. Such claims were echoed in other cities and towns (Fyfe and Bannister 1996). In the event, the evaluations carried out in Sutton and Brighton found little evidence to support these claims as there was no discernible increase in people reporting a greater use of the town centres since the introduction of the cameras (Squires and Measor 1996; Mahalingham 1996).

We have seen that, in trying to account for the rise of mass surveillance, it is necessary to move beyond the limited confines of concerns of crime and disorder and consider the particular configuration of economic, social, political and legal trends which has given rise to British citizens becoming the most surveilled population in the world and it is to documenting this that we know turn.

—3—

The Ever Present Gaze:
CCTV Surveillance in Britain

An Everyday Story of Video Surveillance

Thomas Kearns' day starts as usual. At 7.15 a.m. the sounds of BBC Radio Four, emanating from his clock radio, penetrate his slumbering consciousness. He wakes quickly, showers and dresses in his best salesman suit which flatters his 38 year-old frame. His ten-year-old son and four-year-old daughter are washed and dressed by the time he joins them for breakfast. At 8.15 he kisses his wife goodbye and shuts the front door of his apartment behind him, children in tow, to dispatch them to school and nursery, before embarking on another office day. They head towards the lift along the concrete walkways and are captured on a covert video surveillance operation, set up by the local authority, aimed at identifying residents who are dealing in drugs from their premises (1) (N.B. the numbers in brackets will be used to identify systems in our further analysis). As they wait for the lift their presence is monitored on the concierge's video system twelve floors below, as is their descent for there is also a camera in the lift and their predictable daily routine is preserved on tape to be stored for twenty-eight days, or longer if necessary (2). As they walk from the lobby of their apartment block to the car, it is not only the concierge who monitors the Kearns' departure, but Mr Adams on the fifteenth floor, who has tuned his television to receive output from the Housing Estate's cameras (3).

Thomas drives out of the estate on to the dual-carriageway and, although vaguely aware of the sign that declares 'reduce your speed now – video camera in operation', still drives at ten miles an hour over the speed limit and trips the automatic speed cameras (4). By 8.30 he has dropped his daughter off at the CCTV monitored nursery (5) and is heading towards his son's school. He stops at a red light, which is as well because had he jumped it, another picture would have been taken to be used as evidence in his prosecution (6). As they wait in the playground for the buzzer to signal the start of school, they are filmed by a covert camera secreted in the building opposite to monitor the playground for signs of drug dealing (7) and their goodbye kiss is also captured on the school's internal CCTV system which monitors every entrance and exit (8). Noticing that his fuel tank is nearly empty, he drives to the petrol station and fills up. He knows that he is being filmed as the a large sign at the cash desk declares: 'These premises are under 24 hour video surveillance' (9).

He leaves the garage and approaches the station, and quietly curses as he is stopped by the barriers at the railway level crossing. His location is caught on one of the four Railtrack cameras monitoring the crossing specifically to ensure that the intersection of road and track is clear when the train crosses (10). A few minutes later he is parked in the car park opposite the station under the watchful eye of another set of cameras (11).

As usual, Thomas buys a newspaper at the newsagents. and is filmed by their in-store security cameras as he does so. No one is monitoring the images from the two cameras but they are taped on a multiplex video recorder which records the images from both cameras on one tape, and enables any incident to be reviewed should it be necessary (12). Before buying his ticket he makes a telephone call from the public call box on the station forecourt to remind his wife that he will be late home. Unbeknown to him he is filmed by a covert camera installed by British Telecom to try and catch those who vandalise their telephone boxes and hoax callers to the emergency services (13). His call made, he buys his ticket, walks to the platform and waits for his train all of which has been recorded and monitored by the thirty-two cameras operating at the station (14). On arrival at his destination, he walks the short distance to his office and smiles at the camera monitoring the reception area (15). He is, however, unaware that his movements are being recorded by a number of covert cameras hidden in the smoke detector housings as he walks along the corridor towards his office (16).

At lunchtime, he is going to visit his sister, who has just given birth to a healthy baby boy. He leaves his office and heads for the High Street. His movements along the streets are watched by three operatives in the town hall's CCTV control room (17). His first port of call is the streetside automatic cash dispenser, he makes his withdrawal and his face is captured by a covert camera hidden inside the cash machine (18). He crosses the road and enters Marks and Spencers to buy his sister some flowers and himself a new raincoat. Should the CCTV operative so wish, his every turn could be tracked on the 35 camera in-store security system. At the till he writes a cheque for £45.75 but he doesn't notice a camera zooming in on him to ensure that the store has good pictures of his face should he be touting a stolen cheque card (19).

Outside, he hails a taxi for the two-mile journey and, as they cross a major arterial road, the taxi's number plate is photographed by the Metropolitan Police's new CCTV based automatic licence plate recognition system (20). On arrival at the hospital he is photographed by two cameras covering the main entrance and again as he enters the maternity unit (21). Having carried out his family duties, he walks to the nearest Underground station; here his progress will be recorded on video from the moment he enters the station to the point he boards his train (22). He alights at Heathrow Airport to meet some prospective clients who have flown in for a meeting the following day and, of course, his movements are monitored by dozens of security cameras (23). He escorts his guests to the airport hotel, and then to the car park where a hire car is awaiting them. They drive out of the car park and the number plate is photographed automatically. It is then checked against the computerised database of all cars using the airport car parks (24).

They are heading to Chelsea Football Ground in South London where Thomas, as part of his sales routine, is treating them to a Premier League match. En route they are fleetingly caught by the town centre CCTV systems operating in Southall, Ealing and Hammersmith (25). They are photographed as they enter the stadium and while they are seated their faces scanned and checked against a pictorial database of known hooligans (26). After the match they drive across the river to a bistro in Streatham. As they are unfamiliar with the area they drive slowly down Bedford Hill looking for the correct turn-off. They are filmed on a mobile camcorder, deployed by a detective from the local vice squad in an effort to prevent 'kerb crawling' in this 'red light district' (27). The officer loses interest when they turn off.

Thomas is relieved when they find the restaurant and even more relieved when dinner is over and he awaits the 11.14 from Clapham Junction Station where his presence is recorded on the station's cameras (28). He returns home just before midnight, pours himself a drink and sits down to check the post. His heart sinks as he opens an official-looking letter with an even more officious content. The local police, he is informed, have photographed his son associating with a teenage gang, and wish Mr Kearns to come to the police station to view the video (29). Thomas downs his drink and, as he heads to bed, wonders what on earth his son can have done wrong to warrant being photographed by the police.

From Fiction to Fact: The Reality of Routine Surveillance

At the end of his, admittedly long and busy day, Thomas had been filmed by over three hundred cameras on over thirty separate CCTV systems. While this contrived account is of course a fictional construction, it is a fiction that increasingly mirrors the reality of routine surveillance. In Britain in the late 1990s it is unlikely that any urban dweller, in their role as shopper, worker, commuter, resident or school pupil can avoid being passively or actively monitored by camera surveillance systems. It is now necessary to put substance to the fiction and to document how, across a range of settings the cameras are indeed becoming ubiquitous.

Residential Surveillance: Systems 1, 2 and 3

The surveillance of residential areas is now commonplace particularly on 'council estates' run by local authorities. For example the London Boroughs of Islington, Hackney, Newham and Wandsworth have all installed surveillance cameras on housing estates. And a similar picture can be found on council estates in other major cities, such as Hull, Bristol and Birmingham; according to one Department of the Environment Report: 'It is not unusual to find nine or more cameras in a block all constantly used for surveillance through a monitor network' (DOE 1988).

These concierge systems tend to be limited to monitoring the communal areas of multi-storey blocks, such as entrance, reception areas, lifts and car parks, and the pictures are monitored by local authority employees. However, in both Newcastle and Nottingham, the local council have placed entire residential areas under police surveillance, in both cases in rundown areas with their associated high levels of unemployment, poverty and crime. In Newcastle's West End scheme the first phase saw the introduction of fifteen cameras mounted on 'vandal proof' poles in residential streets monitored from a dedicated police control room. The fifteen cameras in Phase One will be extended to a maximum of ninety-six (see Graham 1998: 95–6). In Nottingham, on the Bestwood Estate, a low-rise development consisting of mainly semi-detached council houses, a four-camera system costing £109,000 is monitored by local authority staff but with a dedicated slave monitor in the local police station (*CCTV Today*, May 1997: 3).

In the main, observation of the images from residential CCTV systems is limited to police or local authority personnel. However, on one local authority housing estate in Doncaster, South Yorkshire, residents can also tune into the CCTV system as a spare channel on tenant's TV sets has been programmed to receive output from the CCTV security cameras monitoring the public areas and car parks of the estate (*Yorkshire Post*, 11 April 1996). In contrast, other local authorities are increasingly utilising covert cameras on estates, in an effort to provide evidence against anti-social tenants. In Hull, for example, private detectives, employed by the local authority secreted a covert camera in a wall panel outside a council flat on the Bransholme Estate. The private detectives filmed more than sixty hours of video footage in an effort to provide evidence that the occupant was dealing in drugs from the premises. The evidence was not being used for the purposes of criminal prosecution, but to be used in eviction proceedings. The court was shown a 76-minute video of edited highlights and the judge ruled that 'viewing the evidence as a whole, I am wholly satisfied that illegal drugs are being sold from this property' and duly granted the council possession of the flat. It would appear that this is the first time a local authority has evicted a tenant without relying on a related criminal conviction (*Hull Daily Mail*, 5 September 1997).

Figure 2. One of the fourteen cameras watching over the town centre of Bridlington, East Yorkshire.

School Surveillance: Systems 5, 7 and 8

In June 1996, as part of the Home Office City Challenge Competition, the government announced funding for over 100 schools to implement CCTV systems. The
grants ranged from £4,000 to Derwendeg Primary School in Caerphilly, Wales,
to £105,000 for Sarah Bonnell School in the London Borough of Newham. In
December 1996, government minister Gillian Shepard, the then Education and
Employment Secretary, announced a £66 million package for school security, which
included provision for the installation of CCTV. For example, government funding
enabled Wolverhampton Grammar School to install sixteen cameras around its site.
During the day the cameras can be monitored by school staff and at night the pictures
are relayed to a central, council run CCTV monitoring station. One innovatory
aspect of this scheme is the provision of an audio link so that 'if an alarm is tripped
. . . a verbal warning can be given to the potential miscreants while they are being
tracked by the cameras.' (*CCTV Today*, September 1997: 45). A number of nursery

schools were also provided with funding under the City Challenge Competition, although others have introduced CCTV on their own initiative. At the Tumble Tots Nursery in mid-Glamorgan, South Wales, for instance, four CCTV cameras have been introduced in each of its four play areas. The original intention was to use the video system to record children in natural play for teaching purposes. However, its role has expanded to include identifying the cause of possible accidents, verifying the identity of people collecting children as well as enhancing the security of the building (*CCTV Today*, July 1995: 33). Schools have also been subjected to covert video surveillance. In 1996 Hull West Crime Prevention Panel announced a scheme in which a mobile covert camera would be deployed to overlook the city's schools playgrounds to provide evidence against, and deter school drug dealing (*Hull Daily Mail*, 3 October 1996).

Road Traffic Surveillance: Systems 4, 6 and 20

Since 1992, speed cameras and red light enforcement cameras have increasingly been deployed on the national road network. By 1994 just over half of all police forces were using speed cameras. In 1996, a survey of ten police forces found they had 102 speed cameras, which were rotated between 700 sites (Hooke et al. 1996). Since 1993 there has been a massive increase in the number of prosecutions. In 1993 there were 6,390, in 1994 20,630, in 1995 36,916 and in 1996 49,560. These cases represent only the tip of the iceberg since they were the ones serious enough to warrant endorsement, disqualification or were contested. The majority of more minor infractions are dealt with by way of a fixed penalty notice which merely involves the payment of a fine and can be dealt with entirely by correspondence. In 1993, evidence from speed cameras resulted in 25,767 fixed penalty notices being issued and paid. In 1994 the figure was 95,510, in 1995, 170,014 and in 1996, 212,000 (Wilkins and Addicot 1998: 13). In addition, in 1996 there were a total of 52,772 prosecutions and fixed penalty notices issued for traffic light offences as a result of automatic camera devices.

In July 1997 the Metropolitan Police, which is responsible for the policing of the whole of the London region with the exception of the square mile of the City, announced it was to introduce an automatic licence plate recognition system in an effort to combat terrorism and violent crime (*Independent*, 22 July 1997). This was prompted by the 'success' of a similar system launched by the City of London police in February of the same year. By integrating digital camera and computer technology, the system is capable of automatically reading vehicle number plates as they pass into the 'Square Mile' of the City of London. The numbers are then stored on computer, and matched against a database of 'suspect' or wanted vehicles. The system is capable of handling 300,000 vehicles an hour (*Sunday Telegraph*, May 4 1997).

Car Park and Petrol Station Surveillance: Systems 9, 11 and 24

Before 1987 there were no local authority-owned car parks covered by CCTV cameras. In 1987 two local authorities introduced CCTV which had increased to only five by 1990. Between 1990 and 1993 this increased from five to twenty-four. (Bulos and Sarno 1994). The uptake has continued. In 1996 for instance, one local authority, Bromley spent £1 million on installing CCTV throughout its town centre including all of its car parks (*CCTV Today*, January 1996). Private sector car parks have also seen a massive investment in CCTV. In 1997, National Car Parks, the largest car park provider in the country, completed phase three of its ongoing investment in CCTV which had seen a major upgrade of CCTV security at 150 sites throughout the country (*CCTV Today*, May 1997).

In 1994 it was revealed that a robbery of 1 million pounds of cash from a Heathrow Airport car park was not filmed by the security cameras because all the car parks cameras were in fact dummies (*Guardian*, 3 April 1994). By early 1995, however, this security lapse had been remedied as the British Airports Authority installed a 100-camera system over their eighteen car parks. The digital system involves a picture of each car, registration number and driver being taken on entry. The information is then stored on a remotely accessible computerised database (*CCTV Today*, March 1996: 10–14).

Video cameras have also been installed by all the major British petrol stations in their forecourt retail outlets in an attempt to deter drive-away thefts, protect their staff from assault and to deter against robbery. While most of these systems are relatively simple, some companies are starting to introduce more sophisticated technology. In 1996 Kuwait Petroleum (Q8) announced it was trialing the introduction of completely 'unmanned' petrol stations and to protect against credit card fraud it was also installing a digitally based video system. The system will 'capture and store on to disk images of users and their registration details, and transmit them in real time. If for example, a card is recognised at the time of use as being stolen through a card hot list recorded images can be transmitted to the police' (*CCTV Today*, March 1996: 3).

Telephone and Cash Machine Surveillance: Systems 13 and 18

Covert video cameras have been installed in cash machines around the country, including twenty belonging to the Alliance and Leicester Building Society. The main use is to eliminate fraud and bitter disputes with customers over 'phantom' withdrawals. The banks and building societies argue that the video cameras will enable them to immediately identify who actually made a withdrawal (*Independent*, 11 October 1992). In July 1994, it was reported that the Nationwide Building Society and Lloyds Bank had also installed covert cameras at their cash machines on a trial basis. According to the report, the location of the Nationwide's cameras was being kept secret 'but if the pilot schemes are successful they could eventually become standard equipment' (*Observer*, 17 July 1994).

In September 1996 it was revealed that the London Fire and Civil Defence Authority had requested that British Telecom fit miniature covert cameras in public telephone boxes in an effort to identify hoax callers. It would appear that BT routinely use such technology as a 'Spokesman for BT, which operates 13,400 public pay phones nationwide said that any application from the emergency services would be considered on its merits' (*Islington Gazette*, 26 September 1996).

Railway Surveillance: Systems: 10, 14, 22 and 28

Limited camera surveillance has been operating on the rail and tube network for over thirty years but the 1990s have seen moves towards blanket coverage. During 1996–7 Railtrack embarked on a major security initiative with the installation of over 1,800 cameras at sixteen of the Central London mainline stations. The cost of the initiative was in excess of £10 million. In January 1998 it announced a £1 billion station regeneration programme, £40 million of which is to be spent on installing CCTV and better lighting at 800 stations (*CCTV Today*, September 1997; January 1998). British Rail has been operating CCTV cameras to monitor level crossings for the last thirty years and they are now to be found at all major road crossings.

Similarly, in the 1990s the London underground system embarked on a programme to install CCTV across its 250-station network. By March 1996 one company, Sony, had alone installed 5,000 cameras (*CCTV Today*, March 1996: 35). On the Central Line which has 55 km of track, 34 stations and carries 166 million passengers a year, 500 CCTV cameras have been installed and are monitored by one central control room. However, the most important innovation has been the introduction of eighty-five one-man operated trains installed with a 'track to train CCTV system'. The system allows the driver to receive pictures of the platform at each station as it is approached and on arrival to see pictures of the side of the train to monitor the doors and passenger safety (*CCTV Today*, November 1995).

Retail and Commercial Surveillance: Systems 12, 15, 16 and 19

Commercial companies are increasingly using CCTV to protect office premises and as part of integrated access control systems. In 1996 the value of sales of CCTV equipment to the commercial sector stood at £34.7 million or about 30 per cent of the total CCTV equipment market. The retail sector accounted for £38.2 million or 38 per cent of the total. Although it is difficult to estimate the extent of CCTV in small retail and commercial concerns, first-hand observation suggests that many newsagents, corner shops, and smaller high street concerns operate

Figure 3. A poster on the London Underground

camera surveillance. This observation is supported by Hearnden's survey of the use of CCTV by small businesses. His survey only required a response from those who used CCTV and the response rate suggests a minimum of 27 per cent of small business utilised CCTV in some way or another (Hearnden: 1996).

For the major retailers, CCTV surveillance is near ubiquitous. Whether in the high street, town centre or out-of-town shopping malls, retailers now operate highly visible internal CCTV systems to deter against shoplifting, staff assault, robbery and to monitor the workforce, both to prevent staff theft and to provide managerial information (McCahill and Norris 1999). For instance, the 'big five' supermarkets Argyll (Safeway and others), Asda, Sainsbury, Gateway and Tesco with 50 per cent of the market share for food and convenience good sales, have invested heavily in CCTV technology (Beck and Willis 1995: 10). The major out-of-town shopping parks, such as the Gateshead Metro Centre, Sheffield's Meadow Hall development and Dudley's Merry Hill, which attract millions of shoppers annually, have invested heavily in visual surveillance. The Metro Centre, which attracted 160,000 people each day in the 1994 Christmas period, has a CCTV system which cost £500,000 to install, consists of seventy-three cameras and has a security budget which runs to £1 million pounds each year (Beck and Willis 1995: 12; Graham 1998).

Marks and Spencer are one of the leading retailers who have committed themselves to a major investment in CCTV technology. One company alone, Westinghouse, has installed CCTV systems in more than 130 of their stores. The

35-camera system in their new store in Milton Keynes was estimated to have cost £135,000. (*CCTV Today*, September 1995: 46) and in the same year it was reported to be spending the majority of its £30 million security budget on improving its CCTV systems (*Guardian* On-line, 21 September 1995: 4). Some stores have integrated their camera systems with the Electronic Point of Sale systems (EPoS) so when a person carries out a transaction between £42 and £50 (the value of goods most often purchased by people using stolen cheque cards) a camera automatically zooms in and takes a clear picture of their face (*Guardian*, 13 May 1993: G2 p. 2).

This integration of CCTV with EPoS systems was also highlighted in a Spar supermarket which installed a Sensormatic EPoS/EM system. The system works in conjunction with CCTV to record and highlight all suspicious till events known to provide staff with the opportunity for theft. The system can be programmed to highlight up to nine 'exceptions' including voids, no sales, refunds, very low value sales, and, with fraud in mind, all cheque tenders and card transactions. Any unusual till event automatically triggers real time recording of the till and overlays the video pictures with a (digital) copy of the till roll allowing store managers to see each individual item being purchased and the corresponding amount being rung by the cashier (*CCTV Today*, March 1996: 31).

These retail and commercial systems are being augmented with covert cameras used either on their own or in conjunction with overt cameras. In one small-scale survey of retail and industrial security managers, a quarter admitted to utilising covert camera devices in their workplaces (McCahill and Norris 1999). In 1996 David Fletcher, the chief executive of the British Security Industry Association, estimated that employers were spending £12 million a year on covert camera equipment to monitor their staff. Examples of covert surveillance that have come to light include a police officer who was sacked after being filmed stealing £4 from a 'fines' jar; a Post Office worker caught stealing cash in Darlington; a Parcel Force employee who was sacked after a CCTV camera filmed him playing frisbee during working hours; UCI cinemas in Poole in Dorset, who installed a hidden camera in the staff changing rooms after a spate of thefts and vandalism (*Sunday Times*, 15 December 1996; see also *CCTV Today*, March, May, July 1997).

Hospital Surveillance: System 21

In 1993, a Department of Health working party was set up to examine issues in hospital security after a number of high-profile cases involving abduction of newborn infants from maternity units and assaults on staff and patients (*Guardian*, 18 July 1994). Among other measures, the report recommended greater use of CCTV and this is increasingly happening. Five schemes were funded as part of the 1996 and 1997 City Challenge Competition but Hospital Trusts are also financing systems themselves. For instance, the Royal Hull Hospital, and the Hull Maternity

Hospital, the Derbyshire Royal Infirmary, and Lewisham Hospital in South-East London between 1995 and 1997 all installed new systems. In Lewisham Hospital the trust were reported to be going to spend £500,000 over a three-year period phasing in a CCTV and access control system involving the use of more than 60 cameras (*CCTV Today*, March 1997).

Football Stadia Surveillance: System 22

At Stamford Bridge, Thomas and his visitors would have been watched by a total of sixty-one cameras which monitor the 44,000 all-seater stadium (*CCTV Today*, January 1998). They would have also been filmed if they had gone to any other professional football ground in the country. During the 1980s and 1990s the Football Trust, a charity funded by the 'spot-the-ball-competition', financed the installation of CCTV systems throughout British football clubs. The Trust also financed police forces to purchase mobile camera equipment which could be used both in and outside the grounds (see Armstrong and Guilianotti 1998).

The policing of football matches has seen the coupling of CCTV with computer technology in an effort to identify suspected hooligans and those subject to banning orders. At Manchester City's Maine Road ground, the police have developed a 'Football Intelligence System'. This consists of a laptop computer running a 'windows database'. The system collates information and photographic records of suspects and offenders associated with football violence. From a set of personal descriptors entered by the operator, the system will display the pictures of the twelve most likely suspects from a database of 150 'known' offenders. Details can be cross-referenced with entries relating to previous convictions, intelligence information, 'hooligan' associates, and 'gang membership'. Although the system does not provide an automatic recognition system it does allow for the easy storage and retrieval of photographic images which can then be compared with the pictures from the CCTV system. The other advantage of digitalisation is that it allows the rapid transfer of pictures in electronic form along telephone lines. This was exploited by the National Criminal Intelligence Service (NCIS) who have a digital database of 6,000 suspected football hooligans. In the run-up to the 1996 European football championship, the NCIS database was made available to all the participating football grounds through the use of 'photophones' enabling digitalised photographs to be transmitted from one central location to a remote terminal in each stadium (*Guardian*, 10 February 1996).

Police Surveillance: Systems 27 and 29

In an effort to deter kerb crawlers, police in Streatham in South London have started to film offenders as they cruise the streets in a residential Red Light District. After capturing the miscreants on film, the police speak to suspects, take their names and addresses and explain that they will be sent letters and photographs to their homes. 'It is a tactic on our part and should act as a deterrent,' said Sergeant Maurice Morewood of the local vice unit (*Guardian*, 11 June 1996). In 1997 Humberside Police announced they too were to start deploying hand-held video cameras in the Red Light District although they were not planning to dispatch photographs to offender's homes (*Hull Daily Mail*, 10 December 1997).

Earlier in the year, Humberside Police reported that they were issuing hand-held video camcorders to some officers in an effort to tackle youth crime. The cameras would be used to take pictures of youths committing 'small-scale nuisance crimes' on a number of problem estates around the city and, rather than arresting and charging the youths, the videos would be shown to the parents who would thus be enlightened as to their child's behaviour and could take the appropriate action (*Hull Daily Mail*, 10 May 1997).

A similar tactic is also being employed by Scarborough Police who stated that they planned to use footage from their town centre surveillance system of what the local newspaper described as 'teenage tearaways'. The paper continued:

> Youngsters who get drunk and abuse passers-by will be painstakingly recorded on Scarborough's crime fighting surveillance cameras. Police also plan to take the names and addresses of any child who joins a big gang whether they misbehave or not. Their parents will receive a letter telling them their child was among a group found in a known area of gang trouble ... Inspector Malcolm Smith said that young people could be recorded on camera for drunkenness, fooling about, congregating in extremely large groups, and intimidating passerbys and the elderly. If offences were committed, the youngsters would face prosecution. Parents would be offered a chance to see the video evidence.' (*Yorkshire Post*, 5 March 1996).

Town Centre Systems and the Rush to Ubiquity

Town Centres and Street Systems 17 and 25

In 1960, the year Thomas Kearns was born, there were, as far as we can ascertain, no CCTV systems operating in public or semi-public space in Britain. The first documented use of CCTV occurred in 1961 when London Transport installed a camera at one of its stations, although this appears to have been a limited operation. It was not until 1967, when Photoscan became the first commercial company to market CCTV as a means of deterring and apprehending shoplifters in the retail sector, that CCTV cameras started to become a routine feature of shops and stores.

For the next twenty years it was the application of CCTV in the private retail sector which was to dominate, as CCTV became a routine feature in the corner

Figure 4. A typical sign now found in many supermarkets warning customers of the CCTV surveillance – they are often displayed near high value goods such as meat and alcohol.

shop, supermarket and department store (Beck and Willis 1995). Thus, while shoppers were often under the ever-present gaze of the camera, this was in the private space of the commercial store. The blanket surveillance of citizens in fully public spaces was not yet on the agenda, and what occurred in the 1970s and early 1980s was the gradual extension of CCTV from private to fully public space.

The first permanent and systematic use of CCTV outside the private retail sector came in 1975. In an effort to combat robbery and assaults on staff, London Transport introduced CCTV cameras in the semi-public space of the stations on the Northern Line of the London Underground and over the next decade, other, small-scale, systems were introduced on the eastern end of the Central Line and at Oxford Circus. (Webb and Laycock 1992). On the roads, it was congestion rather than crime that gave the initial impetus to the deployment of cameras and, by 1974, in an attempt to speed the flow of traffic on London's streets, 145 cameras were deployed to monitor the major arterial roads of the capital under its Central Integrated Traffic Control system (Manwaring-White, 1983: 91).

The police were not slow to realise that a system introduced for one purpose could be used for another and the facility existed to switch the system to the operations room at Scotland Yard used to monitor public order incidents and demonstrations (BSSRS 1985: 41–2). It was also public order policing which provided the rationale for a further extension in the public domain of central London.

Figure 5. One of the fifteen cameras watching over the town centre of Cottingham, East Yorkshire.

The eight cameras of the permanently installed Lynx system were used to provide a surveillance capacity on the major rallying points for public protest. Cameras were used extensively to film pickets during the miners strike of 1984–5 (Coulter et al. 1985) and football supporters became targets for surveillance, not just in the ground but on their way to a match from a mobile surveillance facility, 'the Hoolivan', which could be deployed outside the grounds (Davies 1996: 186). But this extension into public space was still limited to the monitoring of traffic flow and specific events thought likely to cause disorder and, by implication, of people deemed to be marginal – the demonstrator, the picket and the football hooligan.

It was only in 1985 that the permanent surveillance of public space and of all those who ventured into it became a reality with the opening of a system, covering the promenade of a rather gentile English seaside town – Bournemouth. By the end of the decade there were, as far as we are aware, only a handful of public systems covering town centre city streets in Bournemouth King's Lynn, Coventry, Wolverhampton and Plymouth (see also Bulos and Sarno 1994). However, as was revealed in a 'Digest of CCTV Schemes', published by the Home Office Crime Prevention Centre, CCTV systems were starting to make a limited impact in a whole range of settings. The digest listed 123 systems covering traffic and transport, cycle paths, footbridges, industrial estates, shopping centre systems as well as city centres (Home Office 1990). In 1990 what existed was a series of local, piecemeal,

Figure 6. A street sign in Cottingham, East Yorkshire, alerting the public to the CCTV system – these signs are also displayed prominently in shops and local businesses.

schemes whose impact was limited and, although the idea of CCTV was clearly gaining ground, the mass surveillance of the citizenry was still some way off. By the late 1990s however, CCTV and the routine surveillance of the public was to become the crime prevention initiative of the century. Indeed as Goodwin et al. (1998: 3) have observed: 'The extent of Home Office backing for and reliance on CCTV is indicated by the fact that by 1995 78 per cent of the Home Office budget for Crime Prevention was being used to fund schemes to put CCTV in public places.'

The result of this backing has been the exponential growth of town centre CCTV systems between 1990 and 1998. In 1994 the handful of schemes had increased to seventy-nine (Fyfe and Bannister 1996) and by 1996 Norris et al. could report that all cities (except Leeds) with a population in excess of 500,000 boasted city centre schemes. Between 1994 and 1998, there was a fivefold increase in town centre schemes. Goodwin et al's survey based on Home Office, police and local govern-ment data calculated in January 1998 states there 'were at least 440 town centre schemes in operation for which funding had been allocated . . . [and in] . . . 1994 the schemes were mainly restricted to larger urban areas, but by 1998 CCTV had spread to encompass small and medium sized towns' (1998: 3).

Despite this massive increase, there are still, of course, many areas, whether they be suburban side streets, smaller town centres, railway stations, or shops and offices where the gaze of the cameras has not yet reached. However, the demand for CCTV systems does not look likely to significantly decline in the near future and while the growth rate may tail off, it would appear that the industry is still confident of burgeoning sales. For instance, the market analysts MSI reported that the growth of the CCTV equipment market was 17 per cent in 1996, reaching a total of £115.6 million at end user prices. The growth was expected to be 13 per cent in 1997 and, although double figure growth rates were not predicted for the millennium, there were still 'plenty of opportunities for growth' (Evans 1998). The one key site of this growth was identified by another market analyst, Wesbrey Holdings. At the end of 1995 they reported that, although major city centres and shopping malls were now well served by CCTV, there was a 'dramatic emergent' market with an estimated 'immediate demand of £100m+' consisting of: '400–500 shopping precincts, 1500 towns large enough for town centre CCTV to be actively considered, plus 300 small population centres where systems are probably worth considering. In the other 20,000 urban and rural population centres, advances in time-lapse technology may make "village" systems viable' (*CCTV Today*, September 1995: 9).

As we have demonstrated, the imaginary account of Thomas Kearns' day is supported by the reality. The pervasiveness of the cameras in public and semi-public spaces is approaching ubiquity. Having considered the rapidity of growth of CCTV, in the next section we want to examine two additional features of CCTV systems: their diversity and their mutability.

Formal Diversity

While the growth of CCTV systems has been dramatic and saturation coverage is approaching, it is important to recognise that CCTV is not a unitary phenomenon. True, all systems utilise cameras and recording devices, but beyond this there is a huge diversity between systems which vary in regard to a number of significant dimensions: scope and technological sophistication, ownership, organisation and control, all of which can have an influence on the impact of CCTV in a locale.

Scope and Technological Sophistication

Systems vary in terms of the number of cameras, and camera functionality. Thus, for example, Driffield, a small market town in East Yorkshire with a population of 10,000 has 14 cameras, Glasgow city centre serving a population of three-quarters of a million people has 32 cameras whilst Northampton with a population of 180,000, has 112 cameras and Sheffield has 200 cameras for a population of around half a million. Similarly, some systems rely predominately on fixed camera positions, such as Driffield, making the active tracking of people by operators difficult. Northampton, on the other hand, has twenty-five fully functional Pan Tilt and Zoom

Figure 7. One of many similar posters found in shops and commercial premises throughout the town centre of Driffield, East Yorkshire.

cameras which can be controlled by operators to target and track individuals as they move around the town centre. The systems also vary in their recording capacity: some record continuously, other utilise time-lapse recording. As time-lapse recording reduces the amount of information captured on tape, it considerably reduces operational costs since tapes do not have to be changed so frequently. For instance, by recording at the rate of only one frame a second, a standard three-hour video cassette can capture seventy-two hours of images (Constant and Turnball 1994: 90).

However, the most significant technological variation is between systems that rely solely on human monitoring and those that are exploiting the new digital technologies to couple the cameras to computers. Intelligent scene monitoring and automatic number plate recognition are increasingly augmenting and replacing human monitoring. As we have seen in car parks, the City of London and the retail sector such systems are considerably expanding the surveillance gaze. Put simply, to know if a particular car had entered the town centre of Northampton during a 24 hour period, for instance would require reviewing the output of around ten cameras and take over 240 hours. In the City of London, it is potentially possible to find the answer out in less than one minute as it merely requires a computer search of the database records which store the licence plate details of all cars which have been automatically read and logged by the digital camera system.

Organisation

One of the most important variations is the extent to which the cameras are monitored. Some systems, such as in Driffield or the West Somerset scheme have no routine live monitoring and the tapes are only reviewed if an incident comes to light by other means. Other systems are monitored part-time; for instance the twenty-four camera systems in Lichfield is only monitored for sixteen hours a day. In yet other systems, such as Solihull or Cirencester, monitoring is carried out during the day by dedicated operatives and then the systems are handed over to the police to act as 'caretakers' overnight. Finally, monitoring may be permanent and continuous with between one and three operatives watching the cameras twenty-four hours a day as happens in the majority of large city centre sites such as Liverpool, Newcastle and Glasgow.

It is not just with regard to the length of time for which systems are actively monitored that there is variation but in who does the monitoring. This can range between police officers (City of London), police civilian staff (Tamworth), special constables (Ilkeston), private security personnel (Stratford), local authority personnel (Coventry) or those employed by a trust specially set up for the purposes of operating the CCTV system as in the case of Glasgow's City Watch. The location of the control rooms also varies. Some are housed in police stations, and integrated with the command control and dispatch systems, as in Glasgow while other systems are monitored from control rooms located in local authority town halls or civic centres (Portsmouth) and others still in purpose-built stand-alone local authority premises (Peckham).

Ownership and Control

The location of the control room also tends to reflect differences in who owns and controls the systems. For instance, Newcastle's system is wholly owned, operated and run by the local police force, whereas the Windsor and Maidenhead scheme is wholly controlled by the Local Authority, although the police have a dedicated 'slave' monitor which allows officers to view images from the system in the police station. However, under such arrangements, if they want to take control of the system, a formal request must be lodged with the system operators who will continue to monitor the systems and log events as they are seen. In other areas such as

Warrington and Birmingham the CCTV system is run by a local trust specially constituted for the purposes of installing and operating the system.

Impact

The formal diversity in systems makes generalisations about the impact of CCTV a dangerous business. One cannot simply read off the likely effect and impact that CCTV will have by reference to the installation of cameras and video recorders. For instance, where systems are not monitored, they cannot be used to determine police deployment practices in judging the strength of responses to a reported incident. Even where systems are monitored on a permanent basis, if this is carried out by private security personnel, in a remote site distanced from the police operational control room, the influence on deployment will be mediated by the linkages both formal and informal between the two systems. Similarly, the impact on arrest may vary considerably depending on monitoring procedures. Where the cameras are permanently monitored from a police control room it can be used to direct officers to a range of incidents of low-level disorder which would not have otherwise come to the notice of the dispatcher. Where systems are monitored by private or local authority operatives, whether such incidents will be seen to warrant alerting the police will be a matter of local and individual variation.

Expandable Mutability

If diversity characterises the formal organisation of CCTV systems, mutability characterises its use. This can take three primary forms: intra-organisational mutability, extra-organisational mutability and subjective mutability.

Intra-organisational mutability refers to systems which were installed for one purpose finding quite different roles. Thus, in the Tiny Tots nursery, mentioned above, the system was first installed as a pedagogic device to help students unobtrusively observe children's interactions. However, over time it also became used as a means of identifying health and safety risks, supervising access and monitoring building security (*CCTV Today*, July 1995: 33). In the retail sector, systems installed for the purposes of preventing and detecting shoplifting become simultaneously, in the hands of supervisors, a general managerial tool for monitoring workers performance (see McCahill and Norris 1999). And public systems introduced to provide a deterrent to criminal behaviour become managerial tools for the police to manage demand. In Canada, where video cameras are now routinely fitted to police patrol vehicles, Ericson and Haggerty found: 'The patrol officers we studied believed that the video cameras would serve many purposes. One interviewee remarked that the devices would be useful for "Anything that your imagination could come up with".' (Ericson and Haggerty 1997: 138).

While formal intra-organisational uses expand and mutate, their usage also changes in line with the subjective intent of the observer. Thus a CCTV system whose formal gaze is justified in terms of crime prevention can become a voyeuristic gaze for the amusement of the operative. The most notorious example of the subjective mutation occurred when the late Princess Diana was filmed by the security cameras of the Harvey Nicholls department store. A tape was later discovered in a desk drawer belonging to the head of security, which included 'lingering close-ups' of the Princess. As one store official reported to the *London Evening Standard*: 'Our cameras are designed to go in close to observe in detail shoplifters and other suspicious characters. In this case the person operating the camera zoomed in to get close ups of her cleavage and thighs. He lingered for minutes on her most appealing features' (3 January 1996).

This subjective dimension is also apparent in extra-organisational mutation. Video footage, taken by the police for the purposes of prosecuting dangerous and reckless drivers, can be sold to commercial television and video companies to feature in light entertainment programmes such as 'Police Camera Action' or the video 'Police Stop'. Here the intentions of the progenitors of the original footage are superceded as its use value mutates, first as a means of generating revenue for the police organisation, second as a means of generating profits for private companies and finally as a means of entertainment for the general public.

We have charted the contemporary reality of CCTV surveillance in Britain and hopefully demonstrated that the ubiquity of the cameras does, indeed, warrant us arguing that in Britain, at the brink of the millennium, we are approaching the maximum surveillance society. However, while we are all increasingly under the camera's gaze what this means in practice is that its implications for social control are dependent not so much on the cameras, but on their integration with other technologies, and the organisational environment in which they operate. These themes are explored in detail in part two of the book where we document the day-to-day reality of mass surveillance in three contrasting systems. But before we look at *how* mass surveillance operates we want to examine the way the media has represented CCTV and how this may have impacted on public perception. In popular, media and political discourse there has been one, and really only one, central theme which both explains and justifies the rise of CCTV surveillance – it works. In the words of Michael Howard, the former Home Secretary, 'CCTV is a wonderful technological supplement to the police . . . CCTV spots crimes, identifies law breakers and helps convict the guilty . . . CCTV is a real asset to Communities: a great deterrent to crime and a huge reassurance to the public' (*CCTV Today*, May 1995). It is these claims and how they have been played out in the media which forms the focus of the next chapter.

—4—

The Selling of CCTV: Political and Media Discourses

Public Opinion and CCTV

The introduction of CCTV would appear to enjoy widespread public support. As Ditton has noted, on the basis of surveys conducted by those unskilled in the art of social research, the claim of '"90% in favour" has become the mantra of populist proponents of town centre CCTV' (Ditton 1998: 221). However, while professionally conducted surveys have tended to find lower levels of support, they have only been marginally lower. The earliest public attitude survey, published in 1992, found that in the three sites surveyed, between 85 and 92 per cent would welcome the installation of CCTV in their area. (Honess and Charman: 1992). In Brighton and Sutton, 86 and 85 per cent of those surveyed respectively welcomed the presence of the cameras. (Squires and Measor 1997; Mahalingham 1996). In Cambridge, 64 per cent of those surveyed thought CCTV to be a 'good' or 'very good' idea (Bennett and Gelsthorpe 1996) and, in Glasgow in January 1994, Ditton found 69 per cent of people interviewed 'didn't mind' being watched by CCTV (Ditton 1998: 222).

It is always difficult to account for the variation in findings between different studies. They may indeed reflect real local difference between areas in the amount of support for CCTV or they may reflect general shifts in attitudes over time. More importantly, the differing levels of support may not actually reflect 'real' differences but be methodological artifacts caused by the effects of question wording, question order, or sampling strategies. It is the sampling strategies which are most suspect in the amateur surveys castigated by Ditton. For instance, French claimed 90 per cent support in favour of CCTV being installed in Harlow based on a 1,000 self-completion questionnaire randomly delivered to homes in Harlow. Media support ensured an above-average response rate of 48 per cent. The problem of targeting households and not individuals is there is no control as to who actually fills the questionnaire in, although one expects that it will have an immediate bias towards the older members of the household. Moreover, a 52 per cent non-response rate means that, if those who were less supportive to CCTV did not fill the questionnaire in, then there would be a significant bias for an 'in favour' response.

Many of the locally conducted surveys suffer from the similar methodological weakness, especially in using quota samples which are only conducted on daytime and early evening populations and thus skewing the sample to be unrepresentative of those who use a town centre. In Honess and Charman's study, their 85–92 per cent 'in favour' appears to be derived from a quota sample of daytime town centre users (they are not totally explicit on this point). In contrast, Ditton's 69 per cent 'in favour' involved the random stopping of pedestrians between the hours of 8.00 a.m. and 12 midnight. The result was a sample that was more representative of all town centre users and, because it was conducted at night, it was more youthful and more male.

It is not just sampling strategies that has lead to differences in the estimates of public acceptability. Of particular importance is question context which gives rise to what Ditton terms 'skewed contextualising'. In both Squires' and Honess and Charman's studies, the respondents were first asked about their perceptions of the incidence of crime, whether they or members of their families had been victims of crime and how fearful they were of going out after dark. Having been guided to a frame of reference which is dominated by 'fear of crime' is it surprising that they then responded positively to a measure that is specifically supposed to address those concerns?

Ditton has analysed the phenomenon of 'skewed contextualising' in a study directly aimed at finding out the extent to which the level of public acceptability was influenced by the context in which the questions were asked. One group was first asked three questions in a crime control frame of reference, another group three questions in a civil liberties frame of reference, before both groups were asked: are you 'in favour or against closed circuit television cameras video taping people's movements in this street?' A final group was asked only the last question with no contextualising questions at all. The results demonstrate that the level of public support is dramatically influenced by the question context, and suggests that previous studies may have been considerably overestimating public support as a result of an unintentional methodological bias. The crime control group was 91 per cent in favour, the neutral group 71 per cent in favour and the civil liberties group only 56 per cent in favour. As Ditton goes on to argue, if one applies this to the results of the Glasgow Development Agency survey based on a broadly representative sample of the city's population, by taking away the 20 per cent points 'caused' by the skewed contextualising 'the acceptability rate of 95 per cent should be reduced to a more plausible 75 per cent'. For Ditton's 1994 survey (yes, he made the same 'mistake' too!), the percentage of the population in favour of CCTV would have been reduced from over two, thirds (69%) to under half (49%). So, rather than a majority in favour of CCTV there would actually have been a majority, albeit a small majority, against CCTV (Ditton 1998: 227).

Bennett and Gelsthorpe's study also suggests that civil liberty concerns are much more significant than often alluded to, with one-third of respondents (28.9%) stating that they were worried about the civil liberties implications of the introduction of CCTV. However these concerns do not necessarily translate into opposition to CCTV:

> the majority of people who said that they were worried about CCTV did not believe that CCTV was a bad idea. In other words, public concerns about civil rights issues were not strong enough to make them believe that CCTV should not be installed. Hence, these findings suggest that people were either willing to offset their concerns about CCTV for the additional safety that it brought to their lives or their concerns about civil liberties were simply not strong enough to influence their decision-making either way. (1996: 87)

It is impossible to know the 'true' level of public support for CCTV, however, it would appear that measured by questionnaire items on attitude surveys, general public support stands at between two-thirds and three-quarters of those surveyed, although it may fall to below a half of those actually using city centre space. This has important political ramifications. The strength of public support has been used as one of the main selling points and has been central to government claims as to the legitimacy of CCTV. As the Home Office booklet promoting CCTV *Looking Out for You* declared:

> There is no evidence that the public regard CCTV as a threat to civil liberties. Research conducted for the Home Office in 1992 showed that very few people – 6% of respondents – were worried about the presence of CCTV cameras. More recently a poll in Glasgow showed that 95% of respondents were in favour of CCTV and 7% thought that it infringed their civil rights. (Home Office 1994: 9)

It is, of course, easy to dismiss civil liberty concerns as marginal if only one in twenty people expresses them. Whereas if a quarter, or a third, or even a half express them CCTV becomes an area of more substantial contestation. However, this is to fetishize the results of public opinion surveys and to believe them to reflect the opinions of autonomous and knowledgeable individuals. As Gilliom has noted, this is the assumption of classical democratic theorists who hold that people's opinion's emerge from autonomous experience, stable values and reasoned analysis. In contrast, he argues, drawing on the work of Gramsci:

> perceptions and opinions are formed through the consumption of mass media news and political imagery. The main thrust of this orientation is that we should think of 'the "spontaneous" consent given by the great masses' as not being all that spontaneous . . . Rather, consent to impositions of adverse conditions may be the result of actions taken by elites and systematic 'biases' that favour their interests. (Gilliom 1994:10)

The strength of this view is that it problematises how people come to hold their opinions. Drawing on the concept of hegemony it directs our attention to the way in which power is exercised not just through the coercive apparatus of the State, but through the ideological operation of hegemony and it invites us to question why, in areas of apparent contestation, conflict fails to materialise. We do not want to argue that support for CCTV is a chimera, an illusion fabricated by the manufacture of false consciousness but we do want to argue that public opinion towards CCTV is shaped by the messages it receives about CCTV. How else could the public have an opinion about it? For what people 'know' about CCTV is mediated and largely determined by media representations and political discourses.

The Political Discourse: CCTV Works

> Closed-circuit cameras have proved they can work, so we need more of them where crime is high. (The Prime Minister, John Major, cited in the *Independent*, 27 February 1994)

> Closed circuit television surveillance cameras are becoming a regular feature in an increasing number of towns and cities in response to public demand . . . I am absolutely convinced that CCTV has a major part to play in helping to detect, and reduce crimes and to convict criminals. (The Home Secretary, Michael Howard 1994: 3)

Contrary to the assertions of the Prime Minister and the convictions of the Home Secretary, in 1994 there was no reliable evidence on which to base judgments as to the effectiveness of CCTV. CCTV was introduced in town centres and the government funded the expansion prior to conducting any systematic evaluation of its effectiveness in reducing crime in such locations. What evidence did exist prior to 1994 came from small-scale evaluations on systems in car parks (Poyner, 1992); buses (Poyner 1988); housing estates (Musheno et al. 1979); football stadia (Hancox and Morgan 1975), and the London Underground (Burrows, 1979). As Short and Ditton note, the results of these independent and competently conducted evaluations were 'fairly contradictory regarding the effectiveness of CCTV as a crime prevention method' (Short and Ditton 1995: 11), with some initiatives showing no effect (Musheno et al. 1979) others suggesting high levels of displacement, rather than an overall reduction (Burrows 1979) and others showing clear reductions (Poyner 1988 and 1992).

However, the evidence used by politicians and those wanting to garner support for the introduction of CCTV was not that of the professional and independent evaluator but from 'post hoc shoestring efforts by the untrained and self interested practitioner' (Pawson and Tilley 1994). In particular, fuelled by endorsements from Home Office Ministers, dramatic success stories from the towns which had adopted

CCTV in the early 1990s quickly became part of the mythology of the success of CCTV. Kings Lynn had experienced a 97 per cent reduction in car crime, in Newcastle hundreds of arrests were attributed to CCTV and in Airdrie a 95 per cent reduction in car crime was claimed.

These claims were eagerly reproduced in the promotional literature of companies selling CCTV products, local councils trying to raise the funding to install systems and publicity material to garner support for new systems. And, of course, they were to be transmitted more widely by television and newspapers keen to report on this 'wonderful new' technology.

As Tilley has argued, anyone trying to claim a causal connection between the introduction of CCTV and level of crime would need to be sensitive to the following: pseudo-random fluctuations in crime rates; regression to the mean; floor effects; changes in background crime rates; other changes in the area covered by CCTV; changes in patterns of crime reporting and recording of crime; displacement; and diffusion of benefits (Tilley 1998: 142–3). For the purposes of evaluation, relying on the raw figures, with no indication as to whether crime had also been falling across the district or region as a whole, whether crime was being displaced to other areas, or what was the normal month on month fluctuation for the crime figures, gave results that were simply meaningless.

For example, one set of figures frequently quoted in support of CCTV came from Airdrie after Chief Inspector Graham Pearson told a London press conference that total crime had been reduced by 74 per cent (*Guardian*, 16 April 1993: 6) and later claimed that detection rates had almost trebled (*Independent*, 6 July 1994: 19). These figures gained extensive media coverage and were cited by the Home Secretary (*Guardian*, 19 October 1994), the Audit Commission (1993), and local councils as providing the evidence to justify the introduction of CCTV.

The independent evaluation of Airdrie when it was published two, years later told a different story. While CCTV had indeed reduced crime, it was only by 21 per cent (a third of the amount claimed by the Chief Inspector) and, rather than a tripling of the clear-up rate it had increased by only one-sixth (Short and Ditton, 1996). Even without media and public relations inflation, in crime prevention terms these figures are impressive, especially as there was no evidence of displacement. The findings of other properly conducted independent evaluations of major town centre schemes are more equivocal. The Home Office case study of the Newcastle system provides the clearest support for the Airdrie findings, confirming police claims of a 19 per cent fall in crime, although the 'number of public disorder offences remained unchanged' and 'the effect of the cameras on some offences began to fade after a period of time' (Brown 1995: 26).

In Brighton, Squires and Measors found only a 10 per cent reduction overall and, despite claims that CCTV was helping to 'make the county one of the safest in Britain' (*CCTV Today*, September 1995: 48), violent crime actually increased by 1 per cent and there was evidence that crime was being displaced to the surrounding area (Squires and Measor 1996). In Doncaster, the overall effect of introducing CCTV was a reduction in recorded crime of 6 per cent and there was strong evidence of displacement with outlying townships experiencing a 31 per cent increase in recorded crime after the cameras were introduced in the town centre (Skinns 1997: 30–5).

The Home Office evaluation of Birmingham's City Centre system found there was a 'failure of the camera system to reduce directly overall crime levels' in the city centre. Indeed, robberies and theft from the person actually increased as did theft from vehicles and there was strong evidence of displacement to the surrounding areas (Brown 1995: 34–43). In Sutton, there was no evidence that CCTV led to a reduction in crime rates for, while there was a 13 per cent reduction in recorded crime in the areas under surveillance, crime reduced by 29 per cent in the borough as a whole. CCTV did little to reduce assaults and there was strong evidence of displacement of theft (not including shoplifting) from the streets under surveillance to inside commercial premises (Sarno 1996).

Despite the weight of evidence that CCTV was not the silver bullet that had been promised, the Home Office's enthusiasm and ministerial support, continued unabated with further Home Office City Challenge Competitions announced in 1996 and 1997. Even though the Home Office's own commissioned research raised serious doubts about the effectiveness of CCTV, and these were known early in 1995, negative findings were simply swept under the carpet and the script remained the same:

> CCTV catches criminals. It spots crimes, identifies lawbreakers and helps convict the guilty. The spread of this technology means that more town centres, shopping precincts, business centres and car parks around the country will become no-go areas for the criminal . . . CCTV is a wonderful technological supplement to the police. They do not replace police officers but boost their effectiveness. One police officer in Liverpool likens the 20-camera town centre scheme as having 20 Officers on Duty 24 hours a day, constantly taking notes. In Newcastle alone over 500 people have been arrested as a direct result of the scheme and only three have pleaded not guilty to offences recorded by the cameras. CCTV is a real asset to communities: a great deterrent to crime and a huge reassurance for the public. (Michael Howard cited in *CCTV Today*, May 1995)

In December 1995, the Home Office published their only review of effectiveness to date, *CCTV in Town Centres: Three Case Studies*, which looked at the impact of CCTV in King's Lynn, Newcastle and Birmingham (Brown 1995). This was not, it should be noted, a full-scale, independent or thorough evaluation. It only had a budget of £10,000 (*CCTV Today*, July 1995: 6) and did not engage in primary data collection. Rather it utilised 'pre-existing data that already existed within the participating police forces and local authorities' (Brown 1995: 10). Significantly, it was also to draw on the findings of research commissioned by the Home Office's Police Research Group, at a cost of £20,536 from Honess and Charman of Michael and Associates, into the effectiveness of CCTV in Birmingham City Centre. The findings of this study were not good news to those who believed CCTV to be the silver bullet of crime control. It found CCTV had little impact on the crimes that most concern the public. Robbery and theft from the person continued to rise and there was no significant change in the rates for wounding and assault (Brown 1995: 34–6). Moreover, there was evidence of 'some displacement of offending into thefts from vehicles since the installation of the cameras', and this was even more marked for robbery:

> Prior to the installation of cameras in January 1991, the changes in the rates for robbery and theft from the person for all zones . . . were similar. Since the installation of the cameras, the incidence of these types of offences in areas surrounding Zone A (where the cameras are situated) has increased sharply, and by the end of the study period, the number of offences per month is over three times as high as when the cameras were installed. (Brown 1995: 35)

The Birmingham study was never published in its own right, even though a full report was submitted to the Home Office in early 1995, rather it was rewritten by Brown and included as one of the three case studies sandwiched between the far more positive results from the reviews of King's Lynn and Newcastle. The Home Office press release launching the study made no mention of any negative findings. Instead it trumpeted:

> Closed circuit television is cracking crime up and down the country, a Home Office report shows today. The report examines how the police are using CCTV to beat crime and disorder in Newcastle, Birmingham and King's Lynn town centres. It reveals:
>
> Burglaries down by 56% and vandalism down by 34 percent in Central Newcastle . . . 94 percent public support for CCTV systems and little displacement of crime and in Newcastle positive effects of areas neighbouring CCTV zones.

Moreover, the press release included a glowing endorsement from Home Office Minister David McLean:

> CCTV is now one of the best crime-cracking tools the police have. They are using it to catch thieves, thugs and muggers, to prevent crime and focus police resources more effectively. That is why we launched a competition for £15 million of funding in November. The latest figures show the largest ever fall in recorded crime over a two-year period. I am convinced that CCTV has a role in helping police turn the tables against the criminals. This report should encourage everyone thinking of putting forward private funding or proposal to us.

Not only is the positive gloss a clear case of news management but so was the timing of publication. The report is dated November 1995, but it was originally due to be published in the summer of 1995. In the event it was published on 28 December 1995. It seems probable that, despite the Minister's gloss, publication was timed so that it was distanced from the Home Secretary's announcement in November of the decision to commit another £15 million of public money on expanding CCTV. And, of course, launching a report in the week between Christmas and New Year is certainly one way of ensuring little public or political reaction.

It is interesting to note that in 1996 the Law Reform Commission of New South Wales undertook an inquiry into the legal regulation of surveillance which also included a review of the evidence for effectiveness. It drew heavily on UK sources and particularly the work of Brown (1995). They concluded:

> Although the Commission is not itself engaged in evaluating the efficacy of CCTV, it notes that there is little evidence from which to conclude that the enormous expense of establishing such a system will, of itself, provide local authorities with the panacea to crime and anti-social behaviour. Such authorities would need to question whether other means of controlling crime, such as increasing the numbers of beat police, might not achieve similar results at lower cost. (Law Reform Commission 1997: 34)

The Media: Television's Love Affair with CCTV

Television is a visual medium. CCTV is a visual medium. They were made for each other. Add one other ingredient, crime, and you have the perfect marriage. A marriage that can blur the distinction between entertainment and news; between documentary and spectacle and between voyeurism and current affairs.

Crime drama has of course long dominated the output of television schedules, whether in the form of films, drama series or soap operas (see Reiner 1992; Sparks 1992). And of course it has long been a favourite topic of the documentary and current affairs departments. However, in the 1960s a new type of programme was launched, 'Police Five'. It was only five minutes long but, through the use of reconstruction and photofits, the audience was invited to help the police solve crime directly and phone in with information. In 1984, the format of 'Police Five' was radically revised and extended when the BBC launched 'Crimewatch', which has run monthly, for ten months each year and is now into its fifteenth series. The programme format has remained fairly stable. There are three reconstructions of unsolved crimes, interspersed with a round-up of less serious incidents and a Photocall which asks viewers to identify suspects from CCTV footage of suspects in banks, building societies and other commercial premises. As the presenters of the programme explained: 'We discovered there was a rich fund of photographs of suspects, of escaped prisoners and of criminals caught in the act by security cameras. They made good television and television made good use of them' (Ross and Cook 1987: 111).

For all the crimes covered in the program the public is asked to phone in with details surrounding a crime and hopefully name the perpetrators. The use of CCTV footage therefore became firmly entrenched in the new form of 'infotainment' crime programming. In 1984, when 'Crimewatch' was launched, CCTV systems in public spaces were only just starting to emerge and thus in the early years the programme's Photocall relied almost exclusively on footage from commercial private security cameras.

The success of 'Crimewatch' heralded another development, the launch in 1988 of 'Crimestoppers' in the Metropolitan Police area and shortly afterwards extended throughout the country. 'Crimestoppers' is run by a registered charity, the Community Action Trust whose aim is the 'advancement, promotion and preservation of public law and order'. While 'Crimewatch' is a national programme, 'Crimestoppers' is locally based and consists of short advert-like broadcasts, about one minute long, and like the Photocall slot on 'Crimewatch', broadcasts sequences from security cameras and asks the public to ring in and identify the culprits. Unlike 'Crimewatch', 'Crimestoppers' offers rewards and encourages the anonymous reporting of information, and even has provision for those wanting to collect their rewards to do so without revealing their identities. While 'Crimestoppers' has traditionally relied on footage from banks and commercial systems it is also drawing on the images taken from public CCTV systems. For instance, in Leeds a partnership between the *Yorkshire Evening Post* newspaper, the City Council, and 'Crimestoppers' has set up 'Leedswatch', which involves using footage from the city's new CCTV system. These are broadcast in the 'Crimestoppers' television slots, and stills from the footage published in the *Yorkshire Evening Post*'s 'Fight Back on Crime' column. The newspaper offered a £1,000 reward for the first person to identify a suspect which led to a successful prosecution (*CCTV Today*, January 1997 p. 3).

While the early use of CCTV footage in 'Crimewatch' and 'Crimestoppers' programmes was little more than a sophisticated 'wanted poster', in the 1990s a whole raft of prime-time TV programmes was launched which exploited the entertainment potential of CCTV footage more unashamedly. 'Police Camera Action!' for instance, in which 'Alistair Stewart uses real-life footage to expose the nation's more wayward and selfish road users' (*Guardian*, the Guide: 96) was little more than an assemblage of video footage of police car chases, dangerous driving and accidents, selected on the basis of their spectacular or slapstick appeal. This was crime as a spectacle and nothing more. Other programmes such as BBC's 'Crime Beat' and ITV's 'Eye Spy', both shown weekly in prime-time slots, tried to present a more serious gloss. 'Crime Beat's presenter Martin Lewis earnestly announces in its opening credits that it is 'the program that looks at the role of security cameras in all our lives'. At the end of the first edition of 'Eye Spy' the presenter, Selina Scott, declared:

> That's nearly all for this first edition, but I hope you'll join me again soon for more real life stories caught on camera. We'll be revealing how armed police in the front line use video to convict dangerous criminals: the have-a-go-heros – we report on the extra-ordinary acts of courage by ordinary people: inside the world of crime – cameras reveal what really happens when your car becomes a target.

'Crime Beat' and 'Eye Spy' are presented in a thirty-minute magazine format and fuse elements of voyeurism, public service, documentary and entertainment. Typic-ally, in each programme, we might have a report of the 'success' of a new town centre CCTV system, a feature on video surveillance in some specialist area of policing such as an undercover squad or traffic police, a report on a new techno-logical development such as night-vision cameras, and finally a 'Crimestoppers' style photocall. But it is live video footage of criminals 'caught on camera' which provides the lynchpin of the shows and in selection, presentation and content 'Crime Beat' and 'Eye Spy' are celebratory. They celebrate the power of the cameras to reduce crime as Martin Lewis declared: 'Most criminologists and crime fighters agree that the biggest single impact on crime and disorder is the rapid spread of surveillance cameras . . . There is no question that CCTV helps solve crime.'

This effectiveness message is reiterated both visually and through the script in both the programmes. Footage of suspects brawling, trying car doors, and breaking into shops is shown but the punchline is nearly always the same 'and they're caught', 'but he was only part of the way home before the police arrived', 'they were both caught and received lengthy prison sentences'. These infotainments come to resemble the discursive structure of fabular heroism noted by Sparks (1992) in his analysis of the moral world of crime stories. The police always get their man, well nearly always. If they do not, the audience can be asked to participate in the 'fightback against crime', to become 'active citizens' as 'Eye Spy' declares: 'Now it's your chance to turn detective. On 'Eye Spy' we will be asking for your help to fight crime . . . Can you help the police to find this man filmed by a security camera?' ('Eye Spy' 1995).

The message is complete: CCTV works because it deters crime, if it does not deter crime it enables the police to be deployed and apprehend a suspect, and if it does not result in immediate apprehension, in the absence of the police knowing the identity of the culprit, then the public can provide it. And the proof is there before the viewers' very own eyes. For all the words and scripted statements in praise of CCTV, it is perhaps the continuous repetition of the visual narrative structure of success which make such programmes so seductively powerful in promoting CCTV. But of course this narrative structure tells us almost nothing of the routine operation of CCTV hour by hour, day by day, week by week. What is shown is just a minuscule fraction of what is in excess of 17 million hours of video footage recorded on camera each week. The footage shown has been carefully selected by the police or local authority, mindful of the public relations implications of broadcasting footage from CCTV systems. Thus the extracts show only the morally unambiguous interventions in line with public and police conceptions of 'real police work'. The more contentious, yet routine, aspects such as the surveillance of political protesters, the deployment of police officers to move on 'troublesome' youth, or the use of the system by private security guards to exclude children from shopping malls are of course not shown.

The portrayal of CCTV in 'infotainments' perhaps provides an important element in understanding its popular appeal for, while being entertained, the message, sometimes overt and at times sublime, that CCTV works is constantly reinforced. But it is not just nationally networked television programmes that have promoted this positive image, newspapers, particularly local newspapers have also played a central part.

The Media: What the Papers Say

In their classic analysis of the media reportage of 'Mugging', Hall et al. argue that not only does the media: 'Define for the majority of the population what significant events are taking place but also, they offer powerful interpretations of how to understand these events' (1981: 340).

This analysis invites us to question why CCTV comes to be such a 'good' story and therefore seen as a significant event and also how the media construct the understanding of these events. For Hall et al. news texts implicitly have an educative function, which is achieved through both their form and content. This educative function suggests a preferred reading of the meaning of an issue. As issues can be set in alternative discursive frameworks, the questions become: which discourse is prioritised and in whose interests does it operate? This immediately raises the issues of relationship of the media to the wider structures of power.

In the case of CCTV it is clear that there are a variety of discourses within which it can be set; for instance, discourses about 'crime control', 'effectiveness' and 'community safety' or those stressing 'civil liberties' and 'privacy'. Which discourses are prioritised within a news story and how tensions are resolved between competing discourses thus become central to understanding the 'preferred reading' of the text. As we shall see below, these priorities and resolutions are not arbitrary but tend to reflect the interests and values of the powerful coalitions which were actively seeking to promote and implement CCTV systems. However, as Hall et al. have argued, we cannot see the media as merely the puppet of dominant interests, rather it is necessary to focus on the 'routine structures of news production to see how the media come in fact, in the "last instance", to reproduce the definitions of the powerful, without being, in a simple sense, in their pay' (1981: 340). To understand this process it is necessary to attend to two, issues. First, the manner in which news is shaped by journalistic imperatives, which determine 'news-worthiness'. Second the organisational pressures of routine news production which structure the relationship with 'sources' which lead to ascendancy being given to the 'primary definers'. The relationship between primary definers and reporters allows 'institutional definers to establish the initial definitions or *primary interpre-tations* of the topic in question. This interpretation then "commands the field" in all subsequent treatment and sets the terms of reference within which all further coverage of debate takes place' (Hall et al. 1981: 342).

CCTV and News Values

There is no simple correspondence between events occurring in the world and their coverage as news. Every day there are thousands of potential stories waiting to be told and yet only a handful of them end up on the pages of our national and local newspapers. Many fail because there are no channels of communication through which journalists can be made, or make themselves, aware of their existence. Even when events are made visible, unless a story can be transformed into a 'conventional journalistic form' and identified as containing 'newsworthy material according to implicit rules of relevance' it is unlikely to get into print. However anyone familiar with the pages of many national and local newspapers in the mid-1990s in Britain could note that there was increasing incidence of CCTV stories.

In one national daily newspaper, the *Guardian*, in 1993 there were only 15 stories mentioning CCTV; this increased to 46 in 1994 and 50 in 1995. At the local level there was also an increasing focus on CCTV stories. In the *Hull Daily Mail* (HDM) for instance, in 1993, there were 11 stories, in 1994 20 stories and, in the first three months of 1995 alone 17 stories. Similarly in the *Windsor Observer* (WO), which is published twice weekly, there were 5 stories in 1995 and in the first eight months of 1996, 16 stories. How can we account for this sustained privileging of CCTV stories particularly at the local level?

Put simply, stories about CCTV make good copy. They do this because at the outset they are in line with the rules of relevancy which construct them as having 'news value' and therefore as newsworthy.

As Chibnall (1981) notes, the rules of relevancy governing newsworthiness are associated with audience expectations and legitimised in terms of audience desire. For the provincial and local press this means casting themselves as providing something different to the national broadsheets, which at the top end of the market at least, focus on affairs of state, international relations and the few sporting clubs that dominate the elite super-leagues and premier divisions. While a news story may have national or even international significance, the news value for the local press is almost exclusively determined by its ability to be couched in parochial terms. And of course the proposals to place CCTV cameras on town centre streets is unquestionably a local story which has salience for all the local citizens who venture into the town centre because they will be on film.

Newsworthiness is not only determined by its parochial relevance but by its potential to provide an ongoing story. This provides both easy copy to fill the pages of future editions and also facilitates reader commitment by presenting them with a narrative structure in instalments. For instance, the *Hull Daily Mail* ran the following six stories in the first seven months of 1994 on the plans to introduce CCTV into the market town of Beverley, just north of the city.

> Spy cameras plan to curb town crime (12 January 1994)
> Town focusses on TV spy cameras (22 February 1994)
> Eyes will be glued to city's anti-crime TV success (16 May 1994)
> Spy cameras look the part say traders (20 May 1994)
> Sites earmarked for the TV spies (24 June 1994)
> Group may manage town centre [CCTV system] (12 July 1994)

Similar series of stories were run about all the regional town centre bids, from Driffield, Goole, Bridlington and Hull itself and, in total, there were eighteen stories on the preparation for the Challenge Bid from January to July 1994.

That CCTV stories gained wide coverage in the local press can partially be explained by their parochial and ongoing potential but they also fit easily with other aspects of newsworthiness. Chibnall has suggested that these tend to prioritise the present over the past, the unusual over the normal, the dramatic over the mundane, the simplistic over the complex, personalities rather than structures and results over process (Chibnall 1981: 86). And to these we could add three further elements which enhance local news value: stories which can enlist the views of local elites, those that have the potential for conflict and generally those which can be presented negatively (see Hall et al. 1981; van Dijk 1998).

The activities of those engaged in bidding for government funding under the City Challenge competitions automatically succeed on the first criteria of newsworthiness. They are about immediate present rather than the distant past. Thus reports are presented as 'at yesterday's council meeting' or 'Speaking at last night's meeting of the chamber of commerce . . .' Similarly, all proposed developments and innovations are, by their nature, implicitly unusual, if only in the local context, and thus sufficient to justify their claim to newsworthiness. Hence, 'Bus station cameras step nearer' (HDM, 10 December 1990) and 'Town cameras a step nearer' (WO, 24 September 1993) where both stress the imminent arrival of a new scheme.

CCTV news stories also lend themselves to dramatisation. By placing them in the context of the 'battle against crime', certain aspects of CCTV's operation and effects can be highlighted for dramatic effect: 'TV will "spy" on bus thugs' (HDM, 21 December 1990) or 'Eye-in-the-sky will drive out town centre rowdies' (WO, 16 June 1995). Moreover, reportage on CCTV appears to have little difficulty in reducing complex issues to a common sense simplicity such as 'Good citizens have nothing to fear' (*Maidenhead Advertiser* (MA), 17 March 1995) or 'CCTV will be a great help' (WO, 19 April 1996).

The personalisation of the stories can also be achieved with minimum effort. In the run-up to a scheme becoming operational, victim accounts calling for cameras to be installed to prevent future attacks provide good copy thus: 'Shopkeeper's Camera Plea' after a spate of robberies at his shop (HDM, 31 June 1996) or 'Darren this week urged the town's councillors to speed up plans to install close circuit TV to protect others' under the headline 'Attack Victims Fight for Life' (WO, 20 December 1995). In this way, relatively mundane stories of 'everyday crime' which would probably warrant little, if any, news space are reshaped in the light of CCTV to give them news value.

CCTV stories also readily lend themselves to reporting the views of local elites many of whom actively support its introduction: 'Town centre bosses back plan', or 'police chief backs CCTV' (HDM, 5 May 1993). Stories can also be cast in terms of conflict over the effects or operation of the systems – 'Police dismiss fears of rise in village crime' (WO, 20 March 1996) or 'New code to allay public CCTV fears'.

Once a system is in place stories about 'results' present another source of easily obtained newsworthy copy, for instance: 'CCTV gets credit for 26 arrests' (WO, 12 April 1996); 'Spies in the sky yield 31 arrests' (WO, 26 April 1996). Further, one of the features of local news coverage once town centre systems are up and running is the proliferation of stories which ask readers to 'put names to faces' who have been 'caught in the act'. The selection of these stories is not just determined by the general news values which prevail but is influenced by 'at least five sets of informal rules of relevancy in the reporting of violence'. These guide journalists treatment of violence by asserting the relevance of:

1 Visible and spectacular acts.
2 Sexual and political connotations.
3 Graphic presentations.
4 Individual pathology.
5 Deterrence and repression.
  (Chibnall 1981 cited in Kidd-Hewitt 1995: 15)

The story 'Attacker is caught on camera' (MA, 31 May 1996) featured three photographs from the town centre CCTV system in which 'the attacker is pictured with a woman and another man in two, photographs and in the final one "he carries out a violent attack on the man in the phone box"'. Strangely, this incident was not reported to the police by the 'victim' and the police are now asking for 'anyone with information about the incident or who recognises the people in these photographs' to contact them. In 'Are you in the white T-shirt?' (MA, 2 August 1996), a single picture for the Maidenhead town centre system is reproduced after an 'assault in Queen Street which left a man with a broken collar-bone and fractured cheekbone'. In this story the text is careful not to attribute the assault directly to the man featured in the photographs, presumably because there is no photographic evidence of him actually carrying out the attack, but requests 'If anyone knows who the man in the picture is, they can contact the police on . . .'

In both these stories, three of Chibnall's five rules of 'relevance' are present. They are about visible and spectacular acts, they are capable of literally graphic presentations through the use of photographs and they appeal to elements of both deterrence (if you do wrong you'll be caught on camera like this man) and repression (with your help we can identify, catch and punish those responsible).

CCTV stories lend themselves to being transformed into having news value in such a variety of ways that even the most inexperienced journalism student should be able to construct an account that would satisfy the requirements of a 'good story'. However, just because CCTV stories have the potential to be transformed into having newsworthiness does not account for the preponderance of news space devoted to them or the content of those news stories.

The Sources

While journalists are responsible for 'reporting' the news, others try and shape it. The last decades have seen a mushrooming in public and private sector organisations of public relations departments with their 'press officers' responsible for promoting the image and interests of the organisation. They do this by facilitating the take-up of positive stories and the swift management, containment and rebuttal of the negative. At the local level the importance of 'managing the media' was made explicit in the Home Office guidelines for local authorities seeking to implement CCTV published in 1994. The glossy, 46-page booklet with a foreword by the then Home Secretary, Michael Howard, exhorted local initiators to 'give careful consideration to your publicity campaign, which may be crucial to the success of your system' (Home Office 1994: 32). In particular, the booklet noted that: 'If there are local concerns about intrusions of privacy or infringements of civil liberties these should be worked through before the system is put into operation, to maximise public support for it.' However the legitimacy of such concerns was not addressed by the booklet, merely the manner in which they could be neutralised: 'Any public concern about CCTV needs to be set alongside concerns about freedom and safety to shop with the assurance which CCTV can provide' (ibid.: 9).

The importance of the local media in contributing to the generation of public support was implicit in the advice that a 'representative of the media, for example the editor of the local newspaper' should be invited to sit on the multi-agency working party constituted to promote the idea of CCTV in the locality (ibid.: 12). And the purpose of this was not only to facilitate a channel for feeding potential news stories to the press, but to ensure favourable coverage which was in line with the values of the system promoters:

> Get the local press on your side early and get a key player on your committee from the start. Ensure they realise what your objectives are, and focus them on the shopping/ walking element . . . it is also useful to give a high profile to all convictions secured as a result of CCTV. Local press and TV should be constantly reminded of the numbers who plead guilty and are convicted because of the cameras. (Home Office 1994: 32–3)

The Home Office explicitly recognised that the potential for a critical and adverse media comment was best managed by a policy of incorporation. However, to understand how amenable journalists were to this strategy it is necessary to consider the general structural dependence of journalists on their news sources. For Hall et al., the dependence on a few institutional sources, in this case the police and local authority councillors and executive officers, regardless of the existence of a strategy of incorporation, would have resulted in their elevation to the status of primary definers. For as Chibnall notes this dependence leads to a 'complex process of socialisation by which a journalist's frame of reference, methods of working and personal systems of perceptions and expectations are brought in line with his sources' (1981: 88).

In short, journalists are assimilated into the values of their primary definers. Some more recent accounts of news production have qualified what was seen as the over-determinism of the 'dominant ideology and primary definition model preferring a 'field of contestation' model (Skidmore 1995) but as Schlesinger and Tumber (1994) note that despite the shortcomings of Hall et al's position 'there is still undoubtedly a strong case for arguing that the organisation of journalistic practice generally promotes the views and interests of authoritative sources. This is a paramount finding of much of the sociology of journalism' (1994: 20).

CCTV as a Local Story

While the national print media and television programmes have set the broad agenda of the debate about CCTV it is through media reports at the local level, especially local neswpapers, that citizens get information about the development and implementation of specific schemes. As Smith (1984) has argued the role of local media has often been overlooked in the debates about the dissemination of crime news. However as Piepe et al. (1978) have shown it is the provincial press which is the preferred source of information about local affairs and Smith found local newspapers were the single most important source of knowledge about crime (Smith 1984: 290 fn 2).

In this context, we want to examine the coverage by three weekly newspapers given to the emergence of one system in the affluent home counties towns of Windsor, Eton and Maidenhead. We cannot claim anything other than opportunism for the choice of this system. By good fortune we were given a copy of the complete press cutting file and, as it would have taken weeks to compile such record for any other site, the opportunity to use it seemed too good to miss. Nor can we make any strong claims as to the typicality of the reportage of CCTV in the area although our archive of over 500 news stories culled from a variety of local and national newspapers provides plenty of supporting examples. Moreover, a similar analysis of local newspapers conducted by McCahill (1998b) of CCTV reportage in a poor and recession-hit northern town also found a heavy reliance on primary definers and discursive practices aimed at emphasising the positive aspects of CCTV.

The possibility of installing cameras in the towns of Windsor, Eton and Maidenhead was first mooted in 1993 and the final system now comprises sixty cameras covering the three towns operated and observed from one control room. According to the local publicity leaflets there were three lead organisations: The Royal Borough of Windsor and Maidenhead, Thames Valley Police and the Chamber of Commerce. Three weekly papers, which cover the area, the *Windsor Observer* (WO), the *Windsor and Eton Express* (WEE), and the *Maidenhead Advertiser* (MA), published between February 1995 and August 1996 fifty-eight stories which made reference to CCTV although we have also added two, additional stories from 1993 to this main sample.

In these sixty stories ninety-one voices were heard, however as Table 4.1 shows the voices came from a very narrow range. We can see that the media coverage is dominated by the sponsors of the scheme with 86 per cent of voices cited in all the news stories belonging to those involved in the partnership set up to promote and oversee the system. Unsurprisingly, their voices were supportive, welcoming and uncritical of the use of CCTV. Of the citizen contributions, the overall number is skewed by one 'vox pop' article in which the 'Advertiser took to the streets to ask residents and shoppers: is this the answer to local crime or is the borough turning into Big Brother and encroaching on our Civil Liberties?' The feature ran under the headline 'good citizens have nothing to fear' and six citizens were quoted. With the exception of one respondent they were reported as welcoming CCTV and having little concern with civil liberty implications (MA, 17 March 1995).

Table 4.1 Organisational Role and Frequency of Citation in CCTV News Stories

Status of voice	No. of times cited	Percentage of of all voices	Cumulative percent
Local councillors	28	31%	31%
Police	23	26%	57%
Council Officials	19	21%	78%
Citizens	8	9%	87%
Business	7	8%	95%
Independents	3	3%	98%
Others	3	3%	101%
Total	91	101%	

* The total percentages may not add up to 100 due to rounding.

In the sixty stories, only three independent sources, not concerned with the implementation of the system, were heard. Two, were cited in one article in 1993 reporting on a 'special presentation in Windsor Guildhall'. They were Nick Tilley, the co-author of the Home Office booklet *Looking out for You* and Barry Loftus the manager of the King's Lynn system. Nick Tilley was reported as stressing 'CCTV systems had to be well managed, claiming other surveillance projects had been less successful and were open to the abuse of the public's civil liberties.' The report also told how 'a similar CCTV system in King's Lynn, Norfolk, slashed crime by 91 percent' and Barry Loftus was reported to have said 'police had made over 200 arrests as the direct result of CCTV 18 months ago' (WO, 15 October 1993). The only other 'independent' expert was cited in an article in February 1996. Hilary Nevile of the Crown Prosecution Service was reported as saying 'they too were looking forward to the introduction of CCTV, which would help with evidence, identifying an offender and establishing that the actual crime occurred when cases are taken to court'. She added: 'in other towns where CCTV has been brought in it has resulted in more crimes being detected and more cases coming to court. Initially we are expecting quite an increase in work then, hopefully, with people aware the cameras are about, a drop in crime.'

It is not just local elites that dominate the local media coverage but a few individuals who dominate within these groups. As Table 4.2 shows, between them five key individuals account for just over one third of all the voices heard on the subject of CCTV. Three are council officials responsible for implementing, installing and running the system, one is the senior police officer of the area and one is a local councillor. Of the other voices heard, four are councillors, three are police officers and one is a businesswoman. Between them, these thirteen individuals accounted for over half of all the voices heard on the subject of CCTV.

Table 4.2 Identity and Frequency of Individual Voices Cited in CCTV News Stories

Name of speaker	No. of times cited	Percentage of all voices	Cumulative percent
Supt. Bryan*	7	8%	8%
Tony Street	7	8%	16%
David Perkins	7	8%	24%
Councillor Jamison	5	6%	30%
John Russell	4	4%	34%
Sergeant Amery	4	4%	38%
Councillor Kendell	3	3%	41%
Councillor Mair	3	3%	44%
Councillor Stallag	2	2%	46%
Councillor Glikston	2	2%	48%
Sergeant Harvey	2	2%	50%
Sergeant Hincliffe	2	2%	52%
Mrs Ahmed	2	2%	54%

* Supt. Bryan is the local police commander; Tony Street is the Council's head of engineering; David Perkins is the Council's CCTV Administration Manager; John Russell is the Council's Community Safety Manager; Mrs Ahmed is a local businesswoman.

We can see then, that the local story of CCTV is dominated by the opinions of a narrow range of primary definers all of whom support the introduction of CCTV. Other voices are simply not heard. In particular, the voices of youth are absent. Although it is difficult to judge from the news reports, it would appear that not a single person under twenty years of age is given a voice and only two people under thirty are cited. This is particularly important as it is youth who are the main targets of town centre surveillance systems and are most likely to come into adversarial contact with police. Moreover, as public attitude surveys have shown, youth is consistently more critical towards CCTV than its older counterparts (Honess and Charman 1992; Bennett and Gelsthorpe 1996).

Women are better represented but still only constitute about 15 per cent of the voices heard and, judging from names alone, there were only three voices from people of ethnic minority backgrounds. Put simply, it would seem that the voices which dominate are those of local middle-aged, middle-class, white men. But it is perhaps the parochialism that is most important here, since critical or at least sceptical voices which could be found at the national level who have the resources and knowledge base to challenge the assertions of the dominant coalition, are not consulted. For instance, groups such as Liberty, Privacy International, the Local Government Information Unit, and university researchers are, by the fact that they are not local, excluded from the discourse.

So far we have concentrated on the way in which the preponderance of CCTV stories can be accounted for by the ease at which they are transformed into 'newsworthy' stories and how the stories are dominated by the opinions of the promoters of the system. However, we have only tangentially touched on the stories themselves. There are three primary discourses which recur in many of the stories. We have termed these, 'emphasising effectiveness', 'downplaying displacement', and 'your liberties are safe with us'.

Emphasising Effectiveness

Of the ninety-one voices who are cited in the texts forty-four of them are explicitly making claims as to the effectiveness of CCTV in reducing crime and the fear of crime. Thus, almost every story carries some reference to the efficacy of CCTV. Indeed, only seven out of the fifty-eight stories fail to make some positive claim and only three are negative.

The reportage of success can be broken down into three primary stages which mirror the historical developments of the scheme: a) it has been a success elsewhere, b) it will be a success here, c) it is a success here.

It has been a success elsewhere:

King's Lynn have experienced a two thirds drop in crime since they installed the cameras. We have chosen to listen to their experience because the town is similar in its make-up to Windsor. (Business Watch Spokeswoman: WO, 24 September 1993)

In my experience of other local authorities that have implemented CCTV, it has had an immediate impact on the fear of crime as well as crime itself. It has proven to be a significant deterrent. (Community Safety Manager John Russell: MA, 17 March 1995)

In other areas of the country, it has led to spectacular reductions in local crime rates. (WEE, 30 November 1995)

The Royal Borough's scheme has been carefully timed to take advantage of the latest technology and designed to benefit from the experience gained by other towns across the country, where CCTV has seen local crime rates drop dramatically. (MA, 15 March 1996)

As we have already indicated, in the absence of any organised local opposition to CCTV the assertions of the primary definers go unchallenged but they also become repeated not as 'opinions' but as 'facts'. In the last two, examples, it is the journalistic 'voice' that is speaking and informing us of 'dramatic' and 'spectacular' reductions.

As the system moves closer to realisation the anticipated reduction in crime is heralded – it will be a success here:

We are confident that when it's up and running in the middle of March it will prove extremely effective. (Sergeant Amery: WO, 1 March 1996)

Much of the auto-crime occurs in the car parks which will be covered by CCTV. We anticipate there will be a reduction in these types of crime. (Inspector Petford: WO, 6 March 1996)

EYE IN THE SKY WILL MAKE US ALL FEEL SAFER (Headline: WO, 7 February 1996)

As soon as the system is installed, success stories move from speculation about its effectiveness to concrete illustrations that it is a sucess here. Both the *Windsor Observer* and the *Windsor and Eton Express* ran a story about the 'First Arrest via CCTV', and the *Observer* declared: 'Even though the cameras are not yet fully operational they spotted two men at the back of the Castle Hotel on Tuesday evening. They (the police) arrested one of the men for interfering with a motor vehicle.' The *Express* stated: 'Sergeant Ken Amery said yesterday the arrest was an extremely pleasing first result for CCTV. He added: "It shows how it can work. It also gives a warning to any law-breakers they are being watched."' (WEE, 29 February 1996).

However, we are told midway in the story: 'The suspect has been released on police bail pending further enquiries'. This is not commented upon further despite the fact that it would suggest that either the police had arrested an innocent man, or that the cameras had failed to provide evidence with which to charge him. Despite these anomalies, for both papers, this was a dramatic example of success as the *Windsor and Eton Express* declared under the headline 'Caught on Camera' that 'Crime busting CCTV cameras have notched up their first success, police revealed this week.' This strategy of announcing success was repeated by one of the other local papers, the *Maidenhead Advertiser*. On 15 March, three days before the official opening of the system, it declared, 'Crooks nabbed on film during highly successful trial runs' and went on to enthuse 'Spy-in-the-sky's a security hit'; it continued:

The Borough's new closed circuit television system has drawn first blood in the fight against crime, catching criminals on film before the network is fully up and running . . . The spy cameras start rolling on Monday . . . But they have already witnessed dozens of crimes.

Thus, even before the scheme was operational it was declared a success. In the following weeks the three local papers seemed to lose no opportunity to declare the scheme successful:

CCTV gets credit for 26 arrests (WO, 12 April 1996)

The crime-busting CCTV cameras have proved so successful . . . Sergeant Bob Harvey has revealed the Royal Boroughs 'eyes-in-the-sky' have notched up 26 arrests since they went live at the end of last month (WEE, 18 April 1996)

CCTV gives a big boost to crime fight – Spies in the sky yield 31 arrests (Headline: WO, 26 April 1996)

45 arrests thanks to TV cameras (WO, 24 May 1996)

The 63 cameras in Maidenhead and Windsor have led to the arrest of 60 people for offences including violent attacks, drug dealing and car break-ins in just three months. (MA, 21 June 1996)

One could forgive the critical reader for believing that success was pre-ordained from the moment the council agreed to fund the system since this success is being determined not by any objective yardstick but by the uncontested claims of the system promoters. However, once the first arrest had been made, the system was 'a success' and the measure of success became the number of arrests in following weeks. This is significant because there are no criteria by which to judge the meaning of this 'success' or what would have constituted failure. Would, for instance, thirty arrests in three months have constituted a success? or fifteen? or five? Presumably they would have because the criteria of success that the local news journalists use are the self-justificatory ones of the system promoters. Moreover, the uncritical acceptance and publication of arrest figures obscures the issue that 'arrests' are not 'charges' and neither are they 'convictions'. Nor are they synonymous with reductions in the 'real' (as reported by victim surveys) or recorded crime rates. While any of these indices would provide a more robust measure of efficacy, they are not congruent with the temporal frame of newsworthiness which demands that news is about the here-and-now.

In terms of their discursive structure, many of the articles operate using an abstract evaluative structure which takes the form of an 'ideological triangle' so as to:

1 Emphasise CCTV's good properties/actions.
2 De-emphasise CCTV's bad properties/actions.
3 Mitigate CCTV's bad properties/actions.
   (Adapted from van Dijk 1998: 33)

The limited range of voices heard and the incorporation of the local journalists into the definitional stance of the primary definers, means that, in the main the de-emphasising of the bad properties of CCTV is achieved through absence. They are simply not alluded to and therefore no mitigation is required. However, when they are, the three points of the 'ideological triangle' work in conjunction to produce a 'preferred' reading.

This was most forcefully illustrated by the only article which explicitly mentioned independent research as to the effectiveness of CCTV: the report which is not specifically identified in the text is *CCTV in Town Centres: Three Case Studies* (Brown: 1995). The news story consists of a headline, a sub-head, and thirteen paragraphs and contains nearly 280 words including the headline. The findings of the research report are mentioned explicitly in two , paragraphs. The first, which is the second main text paragraph states:

> A study by the Home Office's Police Research Group found some crime was forced in to other areas. It also found crime still fell in areas beyond the view of the cameras.

The second, which is the tenth paragraph of the story states:

> But the Home Office studies, carried out in Newcastle, Birmingham and King's Lynn town centres did find overwhelming public support for CCTV. (MA, 5 January 1996)

These are the only two, paragraphs specifically about the report. It should be noted that the second paragraph is factually untrue. The 'studies' did not report 'over-whelming public support', indeed the studies were about effectiveness not public attitudes (see Brown 1995). Whether the journalist was mistaken, misled, or intentionally set out to deceive we do not know, however the effect is to emphasis the positive aspects of CCTV.

Turning to the first paragraph. The main point to note is that the negative findings of the research are dealt with in one thirty-word paragraph. This compression means there is no elaboration of the negative findings and they are consequently de-emphasised. In contrast, the local proponents of CCTV are allocated seven paragraphs.

If we examine the text of this first paragraph we can see the issue of displacement is addressed by 'some crime was forced into other areas'. The next sentence cryptically tells us that 'crime still fell in areas beyond the camera's range'. What this means is not clear, and might be treated as a negative proposition, the cameras are ineffective because crime reduces in areas without them or a positive proposition – when you put in cameras you also get a 'diffusion of benefits'. Whatever its meaning, the brevity and ambiguity both serve to de-emphasise two negative points about CCTV, i.e. that it may have little impact on crime and it leads to displacement. The issue of displacement is the one that takes up the majority of the remaining paragraphs and is mitigated and de-emphasised. First, the community safety manager John Russell is quoted as saying:

professional criminals might not be scared off but 80 per cent of crime was opportunistic and carried out by amateurs. The opportunist will not be displaced and will be caught on CCTV and through good Neighbourhood Watch. Perhaps some criminals adopt methods which are slightly more difficult to detect but they are a minority.

Thus the issue of displacement is sidelined to the marginal and only relevant in a small minority of cases. However, this has not completely dismissed the possibility of displacement but, should it arise, its affects will be mitigated because as:

> Chief Inspector Bob Jones of the Windsor and Maidenhead police said officers would be prepared for any displacement of professional criminals. We will certainly be ready for them.

But most important is the way in which the story is structured through its headlines and first paragraph.

CCTV WILL HELP CRIMEFIGHTING
Security camera report
rubbished by town bosses

TOWN Hall chiefs have dismissed
research which raises questions over
the long term effectiveness of security
cameras in town centres
A study by the Home Office . . .

Before the findings of the study are even mentioned we are told that it has been 'rubbished by the town bosses' and despite the report's findings, the journalistic voice confidently declares that 'CCTV will help crimefighting'. The prioritising of the dismissal of the report is not only achieved through the text but also by the layout. The head and sub-head are in a larger bold typeface and the first paragraph stressing how the research has been dismissed is in larger typeface than the rest of the text.

Downplaying Displacement

The one potentially oppositional discourse which found a voice in the three local papers, was the issue of displacement. The scheme only covered the town centre of Windsor and this left the surrounding villages outside the scheme. These concerns found an early voice in the debate about the introduction of CCTV. A report in the *Windsor Observer* of a public meeting to discuss the possibility of CCTV noted the 'Members of the audience warned that concentrating security on town centre would leave other centres of the borough unprotected.' While there was the occasional reference to the issue of displacement it was only as the system was about to become fully operational that the issues became a 'hot potato'. As the *Observer* reported on 15 March 1996, three days before system went live:

> A councillor fears the Royal Borough's CCTV project could drive criminals away from Windsor and Maidenhead and into Old Windsor.
>
> Old Windsor Councillor Harry Parker says he fears his villagers are going to be the victim of car crime and petty vandalism as villains shy away from areas with television cameras.
>
> He said 'This is going to be a real problem not just for Old Windsor but for villages such as Datchet, Cookham and Wraysbury.
>
> Ideally we would like CCTV for all these areas but there is no way that the Royal Borough can afford to finance such schemes.'

It is important to note that when one of the local elite raises a serious issue of concern about the operation of CCTV it does get news coverage and the issue of displacement therefore can become a 'field of contestation'. However, the issue of displacement is ideologically ambiguous. On the one hand it suggests that there may be negative consequences for some groups from the introduction of CCTV in a district if crime is displaced from one locality to another. On the other hand, it does not undermine the basic assumption as to the effectiveness of CCTV. As one local councillor was reported as saying: 'It may drive crime elsewhere but so be it. Our responsibility is to the people in this borough' (MA, 17 March 1995). At the local level 'displacement' presents itself as a classic political argument about the distribution of a scarce collective resource, in this case, security through the deployment of CCTV. Thus, while individual councillors may either celebrate their gains and others bemoan the potential costs, the solution to the problem is more cameras. But, in the absence of blanket coverage, if the introduction of cameras to one area merely shifts the problem to another within the same political community, the distribution or, more correctly, the potential redistribution, can become a major political issue which cannot be ignored by local political elites with the responsibility for community-wide provision of services. In dealing with this issue we can see how the local news media implicitly served the interests of the primary definers. The week after councillor Parker raised his concerns, the *Windsor Observer* ran the following story:

POLICE DISMISS FEARS OF RISE IN VILLAGE CRIME.

Police have dismissed fears that the Royal Borough's closed-circuit TV security system which swung in to action this week, will push criminals out of town centres and into villages.

Councillors and residents are afraid that criminals will target villages such as Holyport, Bray and Cookham rather that risk being caught on the cameras which monitor the centres of Maidenhead, Windsor and Eton.

But Supt. Richard Bryan says the fears are unfounded.

He said 'CCTV provides us with a good opportunity to sort out some of the problems that have gone on in the town centres.

I do not accept the displacement argument. The experience in other areas where CCTV is deployed is that opportunistic crime stops. It does not move to other areas.'

If the shift in emphasis did change, said Supt Bryan his officers would be ready to deal with it.

(The article continued for 8 paragraphs outlining general details of the new scheme.).

As we saw earlier when voices questioning the values of the primary definers do find their way into the news text, the discursive strategies through the operation of the ideological triangle come into play. Whereas councillor Harry Parker's concerns originally ran as the bottom half of a small news item under a small headline of 'CCTV system goes live', the response is a full half-page article, the headline of which is twice the size of the original article. Further, the focus of the article is on the dismissal of the fears, rather than of their validity. Indeed while the full personal authority of Supt. Richard Bryan is deployed, the councillors and residents remain anonymous and, while they get one paragraph in coverage, he gets six. The discursive strategies aimed at mitigating the potential negative effects of CCTV become even more apparent when it is revealed that officers would be redeployed from other areas to cope with the expected increase in workload that would arise from the introduction of CCTV in the town centres. (MA, 16 February 1996, WEE, 8 February 1996). Not only were the outlying villages at risk of displacement, they were simultaneously having their local beat officers withdrawn. However the only voice heard on this issue is that of the Local Area Commander, Supt. Bryan defending his decision of redeployment on the grounds that:

It would be awful if we identified problems in the community and didn't put the police there to deal with the problems. (WEE, 8 February 1996)

No other voices are cited either of residents or local councillors, neighbourhood watch groups or any others who might have a critical perspective on the withdrawal of their local provision.

Your Liberties are Safe with Us

In the early reporting of the CCTV proposals, civil liberty issues were most noticeable by their absence and restricted to a short mention of 'a strict code of practice' governing the scheme in the *Maidenhead Advertiser* in March 1995 (MA, 19 March 1995). This was to change in November 1995 when a commercial video went on sale nationally in high street shops entitled *Caught in the Act*. The video presented events recorded by security cameras monitored by local authorities and police forces in the UK. It was aimed at the light entertainment market and included footage of members of the public filmed in compromising situations, and without their consent. The release of the video caused political furore, with MPs from all parties demanding government controls on the release of video footage from public surveillance systems (*Guardian*, 28 November 1995; *Yorkshire Post*, 29 November 1995). In the event, the video was withdrawn from sale the day after it was released when it was argued that it was in breach of the regulations of the British Board of Film Classification. More seriously, Carlton Television were threatening legal action for breach of copyright, as footage which they owned had featured on the video without their consent (*Guardian*, November 29 1995).

It would appear that the release of *Caught in the Act* provided the catalyst for framing the news story in terms of civil liberties and, over the coming months the headlines declared 'Eye-in-the-Sky protest sparks council pledge: Tapes are for police eyes only' (WO, 1 December 1995); 'Tough rules are planned to ensure that new security cameras to defeat crime are not abused' (WEE, 25 January 1995); 'Borough Pledge on town TV Security' (MA, 26 January 1996).

The discourse of civil liberties follows a similar pattern as in 'emphasising effectiveness' and 'discounting displacement'. Firstly, the only voices which are heard are the system promoters and these are dominated by the CCTV Systems Manager and the Council's Head of Engineering Services. In their role as 'primary definers' the issue of civil liberties is transformed into how civil liberties are preserved by the code of conduct. For example:

> Tony Street, head of engineering services confirmed that the network had been designed to protect the rights of privacy of the public. (MA, 15 March 1996).

In a quarter-page article under the headline 'NEW CODE TO ALLAY PUBLIC CCTV FEARS', the only voice heard is that of Mr Perkins, the Systems Manager, in which he is reported as saying:

> 'The code is basically our bible. It explains how we operate and manage the system. We view having this code as vital to the success and integrity of the system.' He said the Royal Borough's code of practice went into even more depth than a national draft code

published this month in response to the growth of CCTV throughout the UK. He added: 'It is not a rigid document and will be updated if necessary as the system evolves.' The Royal Borough has also decided to bring in independent auditors twice a year to measure the system against the code of practice.

Mr Perkins said, 'We want to be whiter than white and to retain public assurance, it is vital to get a regular clean bill of health. It's a very sensitive area. People are concerned about CCTV infringing on their civil liberties. We don't allow anyone into the control room except for a purpose. Staff undergo vigorous training and security checks. Tapes are strictly controlled and are never released for sale.' (WO, 21 June 1996)

The issue here, regardless of the adequacy of the code, is that its appropriateness is never subject to critical scrutiny. In this, and all the other articles dealing with 'civil liberties' issues, the definition of the problem is framed entirely by the concerns of the 'primary definers'. The contents of the code of conduct are never questioned and other parties who may have a critical stance are not consulted. For instance, a central civil libertarian concern is the extent to which the cameras will be used to surveille demonstrators and political activists and whether any resulting images will be passed to the police or security services. These issues are not addressed by the local code of conduct, nor are they raised in any of the news stories.

The irony of accommodation between the local media and the primary definers is best brought out in relationship to the reportage of the code of conduct's regulation of the uses to which the video footage may be used. Two, stories explicitly quote Tony Street, head of the Council's Engineering Services Department as saying:

It will operate under a strict Code of Practice and video tapes will not be released to any other organisation or used for a purpose other than police prosecutions. (Tony Street quoted in the WEE, 30 November 1995)

All video tapes will be strictly managed and won't be released for any purposes other than as evidence in court actions. (MA, 15 March 1996)

However, on 31 May 1996, the *Maidenhead Advertiser* released still pictures from the Maidenhead town centre cameras of three people, one of whom was alleged to have been involved in a violent attack. The attack had happened over five weeks earlier and had not been reported to the police. However the police urged that: 'anyone with any information about the incident or who recognises the people in the photographs, taken from the CCTV video should contact . . .' In the following months other 'faces' of people believed to have been involved in criminal acts were also published along with requests for identifications from the readers.

Whether this is a sensible policy is not at issue, but the public pronouncement that the tapes 'won't be released for any purposes other than as evidence in court actions' would appear to be rather hollow. Clearly they are also being used for the purposes of identification of bystanders, victims and alleged offenders. Although this is a direct breach of the codes of conduct, unsurprisingly it is not something to be raised by the local media, especially when it would interfere in such self-congratulatory copy as:

> Readers ID vandal as seen on CCTV . . . A still from the video was last week published in the Advertiser asking readers to contact the police if they recognise him. And last week a Chippenham man was arrested and cautioned for causing criminal damage. 'Its a big thank to the paper and the members of the public for paying attention' said PC Dave Turner of the Maidenhead Police. (MA, 9 August 1996)

While we do not assume a simple correspondence between the positive portrayal of CCTV in the media and public attitudes and beliefs surrounding CCTV, it would be implausible to believe there is no relationship. For how else do the public 'know' about CCTV systems? Few have any direct experience of CCTV beyond perhaps being able to see a camera in their high street. As Honess and Charman found, 'a substantial number of respondents referred to television programs such as 'Crimewatch' as a source of information about CCTV' and that 'public acceptance is based on limited, and partly inaccurate knowledge of the functions and capabilities of CCTV systems in public places' (Honess and Charman 1992: 6 and 25). Under these circumstances it is hardly surprising that there has been little public opposition to CCTV, since the information contained in political and media discourses has more resemblance to promotional advertising than that of critical and independent journalism. For such a critical stance to occur it is necessary to debunk the idealised gloss represented in the partial media accounts. This requires a detailed examination of how CCTV operates, and it is to this that we now turn.

Part II
The Unforgiving Eye

Introduction: Watching the Watchers – Theory and Method

CCTV and the Panopticon

As Lyon has argued, the sociological response to the general issue of surveillance has been dominated by images of the Panopticon (Lyon 1994). This has been especially true of CCTV surveillance which naturally invites comparisons with Bentham's nineteenth-century design for the new model prison, with its central observation tower, allowing the guards to see everything without ever being seen themselves. And as Lyon has also noted (1994: 62), it is Foucault's reading of the Benthamite project which has been most influential, locating the Panopticon with the birth of disciplinary society and the production of docile bodies (Foucault 1977). However, the extent to which the operation of CCTV mirrors panoptic principles needs to be carefully considered. Just because CCTV systems utilise visual surveillance and rely on centralised monitoring, both key elements of the Panopticon, this should not lead to the automatic assumption that in its operation and effects it is identical. The Panopticon implies far more than these two elements and it is necessary to tease out the important similarities and differences.

For Foucault the Panopticon represents an architecture of power which induces conformity because: 'He who is subject to a field of visibility, and who knows it, assumes responsibility for the constraints of power; he makes them play spontaneously upon himself; he inscribes in himself the power relations in which he simultaneously plays both roles; he becomes the principle of his own subjection' (Foucault 1977: 202). Undoubtably this provides one element in the political and practical appeal of CCTV; it facilitates individual self-control through anticipatory conformity. As Fyfe and Bannister note, the power of CCTV, like the Panopticon, is not vested in surveillance by a particular individual such as a police officer or security guard, but by 'the electronic gaze of the camera' which, following Foucault, they argue, induces a 'state of conscious and permanent visibility that assures the automatic functioning of power' (Fyfe and Bannister 1996: 5; Foucault 1977: 201). But the extent to which CCTV produces an 'automatic functioning of power' is questionable. While Fyfe and Bannister recognise that city streets are not the same as the bounded institutional spaces of the prison and the asylum, they maintain that the panoptic techniques of 'permanent, exhaustive, omnipresent surveillance, have, with the introduction of CCTV cameras, infiltrated public spaces of city centres' (1996: 5).

While we do not disagree that introduction of CCTV to public space represents a move towards panopticonisation, we need to recognise that the totalising vision of the panoptic prison is not simply reproduced on the streets with the introduction of cameras. Unlike the fluctuating and transitory populations of city centre streets, the inmates of total institutions are 'captive' and cannot escape the surveillance gaze, and their incarceration serves as a permanent and powerful reminder of the subjugation. The street population is not so powerless, and anticipatory conformity may be a strictly temporal and spatial phenomenon, with those individuals with deviant intentions shifting the time and place of their activities to outside the camera's gaze. Further, the 'automatic functioning of power' requires that those subjected to surveillance are aware of it. However research into the impact of CCTV in a number of areas has shown that many of those using city centre streets are oblivious of the cameras. Studies by Honess and Charman (1992), Squires and Measor (1996) indicate that only between one third and two thirds of the population using streets with CCTV actually know they are being monitored.

The relevance of the Pantoptican as a model for understanding CCTV needs to be qualified in other ways. Following Bentham, Foucault argues that the strength of the Panopticon design is through inducing anticipatory and, eventually habituated, conformity, making direct physical intervention rarely, if ever necessary. This 'economy of power' allows for a reduction in the number of people who exercise it while:

> increasing the number of those on whom it is exercised. Because it is possible to intervene at any moment . . . Because, in these conditions, its strength is that it never intervenes . . . Because, without any physical instrument other than architecture and geometry, it acts directly on individuals; it gives 'power of mind over mind'. (Foucault 1977: 206)

Whether this is literally true of the operation of panoptic institutions we doubt; resistance and direct coercion have always been features of such regimes. But as a statement of the principle behind the Panopticon it does illustrate how the primary mechanism for inducing conformity is mental rather than physical. Even so, this should not be taken as indicating the irrelevance of direct physical intervention which can be deployed against observed deviants to coerce them back to conformity. In the Panopticon, because the certainty of detection, and therefore intervention, is so high inmates may soon learn the futility of resistance and the necessity of conformity.

The extent to which this is true of CCTV in public spaces is debatable because intervention may not be automatic but contingent on a whole host of social processes: whether the screens are being monitored, and if they are whether an incident is seen and then recognised as deviant; if it is seen, whether it produces a response and the nature of that response. These issues have been noted by a number of commentators. For instance Bulos and Sarno argue that CCTV's role in increasing detection and clear-up rates will be affected by operator attentiveness which will depend on 'the duration for which operators are employed, the number of breaks for operators on each shift, and the length of shifts.' (1994: 44). Similarly Groombridge and Murji note that, while the cameras recorded the abduction of baby Abbey Humphries from a maternity unit, what was 'seen' was a '"nurse" with a child not an abduction' (1994).

As we have already noted, the majority of the populace in some city centre systems are unaware of being watched, and, even if they are, the effects of alcohol-induced sociability may render considerations of the likely response marginal. This suggests that physical intervention will still have to play an important part in the operation of power. Indeed, the advocates of CCTV, such as former the Home Secretary, Michael Howard,while stressing the deterrence functions are also keen to promote its capacity to direct and deploy appropriate responses for the detection and identification of offenders (Home Office 1994: 3).

But it is not just in its monitoring capacity that the Panopticon becomes such a revolutionary mechanism of power, it also is based upon and facilitates the codification of knowledge about individuals and their subsequent classification for the purposes of control. In the case of the prison and the asylum, persons have to be officially labelled as deviant or mad for admission, and then, through surveillance and monitoring, they can be subject to further classifications which single the persons out for the need of treatment or training to foster conformity. This classification is premised on creating individualised dossiers on salient aspects of their behaviour. In this way the Panopticon assumes that those subject to its power are already deviants and that all persons have a known identity within the system which allows for the attribution of any behaviour to known, identified and dossiered subjects.

This is very different from the situation encountered by CCTV systems operating in public space. First, the population is not already predefined as deviant, and second, the identity of those being surveilled is largely unknown. This anonymity of the subjects of surveillance means the images cannot be cross-referenced against a dossier of an individual's biography which might contain their moral and criminal histories which could provide the warrant for extended surveillance, and their address, which is important if they are to be traced. But in one respect CCTV offers a powerful extension of panoptic principles not envisaged by Bentham, as the tapes can hold a permanent record of the activities that fell under the camera's gaze. As Virilio (1994: 44) points out, the results of human visual surveillance cannot be replayed or rewound for other audiences such as the public for identification, the police for investigation or the courts for prosecution. In the absence of a named suspect, retrospective (rather than immediate) investigation and intervention is still, even with the existence of clear photographic evidence on the tapes, very difficult. It relies on the modern version of the 'wanted poster' broadcast via television programmes such as 'Crimestoppers' or the publication of pictures in local newspapers and, as such, is resource intensive and tends to be limited to only the most serious crimes.

This inability to 'know' in advance who is already classified as deviant also means that the CCTV operators are faced with a mass of undifferentiated images with, potentially, the whole population being the object of suspicion. Since it is simply not possible to monitor every person's behaviour closely (the act of zooming in on one person automatically excludes attention on another), surveillance in city streets invites attention to questions that are not posed by the Panopticon, namely how selectivity operates in practice.

In this brief theoretical overview, we have tried to articulate the manner in which CCTV systems may be considered to display panoptic features and have argued there are some important differences: the population subject to this disciplinary gaze is non-institutionalised, not dossiered or officially classified, and less likely to display anticipatory conformity. All these features mean that the power of CCTV systems, unlike the Panopticon, is more dependent on its capacity to produce authoritative responses through direct physical intervention. One of the consequences of these differences is a requirement to pay particular attention to what CCTV operators actually do. For instance, how do CCTV operators determine who is or is not worthy of targeted surveillance? Is it based on people's behaviour, and if so what sort of behaviour? Or is it random? Or is it based on a reading of their sociological characteristic, their age, race and gender for example? What type of behaviours are deemed to warrant intervention, and how is such deployment affected given that CCTV operators do not have the capacity to intervene themselves? It is these questions that will form the basis of our analysis but, before we turn to issues of empirical substance we want to briefly consider what the existing research on CCTV has to say about these matters.

CCTV Research

The rapid growth of publicly funded CCTV systems during the 1990s has also simultaneously led to a growth in research aimed at evaluating the impact of CCTV as a crime reduction measure. Much of this research has been 'post hoc shoestring efforts by the untrained and self interested practitioner' (Pawson and Tilley 1994) leading to results which are 'highly unreliable' (Short and Ditton 1995: 10). However, as Tilley has more recently argued, there is increasingly evidence 'from various more or less technically adequate evaluations' (Tilley 1998: 144–5) of the crime prevention potential of CCTV. Here we could point to the evaluations of Ditton and Short (1998), Skinns (1998) and Bulos et al. (1995) all of which show a reduction in crime following the introduction of CCTV. In these evaluations CCTV becomes the 'X' in the 'OXO' method of evaluation (Pawson and Tilley 1994), with the 'O's representing the crime statistics before and after the implementation of the scheme. But the 'X' resembles an opaque 'black box' and the mechanisms by which it produces its observed effects are largely taken for granted.

This is important for a number of reasons. Unless the mechanisms through which CCTV produces its effects in different contexts are understood, it will be impossible to analyse why some systems appear to work at reducing crime and others do not (Tilley 1993) and mixed findings are already starting to muddy the waters (Bulos cited in the *London Evening Standard*, 3 January 1996). But CCTV is far more than just about the reduction of crime; it is about the power to watch and potentially intervene in a variety of situations, whether they be criminal or not. But the question of who and what is watched and what warrants intervention have largely been ignored by existing research which is primarily concerned with crime prevention. The questions are important for three reasons. First, if the targeting of the street population is not random are some social groups more likely to be monitored than others And, as a consequence, are they more likely to be the subject of authoritative intervention and even criminalisation? Second, to what extent, if any, does CCTV operate as an exclusionary mechanism, targeting the undesirable as well as the criminal, with a view to removing them from certain city centre spaces? Finally, does CCTV lead to the 'thinning of the mesh and widening of the net' of social control by being able to capture ever more instances of previously officially unnoticed deviant behaviour, and responding to infractions of ever decreasing seriousness? (Cohen 1985)

To answer the questions posed by both theoretical and practical considerations, it is necessary to turn our attention to an analysis of the social construction of suspicion and its impact on authoritative intervention as evidenced by our studies of the operation of three CCTV control rooms.

Methodology

The Sites

Observations were carried out in three sites between May 1995 and April 1996. One was in the commercial centre of a major metropolitan city with a total popula-tion in excess of 500,000. During the day it was a bustling shopping and business district and, as darkness fell, supported a thriving nightlife based on clubs, pubs and eateries. The next site centred on the market square of an affluent county town with a population of nearly 200,000. It thronged with shoppers during the day but at night was fairly quiet until the weekends, when it would attract revellers from the surrounding area for a night on the town. The third focussed on a rundown but busy high street in a poor inner city borough with an ethnically diverse population of nearly 250,000. We have named these three sites Metro City, County Town and Inner City to reflect their contrasting features.

The systems contrasted in other ways. Metro City cost over £1 million pounds to install, consisted of thirty-two cameras and had running costs of over £200,000 per annum. Although the system was located in the control room of the local police station, it was run by an independent trust responsible for all aspects of its day-to-day operation, including the staffing of the control room and maintenance of the system. In contrast, the County Town system cost around £500,000 to install and had annual running costs in the region of £120,000. It consisted of over one hundred cameras, although the main monitors generally only displayed the pictures from the twenty-five or so cameras focused on the town centre. The Inner City system cost around £450,000 with annual running costs of about £100,000 and had sixteen cameras focussing on the busy high street and surrounds. County Town and Inner City were run by their respective local authorities, housed in purpose-built control rooms in local authority premises, and both had sub-contracted the staffing of the control rooms to private security firms. All three systems had 24-hour-a-day monitoring. In County Town and Metro City this involved three eight-hour shifts and in Inner City two twelve-hour shifts.

The Observations

In total 592 hours of monitoring were observed – the equivalent of 74 eight-hour shifts (although in Inner City twelve hour shifts were worked). All days of the week were covered, as were an equal proportion of early, late and night shifts. On each shift the observer would 'attach' himself to one operative and shadow their work. In total twenty-five different operatives were shadowed. A small notebook was used in the field when appropriate and full field notes, including full descriptions of any targeted surveillance were written up either immediately after they occurred or at the end of each shift. We defined a targeted surveillance as either one which lasted more than one minute on an individual or group of individuals, or where it was initiated from outside the system (by police or private security for example), regardless of whether a target was identified. The field notes recorded key data for each targeted surveillance based on a checklist of salient features. Field notes were also recorded for general observations on the operation and control of the system, operatives' beliefs and values, work tensions, interactions with visitors to the system and included informal interviews with operators and managers.

The field notes of targeted surveillances also formed the basis for filling in the quantitative observation schedule. This recorded four types of data: **shift data** –

including the number of operatives on each shift, the time screens were left unattended, who visited the system, whether and how many tapes were borrowed for inspection and for what purpose; **targeted suspicion data** – including the reason for the suspicion, type of suspicion, how the surveillance was initiated, how many cameras were used, whether the incident was brought to somebody else's attention; **person data** – detailing the age, race, sex and appearance of up to four people for each targeted surveillance, and finally **deployment data** – recording all deployments initiated by the system operatives, how the system was used during the deployment and what the outcome was.

In total this has yielded data on 888 targeted surveillances. In 711 of these surveillances, a person was identified and we have basic demographic data for each of them (age, race, sex and appearance) as well as on another 966 people who were the second, third or fourth, person in a group being surveilled.

In what follows the names of people and places have been changed to preserve the anonymity of those who took part in the research.

−6−

The Watchers and the Watched:
The Social Structuring of Surveillance

Before we examine who watches the cameras and who they watch, it is necessary
to consider the formal, legal and organisational context in which this occurs and
any internal or external controls which might limit or regulate the manner in which
suspicion is enacted.

Controlling the Watchers: External and Internal Regulation

External Regulation: The Legal Context

There is no statutory regulation in English law governing the implementation or
operation of CCTV systems watching over public or private space. An examination
of British constitutional law also indicates the complete absence of a tort of privacy,
with only limited protection offered in such remedies as the law of trespass,
nuisance, and the breach of confidence. According to Feldman (1993: 381) the
absence of a privacy statute can be regarded as characteristic of English civil
liberties law, and as Baxter notes 'where the law is silent on a matter it will be
assumed that the conduct is not forbidden that is to say, a person is free to do that
which is not forbidden' (1990: 20).

Unlike in other European countries there is no right in English law to prevent a
person either taking or publishing one's photographs (Bailey et al. 1991: 484).
This is best illustrated by the case of *Kaye v. Robertson* (1991) in which a famous
actor, Gordon Kaye, was photographed in a hospital room without his consent
after suffering serious head injuries. At the Court of Appeal, the actor's case, based
on trespass to the person, was rejected thus providing him with little manoeuvre in
English law to protect his privacy. He was granted an injunction on the basis of
'malicious falsehood' but the story and photographs were allowed to be published
on condition that the paper did not claim cooperation from Mr Kaye. The judges
in their adjudication stated:

> It is well known that in English law there is no right to privacy, and accordingly there is
> no right of action for breach of a person's privacy. The facts of the present case are a

graphic illustration of the desirability of Parliament considering whether and in what circumstances statutory provision can be made to protect the privacy of individuals. (Glidewell LJ cited in Bailey et al. 1991: 472)

The defendants' conduct towards the Plaintiff here was 'a monstrous invasion of privacy' (to adopt the language of Griffiths J in *Bernstein v. Skyviews* in 1978) . . . It is this invasion of his privacy which underlies the Plaintiff's complaint. Yet it alone, however gross, does not entitle him to relief in English law (Bingham LJ cited in Bailey et al. 1991: 474)

This absence of the right to prevent photographs being published was also upheld in *Mrs R v. Central Television PLC*. (1994). In this case Mrs R saw a trailer of a programme to be broadcast on 27 January 1994 concerning the work of the police in the tracking down of a purveyor of child pornography. The programme wanted to show the exterior and interior of Mrs R's house and the sound of her voice during the arrest of her ex-husband. In October 1992 he had been convicted for indecent assault and sentenced to six years imprisonment, however Mrs R had concealed this fact from her neighbours and her daughter believing it to be in the child's best interest if she were not branded the daughter of a paedophile. The brief facts of the judgments can be summarised as follows:

1 A concealed camera and sound recording equipment were taken in to Mrs R's home without her consent but, with the consent of the police, by a film crew making a documentary on police work.
2 An action in trespass was sought to protect Mrs R's child. A hearing on 27 January 1994 resulted in the TV company agreeing not to broadcast the scenes of the street, the house or Mrs R's voice. The action in trespass was therefore abandoned.
3 It became clear that the face of Mrs R's ex-husband would remain in the broadcast. Kirkwood J, in an attempt to balance the freedom of the press with the interests of the child, concluded that the aim of the programme would not be defeated by obscuring the face of the child's father.
4 Central Television PLC appealed against this and won. Neill LJ concluded that the present case did not concern the court's care of the child, and upheld the TV company's submission to broadcast the programme in full, allowing the scene of the arrest to be shown, overturning the earlier ruling.

Thus even when a photograph is obtained on private property without the consent of the owner, and its publication may be thought to seriously prejudice the welfare of a child, the courts have still held that it may be shown 'in the public interest'. The implications of this for our discussion of the regulation of suspicion are important. The law regulating the taking and publication of pictures in private space is weak and even when it has involved a trespass fails to allow redress. In public space, where the recording of CCTV footage by definition will not involve trespass, does not involve a breach of trust, and is unlikely to be defined as a nuisance (Sharpe 1989) the law is silent on who may be watched, for what reasons, and for how long. It would appear that when citizens enter the public realm of city streets, they relinquish all claims to privacy. In practice this means that even if a CCTV system operated on strictly racial criteria and only focussed on black people, or was used intensively to track a particular individual whenever they entered a town centre and wherever they went within the cameras' view, there would be no basis in law for a challenge.

Internal regulation: Codes of Conduct

In the absence of legal regulation of the operation of CCTV systems the vast majority of local authorities, police forces and trusts responsible for managing schemes have established internal codes of conduct which specify how systems should be used. It is difficult to generalise about codes since there is no nationally agreed standard and, as the LGIU discovered in their review of codes of practice in 1995, they varied widely in their style, content and length (Bulos and Sarno 1996). However central themes could be discerned:

> A detailed analysis of the codes allowed clear identification of the core concerns of the parties operating CCTV system. These concerns included the need for proper and secure video storage, retrieval and use of tapes, with particular attention being paid to the way in which video material could be used for evidential purposes. Almost as evident was the idiosyncratic and partial way in which other matters such as accountability, provision of information, monitoring and evaluation were addressed. (Bulos and Sarno 1996: 17)

Furthermore what constitutes 'suspicious behaviour' or legitimate grounds for extended surveillance is not addressed by codes of conduct or by training as Bulos and Sarno note:

> The most neglected area of training consists of how to identify suspicious behaviour, when to track individuals or groups and when to take close-up views of incidents or people. This was either assumed to be self evident or common sense. The informality of these procedures leaves unexamined the predispositions of operators to consider some people or types as more likely to commit crime than others. . . . Few codes specify the basis on which tracking should occur or what kind of limitation should be placed on the time a camera is trained on a single person or group in the expectation of an incident occurring. (1996: 24)

Each of our three schemes operated under a code of conduct and the general observations made by Bulos and Sarno would apply. Two of the codes are silent as to what constitutes legitimate suspicion and warrants surveillance although they do make some general points about privacy. For instance, one declares that the system 'must pay due account to the rights of privacy enjoyed by every member of society and no use shall compromise this fundamental right'. Fine sounding rhetoric indeed, but ultimately hollow since, as we have already noted, there is no fundamental right to privacy and as we read on we find the statement is not alluding to the tracking and observation of people in public space, but:

> Persons operating the system will not use the cameras to focus through windows of premises and where ever possible such opportunities will be prevented by mechanical or physical stops restricting camera movement. This restriction is intended to preserve the privacy of the public and enhance the integrity of the system.

Similarly in the other site, although the original codes made no mention of any limitations on surveillance, they were revised in the light of the LGIU's model code of conduct published in 1996 and a new paragraph added which stated the system:

> will safeguard the privacy of individuals and not invade the privacy of any individual in residential, business or other private premises, buildings or land unless in direct pursuance of objectives 1.1 to 1.3.

Given that objectives 1.1 to 1.3 relate to the detection, apprehension and prosecution of offenders and maintaining the free flow of traffic, this would appear to give maximum leeway for operators to argue that they were surveilling a person because they were acting suspiciously. Furthermore the limitation, on the surveillance of private property, both residential and commercial, is also exempted on the grounds of crime control.

The third code is more explicit:

> Operators will not linger on members of the public engaged in legal but personal or intimate past-times; nor will they attempt to view inside any private dwellings.

The definition of 'legal but personal' was not defined, but, by conflating the two, it would appear that operators are perfectly justified in tracking and zooming in on someone behaving in a lawful manner, but not if they were, for example, kissing someone else. However the codes did go on to state that the system 'will not be used for general collection of intelligence about the events and people in a particular area'. Although this would not necessarily limit observation it would appear to limit the subsequent recording and documention of individuals who whilst acting lawfully may be of interest to the police. However, in a memo written several months after the system became operational this element of the code seemed to be abandoned. The memo from the police liaison officer, who was the de facto manager of the scheme, was addressed to all the operators, and noted that although there had been a reduction in street robbery since the beginning of the scheme, it was on the increase again. The memo went on to declare:

> The time has come to remind the villains that we are there. Use the cameras to search the streets for likely looking individuals . . . zoom in and out, look for faces, potential suspects, potential victims, move the cameras around from time to time to let them know you're alert. . . . Use the real time recorders when you identify people of whom you are suspicious.

In other words, not only use the cameras as a deterrence but to use them to gather intelligence.

We have seen that the law and the codes have little to say about regulating who should be watched. Therefore it was very much left to the operators to come up with their own modus operandi, which of course meant that who was watched, and for what duration was influenced by the idiosyncracies of individual operators. It is therefore necessary to consider the nature of the watchers.

The Watchers

Like most of those employed in the private security industry, CCTV operatives experienced poor rates of pay and long hours. Rates varied between £2.60 and £4.60 per hour. Hours were also long, ranging from 42 hours per week to 60 hours and operators also had to endure the ardours of shift work. As the field notes from Inner City make clear other elements of conditions of service were also poor.

> The attractions of working for a security company were extremely limited, for this reason such an industry did not attract the most motivated personnel. Who, it could be asked would want to work for a firm that whilst winning a contract which specified a uniform then made their employees pay for it? Two blue shirts necessary for a six-day week cost £5 each, the epaulettes and tie came free. Black shoes were compulsory, but the responsibility of operators. And, as part of the job description was to patrol the car park an outdoor coat was needed but not provided and whilst a torch was provided for night-shift patrol batteries were not. To cap it all the operators had to convince their employers of their employability by producing a clean criminal record which cost them £10.
>
> The chairs they operated from were too low – operators could not see half the cameras above their console when sitting down. The room whilst air-conditioned was frequently too hot which only served to induce tiredness and intermittent sleep. The book-keeping

they were required to do did not force their employer to provide pens and the subject of hourly pay was contentious. Operators kept what they earned to themselves realising that they were on different rates of between £3.15 and £3.75 depending on what the company could get the various individuals to accept on joining. Overtime payments were at the same rate as normal time, no holiday pay was included, no Union was recognised and all worked a seven on three off followed by seven on four off work pattern.

In view of the pay and conditions it is hardly surprising that few had chosen to become a CCTV operative as a vocation, most had been forced into security work after a period of unemployment due to redundancy, ill health or disability. In Metro City all the operatives except one had disabilities, ranging from kidney problems to multiple sclerosis to paralysis. Even so it is difficult to generalise about the operatives, they ranged in ages between early twenties and late fifties, only two of the operatives were female and apart from in Inner City, where half the operatives were black, they were with one exception white. But this statistical portrait does little justice to the variations in how the operatives saw their role and the range of commitment and motivation to the job. Hopefully the 'pen portraits' of nine of the operatives below, selected for contrast rather than typicality, should help to convey a sense of the operatives' orientation to their job:

Lenny: One of the oldest and longest-serving operators he had worked in the control room since day one. He was in his fifties, born in Jamaica and married. With his children now grown up Lenny was biding his time to retirement and was not foregoing this warm and comfortable job for anything! Whilst not well-paid it was near to his home and the day shift suited his lifestyle. Following 20 years as a factory machinist redundancy had found him in security work. Five years with one company saw him seek a change and move to his current job where he was quick to impress management with his punctuality and politeness.

Jimmy: A year's unemployment awaited Jimmy when he left the Army, now aged twenty-four this Geordie had found a wife-to-be in London and was using security as a stop-gap before finding work as a courier driver. Uninterested in the job of operator Jimmy worked for two weeks before moving on and in that time manifested only a dislike for his fellow operators and a liking for attractive women to be viewed by the cameras. A dislike of young black males did not make him stand out amongst his workmates.

Barry: A former store manager who, when made redundant found he had few marketable skills to fall back on and so had drifted into and remained with the same security company for five years. Within two years he was offered the Control Room job and was now one of the longest serving operators. In recognition of his longevity and experience he had recently been promoted to the rank of Sergeant. He now earned 25p an hour more than colleagues, was the first line of management and was responsible for ensuring the system always had security personnel on duty. If one of the succeeding shift phoned in sick he had to find a replacement amongst off-duty operators or stay on and work a double shift. An obedient worker, Barry was punctual, meticulous and played everything by the book. Having lost a good job he did not want to lose another.

Conscientious and very polite Barry was articulate about his job, but uninformed about the politics of surveillance or issues of liberty. Pro-police and deferential in their presence Barry had no sympathy for that part of the population he called 'scum' or 'shitbags' and if police were 'forceful' in making arrests he was unperturbed; such tactics were needed against some people. After three years he was preparing to move on to new things, ideally involving training others in CCTV use.

Robert: In his mid-twenties Robert was polite, charming, curious, and good company. Such politeness and deference meant that in his daily dealings with the town's store detectives and police officers he was, according to some of his co-workers too eager to please. The end product was a willingness to surveille anyone whom these two agencies considered 'suspect' regardless of the merit of the request.

He left school at sixteen with a few 'O' levels and spent the next six years working as a handyman before being made redundant and found security work the only job available at the time. Although a 'local' Robert rarely recognised anyone on the screens. In all likelihood a somewhat sheltered upbringing did not see him out on the town too often, but instead marriage at the age of twenty-one. He showed no particular like or dislike towards the young men he followed on camera daily. This made him strangely enough the most impartial of all operators.

Colin: Working six nights a week from midnight to 8.00 a.m. was not ideal hours for an unmarried man in his mid-twenties. But, for someone with few qualifications, it was a job which paid decent money and, in all honesty, there was little else he could do. Colin left school early, did a stint in the Army, followed by a period of unemployment before taking a job as the night CCTV operator. The boredom of night shifts was relieved by a variety of reading material ranging from pornographic magazines to the American survivalists magazine *Combat and Survival*, and by sleep. Which on quiet nights was regulated by an alarm clock set after 2.00 a.m. to wake him before the nightly visit of the mobile security van (3.30 a.m.) and reset on his departure for 7.00 a.m. in time to freshen himself up before the arrival half an hour later of the car parks manager. Should sleeping be a problem Colin had a collection of tapes to watch. Recorded from mainstream or satellite TV there was always some programme or other to catch up on.

Phil: Phil was only twenty-two and in his final year studying for a degree at the local university. Not that his future was going to be dependent on academic repute, he had considered careers in the police, prison service, accountancy and law. Reading a variety of job literature on his one night a week shift he did not in reality know what to do for a career. Meanwhile he had worked on CCTV each college vacation and whenever called upon to relieve absenteeism or illness.

Phil had been a privileged student. A scholarship saw him spend twelve months in an American college and a legacy meant he could buy a three-bedroom house to both live in and rent out to his fellow students.

Despite working alone each Saturday night Phil would always wear full uniform (including tie) all night and was the only operator who did not work to the accompaniment of music radio stations. The only deviant act he allowed himself was a visit from his girlfriend when she had finished waitressing in a town centre restaurant. Because of his conscientious approach and because he worked the night the town was busiest he was responsible for many arrests. He was undoubtedly a good operator who watched anybody and everything and disliked 'scum' and 'scrotes', but he would not be in the job for too long after graduating because he had plans to set himself up as a consultant in the training of CCTV operators.

Simon: in his mid-twenties Simon was one of the youngest operators and popular with both police controllers and other operators. From a middle-class background, and a one-time aspirant to the priesthood he moved away from the seminary to begin a course at university, but was forced to leave having contracted a disibilitating illness. He worked in his family's business and attended catering college but was hampered by his illness. He took the CCTV job to keep busy and kept active with a girlfriend, the use of the family boat, and a car. He was the most disabled of the operators and this meant he found difficulty opening folders to complete documents. The future was not bright for him, with a deteriorating condition a wheelchair seems inevitable, but the building has no wheelchair facilities. Being a staunch football fan and fond of a drink himself he was not one to moralise over drunks and rowdy behaviour he saw on the screen.

Gordon: a fifty-year-old father of two who lived in a council tower block near the Control Room. He was always impeccably attired in full uniform with polished shoes and clean-shaven and did everything by the book. Living nearby permitted him to take his meal breaks at home. However he bemused the other operators by taking extended detours whenever he went to and from home which they believed were attempts to conceal the reality of what he did from neighbours. Certainly he did not want people to know what he did – he told me as much – and became very worried and animated when he learned that the operators would be required to go 'on the road' to publicise the scheme in a variety of city centre venues. He asked not to be on public display and his wish was granted.

Following twenty-three years working as an electrician he had faced twelve months of unemployment before this job came along. Gordon was fastidious about procedures and consequently was not popular with this co-operators – who had titled him 'The Prince of Darkness' because of his obsessive secrecy. Whenever he was referred to in his absence the conversants would wrap their arms around the lower face revealing only furtive eye movements above their forearms. This ridicule was taken further by two of the other operators who, since the scheme's inception, had taken against his bossy manner. Their favorite ploy was to wait until he left the room and to alter the height of his chair and mess up the orderliness of his desk. On return Gordon would say nothing as he meticulously rearranged this papers and silently readjusted his seat. For Gordon the control room was a lonely place but he appeared to take comfort in knowing that he was right.

Bill: After twenty-five years as an electrician and his mortgage paid and children gone Bill worked as an operator just to get him out of the house and to earn money for a drink. This latter pastime proved problematic – according to the other operators Bill had a drink problem which meant he was frequently late for his shifts and sometimes did not arrive at all and if he did often snoozed on the job. However they covered for him and at times wrote his name in the signing-on book even when he was absent all the shift. A quiet manner could reveal at times a wicked sense of humour. Because he made people laugh and because other operators knew Bill would not be in the job very long his absences and general irreverent attitude to the job were tolerated.

George: The most thoughtful and professional of all the operators had a background which combined craftsmanship with care. He had been a skilled engineer and Union shop steward before being made redundant in his early thirties. Soon after he contracted a long-term illness which limited his capacity for further engineering work. An avid reader and generally inquisitive man he was very well informed on politics. Polite and courteous he was also one of the two operators who did not worry about asking police officers who had taken control of the system to hand it back to him. Unhappy with the pay and conditions and the way the Scheme was managed George planned to leave the job unless the operators could join a Union or possibly manage the Scheme themselves in liaison with the police.

The different backgrounds, motivations and orientation to their work inevitably meant that operatives were not always in agreement with their colleagues as to who or what should be surveilled. In the main, any disagreements remained largely unspoken: good working relations required toleration of others idiosyncracies in choosing targets, especially when there were not formal guidelines to fall back on.

However on one occasion they did publically surface in a heated dispute between two operatives about the appropriateness and fairness of the surveillance and the subsequent arrest for a minor, and apparently 'vicitimless' crime.

The early June Sunday morning early shift was dire. There was barely a soul to see amidst the early summer drizzle. Still there was plenty to talk about and an unusual scenario presented itself because for the first time ever Bill was working a shift with Steve. The shift change, at the request of Jon who was having a family celebration the night before and wanted to avoid an early shift, suited Steve who wanted a Sunday afternoon free. The only person this arrangement did not suit entirely was Bert who hearing of the change the previous day told Jon that Steve was a 'supercilious bastard' when they were in training together.

Attempting to jolly the pair on a non-eventful morning I had turned the topic of conversation to crime, it had proved enlightening. Predictably Steve realised his contributions to sound-bites; 'individual responsibility', 'take control of your own life', 'scum who sell Big Issues', 'Yobs from the council estate', it was all good Tory stuff. By contrast in some ways was Bert who whilst suggesting that those who are of no use to society should not be allowed to breed or should be destroyed, at the same time was posing rhetorical issues about crimogenic populations which he admitted he could not answer. But he was articulate and gave a soliloquy of how the Conservatives had ruined the country by their policies in the last 15 years and how all this CCTV system did was catch 'bairns' and 'poor wee souls from the schemes', and how, in his opinion, such surveillance never caught big-time crooks or money fraudsters.

Whilst listening Steve had no opinion which reflected on them both; Steve wants a job at all costs and will never criticise the scheme, Bert could not care less. A life in industry and a pension from it means the money he earns whilst getting him a bit of freedom is not worth sweating over. Whilst other operators (particularly Steve) might strive to get their names next to arrests in the Incident Book, he was not bothered if his never appeared. Over an hour lapsed since we had left this debate when Steve noticed a scenario that made him suspicious and caused him to zoom in on a person. Next to an old and derelict warehouse was a permanently locked gate and rubble-strewn driveway. Over this gate had jumped a man who had two items in his hand. On closer inspection the suspect was aged around mid-20s and poorly dressed in cheap casual sportswear, dirty trainers, with a stubble lower face and unkempt dirty hair. In his hands were a roll of rusting copper wire and a narrow strip of lead about three foot long. Walking to a shopping trolley he had obviously placed strategically by a building skip he placed his treasure in it and off he went pushing it up the street.

Seeing all this Steve immediately shouted to the Controller the sequence of events. The Controller watched the man and after about a minute replied that all units were engaged or in the station; there was no one to send or, I suspected, even she thought the offence so trivial she did not want to send anyone. After another minute she finally deployed a mobile unit. The suspect meanwhile was closely under Steve's surveillance as he searched in a building skip this time picking out pieces of wood until a mobile police unit finally arrived after five minutes to apprehend him as he pushed his wares down the street. The cameras permitted the operator to see the police car and the arrest and then see the vehicle return to where the suspect was first sighted by Steve. Minutes later the enquiring officer returns to the car after looking around the derelict warehouse and the suspect is brought to the station. He is under arrest and is to be charged, not with Theft but, according to the operator, with Entering Closed Premises. It is now 12.04.

Hearing this Bert slowly shakes his head and in what seems a bad mood decides he's going to the toilet, leaving an embarrassed-looking Steve. From the moment Steve spotted this man Bert had goaded him as to his motive. Firstly he pointed out the suspect was just a 'poor soul' who had negligible amounts of metal and could he not leave him alone. In reply to Steve's insistence that theft is theft, Bert accused him of 'glory hunting' and just wanting to put his name in the incident book. Expanding on his disgust Bert explained more, 'I've done it. I've been poor, I've pinched metal . . . Leave him alone he's not kicking car panels in nor nothing like that . . . bah! All for 10p's worth of scrap'. Steve's reply was emotive, 'I've been poor. My kids and I have had to share packets of crisps for meals, but I've never thieved. Theft is crime and is wrong; he's a scummy dirty yob. Besides my job is just to point out and tell police what I see, they decide if it is a crime . . .'

In this impasse Bert left disgusted. When he returned he winked at me and asked Steve if he had put the incident in the book yet. The reply was that it was too trivial an offence and he would not bother. When Bert left at the end of the shift Steve put the details of the arrest and his name in the incident book.

Who was Surveilled and Why?

Each of the systems displayed the images from the cameras on a bank of monitors in front of which sat the operators at a console. The console had a dedicated monitor and a control panel for selecting and operating particular cameras, making dedicated recordings, and housing telephone and radio links for communicating with the outside world. For example, the Inner City system had a bank of 16 colour monitors which displayed the images from the 16 Pan, Tilt and Zoom cameras located in the high street and surrounding roads and a further 20 monochrome monitors which, by using split screens, displayed the images from 47 fixed-position cameras located in and around the nearby car parks.

With such a constant bombardment of images, CCTV operators were faced with an inevitable task of selectivity in deciding which people and activities were worthy of special attention. In Table 6.1 we can see the age and sex of those people the operators chose to focus upon. As any incident could involve more than one person we have two measures: first, the breakdown of all people surveilled and second the breakdown of the primary person surveilled if the surveillance involved more than one person. In fact, of those surveillances where a target was identified 234 (32%) involved a solitary person, 193 (26%) involved two people, and 208 (42%) involved three or more people.

Table 6.1 Characteristics of All People and Primary Person Targeted for Surveillance

Characteristics	All people		Primary person	
	No.	*%*	*No.*	*%*
Sex				
Male	1485	89	660	93
Female	192	12	49	7
Total	1679	101	709	100
Age				
Teen	775	47	270	39
Twenties	705	42	320	46
Thirties +	185	11	107	15
Total	1665	100	697	100
Race				
White	1076	65	483	68
Black	571	34	216	31
Asian	14	1	5	0
Total	1661	100	704	99
Appearance				
Smart	172	10	71	10
Uniform	31	2	10	1
Scruffy/subcultural	214	13	118	17
Casual/indistinct	1245	75	499	72
Total	1662	100	698	100

* Percentages may not add up to 100 due to rounding.

The first point to note from Table 6.1 is that there is little difference in the demographic features of the sample whether measured by the characteristics of the primary person or of all people surveilled and we will therefore confine ourselves in the following analysis to a consideration of the primary person surveilled.

Looking at age, gender and appearance first, we can see that CCTV operators focus their attention heavily on young men, particularly teenagers who account for less than 15 per cent of the population, but constitute nearly 40 per cent of those singled out for targeted surveillance. The vast majority (72%) of those who are surveilled are casually or indistinctly dressed although those who are scruffily or sporting distinctively subcultural attire account for a further 17 per cent of the total.

The extent to which these differences reflect real differences in the behaviour or availability of young men which cause them to be disproportionately the target of operators' suspicion is a question to which we shall return. However, all three areas were busy commercial centres attracting women as both employees and consumers and certainly not devoid of men over thirty. It is therefore apparent from the outset that surveillance in public space is heavily skewed toward young men – women and those over thirty hardly ever enter the frame.

The issue of race is more complex. We can see that whites make up around two thirds of both groups – 65 per cent of all people surveilled and 68 per cent of the primary person surveilled. Black people accounted for about one third of both groups at 34 per cent and 31 per cent respectively. Asians hardly figure at all at less than 0.5 per cent.

This, of course, does not by itself mean that black people are over-surveilled even though they only make up some 2 per cent of the national population. Their over-representation is partly a function of the areas in which the study was undertaken. Metro City has a small ethnic minority population, less than 3 per cent; County Town has 6 per cent, and Inner City has a black population of around 18 per cent with other ethnic minorities totalling 7 per cent.

For Inner City these figures are for the Borough as a whole. However, local authority figures for the area immediately surrounding the CCTV system, which includes a densely populated council estate show that over half (52%) of the residents belong to an ethnic minority. This would suggest the over-representation is partially accounted for by the large number of black people living in the vicinity of the system. On the other hand, the area surveilled by the cameras includes a major bus interchange and is one of the primary shopping streets in a borough with a population which is three quarters white. This, along with our own casual observation which reveals many white shoppers and commuters, indicates the over-representation of black people is also partially a function of operator differentiation.

While it is impossible to arrive at a precise figure for the racial composition of the people using the streets covered by the Inner City system, to err on the side of caution, we will take the local figure and assume that 50 per cent of people using the streets under surveillance are black.

Table 6.2 Race of Primary Person Surveilled by Site of System

Race	Metro City		County Town		Inner City	
	no.	%	no.	%	no.	%
White	275	99	162	85	30	16
Black	3	1	28	15	177	84
Total	278	100	190	100	207	100

The figures for Metro City are too small to be meaningful so we will discount them. In County Town and Inner City there would appear to be clear evidence of over-representation, in County Town by a ratio of 2.5 to 1 and in Inner City by about 1.7 to 1. In other words, in County Town, black people are two-and-a-half times more likely to be the object of targeted surveillance than their presence in the population would suggest and in Inner City over one-and-a-half times more likely.

Why were People Targeted?

For each targeted surveillance we recorded what, at the outset, the incident 'seemed' to be about. For instance, a youth crouching down by the side of a car would be classified as crime related, a group of men involved in revelry at closing time as order related and surveying the scene of a traffic accident as 'Other'.

This category does not imply that the person was involved in any criminal behaviour, merely that the operator had some explicit grounds for targeting the person or incident. A youth crouching by the side of a car is, in all probability, doing up his shoelaces rather than removing hubcaps, and the targeted surveillance may well confirm this. However, this will still be coded as crime related since the operator was treating the behaviour as indicative of theft. Similarly, if the operator tracked a known shoplifter this would also be classified as crime related because they had explicit grounds for their suspicion. If there were no signs from a person's behaviour or they were not a 'known offender', then we recorded the surveillance as for 'no obvious reason'.

Table 6.3 Reason for Targeted Surveillance

Reason	No.	%*
Crime	257	30
Order	192	22
No Obvious Reason	310	36
Other	98	11
Total	857	99

* Percentages do not add up to 100 due to rounding.

We can see from Table 6.3 that between them Crime and Order-related suspicion accounted for just over half of all targeted surveillances (52%). Within Crime-related suspicion, the largest single category of suspicion was for theft (55%), followed by crimes of violence (19%) and drugs (13%). For Order-related suspicion the largest category was unruly and disorderly behaviour (64%) followed by nuisance behaviour (32%). The 'other' category included traffic (21%), city management (17%) and missing persons (5%). Overall, rather than suspicion being based on explicit behaviours related to crime or order maintenance the largest single category (36%) was for 'no obvious reason'.

The important question is whether, in the light of our data which has already indicated the over-representation of certain social groups, the reasons for surveillance are also socially differentiated. Before we try and answer this question it will be useful to examine the 'type of suspicion' that each targeted surveillance was based on. For each targeted surveillance we coded the suspicion as one of seven types listed below:

categorical: suspicion based merely on personal characteristic such as dress, race, membership of subculture group

transmitted: surveillance initiated by someone else e.g. police, store detective or member of the public

behavioural: suspicion based on behaviour, i.e. fighting, public display of drunkenness

locational: suspicion based on a person's location, e.g. walking through a car park with a high rate of theft late at night

personalised: suspicion based on personal knowledge of the person surveilled

protectional: suspicion based on fear for persons safety, e.g. woman late at night at a cash machine

voyeuristic: monitoring based on prurient interest.

Table 6.4 Type of Suspicion Involved in Targeted Surveillances

Type of suspicion	No.	%*
categorical	298	34%
transmitted	273	31%
behavioural	208	24%
locational	36	4%
personalised	30	3%
protectional	20	2%
voyeuristic	8	1%
Total	873	99%

* Percentages may not add up to 100 due to rounding.

We can see from Table 6.4 that categorical suspicion is the largest single type, accounting for one-third of all targeted surveillances. Thus the most frequent reason that an individual is targeted is not because of what they have done, but because of who they are, and operators identify them as belonging to a particular social category which is deemed to be indicative of criminal or troublesome behaviour. More concretely, however, a quarter of all surveillances are related to a person's behaviour, one in twenty to the location that someone was in, and one in thirty to personalised knowledge. One per cent of targeted surveillances related to voyeuristic interest although this is a considerable underestimation of the time spent dwelling on females, as our recording procedures only allowed us to code for one reason the type of suspicion, and women who were lingered over were often noticed as a result of an initial surveillance of men based on another type of suspicion. Thirty-one per cent of targeted surveillance stemmed from outside the system and was therefore based on others' suspicions, mainly store detectives but also members of the public or police.

To explore if suspicion is socially differentiated we need to look at how the reasons for the surveillance and type of suspicion are stratified by age, sex and race. We will deal with age first, the results of which are set out in Tables 6.5 and 6.6.

Table 6.5 Reason for Surveillance by Age*

	Teens		Twenties		Thirties plus	
Reason	no.	%[†]	no.	%	no.	%
Crime Related	59	22	80	26	17	17
Public Order	30	11	83	27	46	45
No Obvious Reason	173	65	115	38	21	21
Other	4	2	29	9	18	18
Total	266	100	307	100	102	101

* The results presented in this table are statistically significant at the $p<0.01$ level.
[†] Percentages may not add up to 100 due to rounding.

Table 6.6 Type of Suspicion by Age*

| | | | Age | | | |
	Teens		Twenties		Thirties plus	
Type of suspicion	no.	%[†]	no.	%	no.	%
categorical	179	67	103	32	15	14
transmitted	39	15	52	16	27	26
behavioural	31	12	121	38	49	46
locational	9	3	15	5	6	6
personalised	6	2	17	5	6	6
protectional	3	1	4	1	3	3
voyeuristic	1	0	7	2	0	0
Total	268	100	319	99	106	101

* The results presented in this table are statistically significant at the $p<0.01$ level.
[†] Percentages may not add up to 100 due to rounding.

Age appears to make little difference as to whether a person enters the frame as a suspect involved in a criminal activity. Around one-quarter of teenagers and twenty-year-olds, and one-fifth of those aged-thirty or above were targeted for suspicion of criminal activity. There are, however, major differences for public order-related offences. As we have already noted those over thirty years old are rarely the subject of surveillance and when they are surveilled, it is most likely to do with public order. In fact they are four times more likely to be the subject of public order-related surveillance than teenagers and three times more likely than twenty-year-olds. On the other hand, two-thirds (65%) of teenagers were targeted for no obvious reason – that is three times the rate for those over thirty (21%) and twice the rate for those in their twenties (38%).

These figures are confirmed by looking at how the type of suspicion is affected by age. Only one in eight (12%) teenagers are targeted as a result of their behaviour, compared with four out of ten twenty-year-olds (38%) and nearly half (46%) of those aged thirty or over. Put simply, for anyone over thirty to be surveilled at all it is most likely to be as a direct consequence of their behaviour. In all probability they have been drinking and are causing disorder or nuisance. If this is not the case, they are largely ignored by the cameras. In contrast, youth is treated as suspicious merely because it is youth. Thus two-thirds of teenagers were subject to categorical surveillance which is five times the rate for thirty plus year olds. We now turn our attention to gender.

Table 6.7 Reason for Surveillance by Gender*

| | Sex | | | |
| | Male | | Female | |
Reason for surveillance	no.	%†	no.	%
Crime Related	138	22	19	43
Public Order	150	24	12	27
No Obvious Reason	302	47	7	16
Other	49	8	6	14
Total	639	101	44	100

* The results presented in this table are statistically significant at the p<0.01 level.

† Percentages may not add up to 100 due to rounding.

Table 6.8 Type of Suspicion by Gender*

| | Sex | | | |
| | Male | | Female | |
Type of suspicion	no.	%†	no.	%
categorical	287	45	9	18
transmitted	109	17	16	33
behavioural	174	27	15	31
locational	30	5	1	2
personalised	27	4	2	4
protectional	10	2	1	2
voyeuristic	3	1	5	10
Total	640	101	49	100

* The results presented in this table are statistically significant at the p<0.01 level.

† Percentages may not add up to 100 due to rounding.

The first point to note from Table 6.7 is that if women are surveilled, which is an infrequent event, it is because they are suspected of being engaged in specific criminal activity. Twice as many women were surveilled for crime-related reasons than men and, while half of men were surveilled for no obvious reason, only one in six females were. This is confirmed when we look at the type of suspicion (Table 6.8) where only one-fifth of women (18%) as opposed to nearly half of men (44%) were subject to categorical surveillance. While some have argued that CCTV is women-friendly – making them feel safer on the streets – this is not the result of a protectional gaze directed by the operator. In only one case of targeted surveillance directed at a woman could it be said to be specifically protectional. Operators simply do not look out for those they think may be vulnerable to ensure that they do not become the victim of mishap or predators, but focus on stereotypical categories of those they think may be likely to offend. Women were also far more likely to be the object of voyeuristic rather than specifically protectional surveillance and, while only five incidents may seem relatively small, it is, as we noted above, an under-representation but still represents 10 per cent of all the targeted surveillances of women.

Table 6.9 Reason for Surveillance by Race*

	Race			
	White		*Black*	
Reason	*no.*	*%†*	*no.*	*%*
Crime Related	115	25	42	20
Public Order	148	32	13	6
No Obvious Reason	163	35	141	68
Other	41	9	12	6
Total	467	101	208	100

* The results presented in this table are statistically significant at the p<0.01 level.
† Percentages may not add up to 100 due to rounding.

Just as age and gender structure the reason for the surveillance and the type of suspicion so does race. Blacks (20%) and whites (25%) are equally likely to be surveilled for crime-related matters, however whites are much more frequently surveilled in relation to public order (33%) than blacks (6%), mainly because they are more likely to constitute town centre drinkers. Blacks, however are twice as likely to be surveilled for no apparent reason. This is corroborated by the type of suspicion to which each were subjected. Three-quarters of the targeted surveillances of blacks were based on categorical suspicion compared with just over a quarter of those for whites. Conversely, few black people were surveilled explicitly because of their behaviour – 13 per cent of targeted surveillance compared with 36 per cent for whites.

Table 6.10 Type of Suspicion by Race*

Type of suspicion	Race			
	White		Black	
	no.	%†	no.	%
Categorical	136	28	157	74
Transmitted	109	23	14	7
Behavioural	174	36	27	13
Locational	24	5	6	3
Personalised	20	4	9	4
Protectional	10	2	0	0
Voyeuristic	8	2	0	0
Total	481	100	213	101

* The results presented in this table are statistically significant at the p<0.01 level.

† Percentages may not add up to 100 due to rounding.

A person's appearance (no tables shown) was also strongly correlated with both the type of suspicion and reason for the surveillance. Those who were scruffily or subculturally dressed were nearly three times more likely to be targeted for order-related matters (46%) than those who were casually dressed (17%) but were no more likely to be targeted for 'no obvious reason' than others. Similarly, the scruffy and distinctively subcultural were targeted less on the basis of categorical suspicion (31%) but more as a result of their behaviour (42%). Interestingly while smartly dressed people were rarely surveilled, accounting for less than one in ten of all targeted surveillances, when they were, it was also predominately for their behaviour (46%) compared with only a quarter (23%) of those who were casually dressed.

We have profiled the statistical features of the surveilled population and demonstrated that it is not a simple sub-set of the street population available for surveillance. In the next chapter, drawing on the ethnographic data from the three sites we want to explore the processes which produce this particular pattern of surveillance.

−7−

Working Rules and the
Social Construction of Suspicion

In an essay first published in 1972, Harvey Sacks argued that the police 'were the occupational specialists in inferring the probability of criminality from appearances people present in public places' (Sacks 1978: 190). With the growth of camera surveillance, in Britain at least, this function is fast being usurped by CCTV operators. For Sacks, the key problem for the police patrol officer was how they could use a person's appearance as an indicator of their moral character and thus: 'maximise the likelihood that those who turn out to be criminal and pass into view are selected, while minimising the likelihood that those who do not turn out to be criminal and pass into view are not selected' (1978: 190).

The problem is identical for the CCTV operator. Bombarded by a myriad of images from dozens of cameras and faced with the possibility of tracking and zooming in on literally thousands of individuals, by what criteria can they try and maximise choosing those with criminal intent? Compared with a patrol officer, they are at both an advantage and a disadvantage. Because their 'presence' is remote and unobtrusive there is less likelihood that people will orientate their behaviour in the knowledge that they are being watched and, by virtue of the elevated position and telescopic capacity of the camera, they have a greater range of vision than the street level patrol officer. However, these advantages must be offset against their remoteness which means they are denied other sensory input, particularly sound, which can be essential in contextualising visual images. Unlike the patrol officer, the CCTV operative is both deaf and dumb. They simply cannot ask citizens on the street for information nor can they hear what is being said.

In a city centre system comprising of twenty-four cameras, the number of images, as measured by frames per second of videotape, entering the system in a 24-hour period is around 80 million. Faced with such an avalanche of images and a limited range of sensory data, how then does the CCTV operator selectively filter these images to decide what is worthy of more detailed attention? The problem is the operative does not have prior knowledge which would enable them to determine which persons are going to engage in criminal activity. It is therefore an occupational necessity that they develop a set of working rules and procedures which seeks to maximise their chances of selecting those most likely to be involved.

For Sacks, the patrol officer achieved this by using the 'incongruity procedure' which contains a number of working assumptions of equal relevance to CCTV operatives. As we shall see, Sacks' account provides an extremely useful description of the localised, situated and contextualised features of ascribing criminal intent on the basis of appearance. However, for our purposes it is necessary to qualify it in two important respects. First, Sacks was not concerned with behaviours which are indicative of suspiciousness – only appearances – nor was he concerned with the identification of candidates for surveillance on the basis of their, known, past criminality. Second, by focussing on the micro-sociological dynamics of the social construction of suspicion he has underplayed the already taken-for-granted assumptions which prefigure the selection process and rule out large sections of the available population. This is hinted at when he notes that the 'normal ecology' becomes a 'normative ecology' (1978: 195) but in this formulation suspicion becomes a property of the area rather than of the observer. We would argue however that, when assessing who is worthy of a second glance, CCTV operators bring with them taken-for-granted assumptions about the distribution of criminality within the population. This revision of Sacks leads us to the first three working rules that operators use for determining who and what to watch.

1 Given the sheer volume of candidates for targeted surveillance, the operators utilise their already existing understanding of who is most likely to commit crime or be troublesome to provide potential candidates for targeted surveillance.
2 Certain behaviours unquestionably warrant surveillance because they are themselves criminal or disorderly. However, there is a range of other actions which, whilst not criminal, operators treat as indicative of potential or recently occurring criminality.
3 Certain people are immediately worthy of surveillance because they are known by operators to have engaged in criminal or troublesome behaviour in the past.

These first three rules are not especially space-time dependent and do not rely on a normative concept of place. They prefigure the other working rules that are more contextually located and in line with Sacks' original statement of the 'incongruity procedure'. However, the rules that follow are not a simple restatement of Sacks' but have been modified to account for the different circumstances faced by the CCTV operative compared with the patrol officer.

4 Operators must learn to treat locales as territories of normal appearances and against this background variation can be noticed. This involves utilising the temporal and spatial variation of activities within a locale to judge what is both 'out of place' and 'out of time'.

5 For operators the normal ecology of an area is also a 'normative ecology' and thus people who don't belong are treated as 'other' and subject to treatment as such.

6 There is an expectation that just as operators treat territories as a set of normal appearances, so others are expected to treat them as such. And thus if a person appears lost, disorientated, or in other ways at unease with the locale, this will indicate suspiciousness.

7 Operators learn to see those who treat the presence of the cameras as other than normal as other than normal themselves.

The Working Rules in Operation

Rule One – *Given the sheer volume of candidates for targeted surveillance, the operators utilise their already existing understanding of who is most likely to commit crime or be troublesome to provide potential candidates for targeted surveillance.*

It will come as no surprise to anyone who is aware of the literature on police suspicion that CCTV operators adopt similar criteria to construct the targeted population: focusing on the young rather than the old, disproportionately targeting blacks rather than whites, men as opposed to women, and the working rather than middle classes (McConville et al. 1991; Norris et al. 1992). Of course, it may be argued that, since those officially recorded as deviant are disproportionately young, male, black, and working class that targeting such groups merely reflects the underlying reality of the distribution of criminality. Such an argument is, however, circular: the production of the official statistics is also based on pre-given assumptions as to the distribution of criminality which itself leads to the particular configuration of formal and informal operational police practice. As McConville et al. argue, the convicted population 'is a subset of the official suspect population. Whilst convicted criminals may be broadly representative of suspects, there is good reason to believe that they are very dissimilar to the "real criminal population" . . . The make up of the convicted population is, therefore, like the make up of the suspect population: a police construction' (1991: 35).

Targeting Youth

As we have seen, young men were the main targets of surveillance. This is not surprising given the attitudes that operators displayed towards youth in general and particularly those identified by attire, location or body language as poor or belonging to the underclass. Like the police, operators often referred to such categories as 'toerags,' 'scumbags', 'yobs', 'scrotes', and 'crapheads'. As the following two examples illustrate operatives need no special reason to ascribe malign intent merely on the basis of age, particularly if youth are in a group:

13.45 – The operator sees and zooms in on four boys walking through a pedestrian precinct. Aged between 10-12 and casually, but fashionably dressed the four in combining age, appearance, location and numbers are suspects for a variety of possibilities. The four gather around in a form of 'conference' and 30 seconds later walk a few yards to their left and enter a shop renowned for selling toys. What the operator sees is not kids entering a shop meant for kids, but sees something else – they are all up to no good and in his opinion have probably just plotted to steal and will be coming running out any minute with stolen merchandise. In anticipation he fixes a camera onto the shop door and tells the other operator to put the cameras onto the street he presumes they will run into.

Using two cameras and two operators the surveillance lasts six minutes before the boys leave the shop – slowly and orderly and without any apparent stolen goods. Now, the operator informs me, he will zoom in on the four as they walk through town in a search for bulges under their clothing, particularly around the waistline – this according to him is where stolen toys would be concealed. But the boys have jeans and T-shirts on and no bulges are apparent. Still, however, the four are followed by both operators to see if they will pull items out of their pockets – they don't. The four then disappear from view as they enter another department store. The operator looks elsewhere, but comments to his colleague 'They're definitely up to no good.'

16.45 – Impending criminal activity is noticed when three males aged 16 are noticed standing around a market stall displaying watches. The operator zooms in with his camera and gets his colleague to do the same with another camera from a different angle. They then wait . . . but the youths merely walk away having neither purchased nor stolen anything. The operator is left to muse, saying 'I wonder why they changed their minds?' (3 minutes, 1 camera)

While youth is generally seen as suspicious and warranting of targeted surveillance, this would still leave operators with far too many candidates to choose from on the basis of the images alone. Two additional features become salient for further subdividing youth into those who are worthy of more intensive surveillance and those who are not: attire and posture.

The following garments were thought by operatives to be indicative of the criminal intent of the wearer: 'puffer' coats (ski-style fashion), track suit bottoms, designer training shoes, baseball caps (ponytail hairstyles only compounded suspicion) and anything that may conceal the head, be it a woolly hat, hood or cap and football shirts or supporter paraphernalia. Any type of loose-fitting jacket could provoke suspicion because in the operators' eyes it may conceal stolen items or weapons, as would a jacket or headgear worn in warm weather. Young females were only guilty by association, i.e. if seen with 'scrote' boys. Otherwise they were not a category worthy of surveillance unless they were good looking. In the following field note extracts the manner in which a person's visual identity is used to further sub-classify the youth population is illustrated:

01.46 – Surveilling the car park the operator finds a suspicious person. This is a white male in his early 20's, casually but expensively dressed. The object of suspicion is the sunglasses he wears. The operator asks himself why does a man need them on at night. Furthermore he is standing leaning against a good (i.e. sporty) car talking to another male. The male compounds his suspicion further by wearing a leather zip-up bomber jacket, designer trainers and a fashionable haircut. The camera is trained on him and his colleague as they get into the car and drive away. As they do so the vehicle registration number is zoomed in on and noted on a note pad the operator has with him. The operator keeps his own dossier on 'flash cars' and their occupants and believes such people are all potential drug dealers. (2 minutes, 1 camera)

03.01 – A male and a female are noted walking across the car park. Both are white and in their mid-20s and whilst she is smartly dressed, it is her male companion who arouses the operator's suspicion. He has about him the stigmata of criminality – he has a coat on with a hood up. The operator knows it is not raining so cannot understand why (the possibility being because it is because it is bitterly cold outside does not appear in his logic). The couple are carefully surveilled as they walk to the railway station, check a railway timetable board and then retrace their steps and walk out of sight. (4 minutes, 4 cameras)

11.50 – A black male aged around sixteen attracts the attention of the operator because of his white cloth cap. Followed and zoomed in on he has no apparent criminality, but as the operator states his attire makes him out to be a 'wide-boy' and therefore worth following. (2 minutes, 1 camera)

00.42 – Two white males aged 16 and dressed casually but with hoods covering their heads on this cold winter night are followed. Their suspicion is founded in two things: firstly, they have the ever incriminating hood up, the other is that they are walking through an open-air car park whilst apparently too young to drive. The operator sees in them a 'result' and as they pass a cluster of parked cars mutters to the screen they are visible on 'have a go, have a go'. They disappoint him. Whilst followed as they make their way they merely walk out of the car park and towards the periphery of the town toward a Council estate. (2 minutes, 1 camera)

There are two issues to note from these examples, first that suspicion is not uni-dimensional. The background assumptions concerning youth are refined by utilising other visual clues that can be inferred from the clothes of a potential suspect and this is read in conjunction with temporal and spatial features of a locale. In the surveillance of the couple in the car park, attire is also compounded by place and time – a young man in car park with his face obscured at three in the morning is unambiguously read as a potential car thief. In the first example, involving the young man with the sunglasses, attire was compounded by accoutrements – a flashy car, and the time. Implicitly, the form of reasoning is based on a reading of the protestant work ethic: who can afford to buy an expensive car by the fruits of an honest day's work if they are out enjoying themselves at nearly two o'clock in the morning?

The second point is that wearing headgear is particularly stigmatising in the view of CCTV operators. First baseball caps, woolly hats and hooded parkas (short coats) were seen as indicative of subcultural affiliation, and thus helped to single out respectable from 'deviant' youth. Indeed, at times when watching the operators, the only distinguishing feature which could justify why one youth, as opposed to another, was targeted for extended surveillance was the presence of baseball caps, particularly if worn with the peak facing backwards. We will return to the issue of hats later, because they are significant to rule seven of the incongruity procedure.

It is not just attire which provides a warrant for narrowing down the suspect population. In all sites, operators believed in a practice known as the 'scrote walk' which was a rather fluid concept reduced to a series of seemingly contradictory clichés:

> Too confident for their own good
> Head up, back straight, upper body moving too much
> Chin down, head down, shuffling along . . .
> Y' know . . . swaggering, looking hard . . .

Suspicion was compounded when a 'scrote haircut' was evident; this could be very short, or very long, or medium length with hair gel or most significantly pony-tailed. But to make identification easier 'scrotes' generally could be identified because they hung around in groups:

19.03 – Four white male juveniles dressed subculturally are noticed looking at shop displays. But as they depart the operator considers they are 'walking funny' a product of large training shoes and baggy jeans, perhaps, but nothing more untoward. On closer inspection the operator realises one of them is known to the system because of an incident concerning criminal damage (i.e. graffiti), but whilst following the four the operator's attention is directed elsewhere. (4 minutes, 2 cameras)

21.45 – The operator notices a character who has come to his attention before. Believed to be involved in all sorts of criminal activities the suspect and his two mates are surveilled and zoomed in on as they stand outside McDonalds. The operators discuss with contempt the characteristics of these three males reserving particular venom for their 'swaggering' and 'scrote way of walking'. However, they have done no wrong for the moment bar offend the operator with their presence and so are left alone after they walk through the town. (5 minutes, 1 camera)

As Kenan Malik reported in the *Independent* on the operation of the CCTV in the West End of Newcastle, the selection of youth was also based on such categorisation. As the operators reported: 'we keep an eye on them to see if they're up to something. They're the type you see . . . They're all scrotes round here – petty thieves, vandals, druggies, there's not much that you can do but keep an eye on them. (*Independent*, 3 September 1995)

The section of youth as potential candidates for targeting rests on the background assumption as to their over-propensity for criminality. This is then refined through the use of visual clues which enables some youths to be identified as belonging to common-sense categories of moral waywardness which then gives the warrant for targeted and extended surveillance. So far we have talked about the processes which mark out youth as the disproportionate targets of surveillance, but as we have seen it is not only youth, but black youth in particular that is over-surveilled.

Colour-coded Suspicion

Racist language was not unusual to hear among CCTV operators and, although only used by a minority of operators, the terms 'Pakis', 'Jungle Bunnies' and 'Sooties' when used by some operatives did not produce howls of protests from their colleagues or line managers. Stereotypical negative attitudes towards ethnic minorities and black youth in particular were more widespread and ranged from more extreme beliefs, held by a few operators, about their inherent criminality to more general agreement as to their being work shy, 'too lazy' to get a job and in general 'trouble'.

Given these assumptions the sighting of a black face on the streets of either Metro City or County Town would almost automatically produce a targeted surveillance.

14.00 – Whilst surfing the cameras and streets the operator sees two young men standing in a pedestrian shopping precinct both looking into a holdall bag one of them is carrying. Whilst this scene is not remarkable what is unusual is that one of the two is black, a rare sight in the city centre. The two are in their early 20's and smartly dressed. After a minute or so one hands to the other a piece of paper which most onlookers would presume was an address or phone number. Finally, on going their separate ways the two indulge in a fashionable 'high-five' handshake. This alerts both operators.

To these two the 'high-five' was suspicious because it was not done with flat-hands and it 'wasn't firm enough'. In fact according to the second operator one of the men had a distinctly cupped hand. Whilst this was explainable by his holding the piece of paper just given him by the other the operators see only criminality – this could be a surreptitious, yet overtly public exchange of drugs. The youth with the bag is surveilled closely as he continues his walk. He not only has a bag, possibly the merchandise, but he is also black – a drug dealer. The suspect then enters a men's fashion store which means that the camera is now trained on the doors whilst the operator awaits a possible hasty reappearance complete with stolen items in shoulder bag. After a few minutes the camera is zoomed into the store and the suspect is visible in a capacity the operators did not consider – he is a sales assistant.

This colour-coded suspicion was intensified when combined with cars, or headgear, or being in places the operators presumed they should not be:

15.00 – A black male with dreadlocks, wearing sports gear, and in his mid-20s is inviting the operators' suspicion and surveillance because he is in the wrong place doing the wrong thing. He is in fact crouched by a bicycle rack fiddling about with a bike. Zooming in the operator looks for evidence of a theft – is he looking around him as he fiddles? no, is he forcing something which won't move? no. He then gets something out of his back pocket – this happens to be a bicycle rear lamp. Fitting it on he rides the bicycle, which is obviously his, safely and legally. (4 minutes, 1 camera)

23.05 – A group of 12 black youths all in their late teens and casually dressed are noted outside a fast-food outlet. They are doing nothing more than eating and talking to various youths, male and female, white and black who approach them. However, on the encouragement of the Manager who describes them as 'our ethnic problem' the operator CCTV system surveilles them and follows them when they move up the street. (20 minutes, 1 camera)

14.34 – As a former police officer of ten years' experience, the operator 'knows' that young black men are 'trouble' when she catches sight of a white escort convertible complete with wheel trims/spoilers and with its hood down and driven by a black male aged in his mid to late 20's she is alerted enough to zoom in on him. The vehicle is parked up and he is chatting to his passenger – a white girl with blonde hair aged in her early 20's. This combination of colour and technology is all too much for the operator who phones the police controller explaining that 'men of that age and that colour only get their money one way and it's not through hard work' and puts the image onto his monitor. On suspicion of being a drug-dealer she zooms in on the registration plate whilst police do a PNC on the vehicle. Whilst not disclosing fully what he had done or is suspected of doing the controller gets back to the operator to tell her that the driver is 'of police interest'. The suspect drives away out of sight unaware of who has been watching and talking about him. (8 minutes, 2 cameras)

In County Town and Metro City the background assumptions are cross-cut by the rule that indicates that those who are by way of appearance statistically different from the norm will be candidates for surveillance. Thus black people in predominately white areas will be targeted and, as Jefferson has shown white people in black areas are most likely to be targeted by the police (Jefferson 1992). In this case, by Sack's original formulation of the incongruity procedure, in Inner City, black youth which is a permanent feature of the locale should be treated as 'normal' and subject to low-intensity surveillance while older, white men should be singled out for special attention.

However, in Inner City, the selection of black youth was not just a matter of operator discretion but a deliberate matter of policy. The first week of operation saw the police officer responsible for setting up the scheme give advice to both shifts on where and what to watch. The priority target was stated to be black youths and the priority crimes drug-dealing and street robbery. This effectively meant that the majority of the cameras were never really monitored, since they covered the more general shopping area, indeed for most of the time only three out of the sixteen cameras were actually watched. For the purposes of target selection, attention was focussed almost solely on a junction which housed a row of bus stops and a number of West Indian shops, one of which, Santana's, a general grocers and late-night store would, from early afternoon to late evening, see groups of youths hang about outside.

Nor can the over-representation be viewed as white operators selecting young black men on the basis of second-hand stereotypes although, as we shall see, some of the white operators targeted blacks with a relish which implied a deep prejudice. Black operators similarly targeted young blacks but their comments directed at the screen were not usually so venomous. The following goes some way to illustrating the point:

Black Operatives

19.20 – The night shift have inherited a job from the day shift – namely, a group of 15–20 black males and females, all in their teens and casually/sub-culturally dressed who are standing in a group outside an off-licence and general store called Santana's which is adjacent to a series of bus stops. Zooming in on this group the operator can see nine black males and four black females. The operator is a black man in his late 50s and not impressed by this assortment saying for mine and the other operator's benefit the police should round em up and get their mums and dads to come and fetch em and shame them. The group are generally standing talking and flirting with the occasional bout of horseplay and dancing, they harass no one. Nearby are standing dozens of people awaiting one of the 12 bus routes which pick up at this point. Even so the camera remains on the group for 30 minutes and notices a group of eight black males in their early 20's who walk through the gathering and continue elsewhere. Two of this group then split off and the operator decides to follow the remaining six, but is thwarted when they walk out of range of the cameras. (51 minutes, 4 cameras)

02.00 – Standing outside the all-night shop are three black males in their 30s. One has the stigma of being a Rastafarian and having a woolly hat balancing on long dreadlocks. The operator is confused and tells his co-operator of his dilemma: why are they still out at night and not buying anything? The answer: 'They don't work they just sleep all day . . .' With mutual disgust the two black operators watch these black men as they stand and talk and then drive away in a car. (5 minutes, 1 camera)

White Operatives

10.04 – The first sighting of young black males produces the day's first surveillance. Two 16 year olds, casually dressed, are noticed standing outside a clothes shop talking. The operator zooms in and notices their sub-cultural attire which for one includes a pair of large designer training shoes. The operator comments to no-one in particular 'I wonder where he nicked those trainers from'. The suspects do not enter the store, but resume their walk. The operator looks elsewhere. (2 minutes 1 camera)

12:57 – An uneventful morning has produced nothing of interest for the operators in six hours. In between reading various newspapers and zooming in on attractive women the conversation turned twice to the main targets of the system – black youths. Explaining how the mornings are both boring and a ' waste of time' the operators explain that really their job was one of ' waiting for the kids'. By 'kids' they meant groups of black youths who congregate outside Santana's and any others they happen to see who walk along the two main streets covered. By mid-day, more in an attempt to break the monotony and silence one operator exclaims how 'we haven't seen any of our regulars yet'. The other agrees but explains their absence in the derogatory, 'They're all still in bed after a night out thievin' and mugging.'

13.45 – Returning to Santana's here are now eight black youths. Two have been followed earlier in the shift, but the other six are not known. This prompts an evaluation from the operator that the big lads are in town. These big lads are black, about eighteen years old, but are not around long as the group boards a bus to the operator's pleasure and advice of: 'get on it and fucking stay on it'. (3 minutes, 1 camera)

12.35 – Five black males are surveilled as they stand outside Santana's. All are casually dressed and two have baseball caps on, one attracts attention because he is dancing to a tune either in his head or audible via an unseen tape machine. The operator is not impressed and somewhat disgusted points him out to his colleague saying: 'Look at him . . . he's always doin' that'. Zooming in closer on the five the same operator offers his thoughts on contemporary youth saying: 'They shouldn't be hanging around . . . they should be out looking for work.' His colleague agrees and the pair sit silently watching the group as they board a bus. The operator however is keen to keep an eye on them and follows the bus two stops and notices them getting off and walking towards a leisure centre. This seems to annoy him as he states: 'I dunno, game of pool, can of coke . . . then passing drugs around'. Slowly shaking his head the operator moves the camera elsewhere. (12 minutes, 2 cameras)

Gender blindness?

While women make up 52 per cent of the general population they only accounted for 7 per cent of primary persons surveilled. Women were almost invisible to the cameras unless they were reported as known shoplifters by store detectives or because of overt disorderly conduct. This accords with Bulos and Sarnos observations as they note the views of female operators on whether they viewed the monitors differently from their male colleagues:

> One replied 'no its exactly the same'. The other two however, made one or two significant comments. Firstly it was considered that she (female controller) looked more on women as potential criminals. The male controllers tended to see criminal activity as a male preserve and tended to ignore or oversee women acting suspiciously. She (female controller) prided her self in being quick to spot women acting suspiciously. Another female controller commented 'they (men) look at women but not for the right reason!' (Bulos and Sarno 1996: 29).

If they were invisible as suspects they were also invisible as potential victims and were unlikely to became targets by virtue of a protectional gaze, indeed in nearly 600 hours of observation only one woman was targeted for protectional purposes – as she walked to and from a bank cash dispenser. In fact the protectional gaze was more likely be focussed on male security guards involved in the transit of cash. Moreover there was evidence that the same attitudes which have traditionally been associated with the police occupational culture surrounding domestic violence continue to inform the operation of CCTV as the following incidents from two different sites show:

> 01.20 – With hardly anyone on the streets anyone who is noticed is worth surveilling. An opportunity to break the monotony is provided by a white female in her late 20s who in black leather attire seems to be dressed for an occasion bordering leather fetish. She is first sighted outside a fast food outlet and moments later she climbs into a car – a mini-cab – from the office next door. Sitting in the rear of the vehicle for only half a minute she then gets out and appears to be walking alone down the street. At this point the operator can zoom in and see her attire – black high-heel boots, black leggings, black leather jacket and ribbed and sequined shirt which evokes a laugh and the comment 'What a scrubber' from him. The object of curiosity then stands still and asks two passing females for something – the two appear to ignore her. Less than a minute later the woman then back-tracks to follow a black male (late 20s). Whilst she follows she then gestures towards the bottom of the street whereupon seconds later another white female of similar age appears and joins her friend.
>
> From the other direction appears a small white male in his 20s who is obviously shouting at the first female as the three now walk together back towards the cab firm outside of which other people are gathered. The animated white male continues his rant

and attempts to strike the female, this does not connect and is not repeated. The operator does not respond to what he considers a domestic incident, but tells me he is going to zoom in on their faces because as the three now are about to get into a cab they might not pay the driver at the end of the journey! The car drives away at 00.51. (7 minutes, 1 camera)

01.05 – The operator notices a couple in the street having an animated row. Both are white and in their late twenties and stylishly dressed as if returning from a night out. This quiet Monday night has produced nothing of interest and these two arguing is the most interesting event of the past three hours. This and the fact that the woman in view is blond and good looking has added to the attraction and so the operator tells the police control room staff (two men) to have a look at the event unfolding.

After a two-minute argument the woman storms off up the street, but does not go out of the man's sight and slumps against a wall looking miserable. The man, meanwhile, climbs into a nearby car, closes the door and waits in the driver's seat, lights off. The impasse lasts five minutes, the female walks slowly towards the car and begins to talk to the man via the driver's window, only to storm off again after a minute. This time the male follows her on foot to continue the row. The operators and police enter into a commentary urging the man not to chase after her and having decided she is hot-tempered and sulky the operator says aloud 'You hit her and we'll be your witnesses'.

The couple continue their debate and this time the female decides to walk off past the man, but as she does so he attempts to restrain her by holding her arm. She pulls back, in the stand-off further words are exchanged and a blow is aimed from the male to the female which strikes her around the upper chest and causes her to stumble. The blow does not look to be a hard one and she picks herself up and walks away. Meanwhile the male returns to his car and once again sits and waits. This time the female walks down the street past the car and continues for 20 yards only to stop, walk back to the car and stand looking into it.

After a couple of minutes of her looking and him pretending not to notice the pair resume their chat, this time via the passenger door. The drama continues when she walks away again, this time the distance is only ten yards then she does an about-turn and returning to the car opens the front passenger door and whilst she sits in it she leaves the door wide open. After a mutual silence (seen by zooming the camera into the car's windscreen) the pair decide to talk again. This time she lasts three minutes before getting out and storming off.

By now other police personnel have appeared to watch this drama Two other officers have entered the room so that six men can now, in pantomime mode, boo and cheer good moves and bad moves. One boo is reserved for the male when he starts up the car, does a three-point turn and drives up to where she is sulking and parking up tries to persuade her to get in. A cheer goes up when he has seemingly failed in this effort and so drives away. But cheers turn to boos when he reverses to resume his persuasion. His words work and to boos, from her audience, she climbs in the car and after a four-minute discussion the stationary car drives away into the distance. (Two cameras 25 minutes).

As these incidents make clear, there is no simple correspondence between the discovery of criminal activity and the resulting deployment and arrest. Lesser assaults when perpetrated by men on men outside nightclubs resulted in police officers being deployed and arrests being made. However, the images from the screen are filtered through an organisational lens which accords meaning, status and priority to events. It will come as no surprise to critics of the police handling of domestic violence (Edwards 1989; Stanko 1985) that the existence of 'objective' evidence led to neither a protective response in the first instance to prevent the assault occurring nor, once it had occurred, a legalistic response to arrest the perpetrator. As Edwards has argued the police have always concerned themselves more with public order than private violence, and this was deemed as essentially a private matter, albeit occurring in public space.

Moreover, this example gives credence to Brown's assertion that the essentially male gaze of CCTV, has little relevance for the security of women in town centres and may indeed undermine it by offering the rhetoric of security rather than providing the reality (Brown 1998). CCTV also fosters a male gaze in the more conventional and voyeuristic sense, with its pan-tilt and zoom facilities the thighs and cleavages of the scantily clad are an easy target for those male operators so motivated. Indeed, 10 per cent of all targeted surveillances on women, and 15 per cent of operator-initiated surveillance were for apparently voyeuristic reasons outnumbering protective surveillance by five to one. Moreover, the long understood relationship between cars and sex provides operators and police with other chances for titillation:

> 01.00 – On the first night shift the operator is keen to show me all his job entails. Eventually I am taken, via the camera, to 'Shaggers Alley', an area of a car park near the railway station which, by virtue of having a large wall covered in ivory and being a dead end to traffic, is the most discreet town centre place for punters who have picked up prostitutes soliciting from an adjacent industrial estate about a mile away. Whilst this location is out of the way to passers-by many a punter and indeed a happy couple not involved in a financial transaction are unaware of the reach of the all-seeing camera whose job is facilitated by a large and powerful car park light which does not leave much to the imagination of the observer.
>
> Clearly visible on this night thanks to the cameras' ability to zoom in and look into cars is a male in his late 20s sitting in the driver's seat with what can only be described as an expression of glee as a female, kneeling on the passenger seat performs fellatio on him. Her hair and head are noticeably bouncing up and down for around two minutes. When the performance is over the woman is clearly visible topless in the front seat. From beginning to end this scenario is put onto the police monitor, the operator informing me that the police officers in the communications office enjoy such scenarios and when bored will sometimes phone to ask him to put the cameras on Shaggers Alley for their titillation. (11 minutes, 1 camera)

The 'appreciation' of such public displays was a regular feature of the night shift in one of our sites and not just confined to those with access to the monitors. Many such encounters could be found on the 'shaggers alley greatest hits tape' which was compiled and replayed for the benefit of those who missed the 'entertainment'.

We have so far concentrated on the how the operator's moral assessment of character is predicated on a pre-given understanding as to who is responsible for the crime problem. This does not mean that other social groups are not targeted but in general they will only come to attention if, through appearance or behaviour, they are specifically calling attention to themselves. Nor does it mean that all youth is targeted. Operators further select on the basis of the working rules contained within the incongruity procedure.

Rule Two – *Certain behaviours unquestionably warrant surveillance because they are themselves criminal or disorderly. However, there is a range of other actions which, whilst not criminal, operators treat as indicative of potential or recently occurring criminality.*

When watching the multitude of screens it is not just particular types of people who warrant surveillance but also certain classes of action. Unsurprisingly if people are noticed engaged in activities that could be construed as fighting, the people are zoomed in on. But as appearances can be deceptive (see Rule 7) and operators are aware that what looked like an assault may actually be a friendly slap on the back, they therefore take cognizance of the contextual features of posture and facial expression to enable interpretation. This is particularly the case with juveniles who are frequently targeted because they appear to be fighting, but on closer inspection turn out to be engaging in 'horseplay' and, as the following incident suggests, at times this may be specifically for the benefit of the cameras:

21.07 – Three black youths casually dressed and aged between 16–18 are noticed as they stand outside Santana's talking and laughing. Zooming in the operator tells me that they are 'behavin' . . . just talkin''. While leaving the camera on them the operators shows little interest in this group until a couple of minutes later, the three run off in three different directions and rendezvous a minute later at a phone box. Moments later they run across the road laughing as one takes punches given out by the other two. Then in mock retaliation the 'victim' pulls his trouser belt off and begins to pretend to strike out at his 'assailants'. The horseplay continues and the operator decides to leave them alone. What the operator does not admit is that the three have been playing with the system and him since they were aware the cameras were on them. (13 minutes, 3 cameras)

While displays of fighting warrant surveillance because it is in itself an offence, two types of non-criminal behaviour are seen as potentially indicative of criminality: they are running and loitering.

Running the field notes contain dozens of examples of people being targeted because they are running and, in general, anyone noticed running will be zoomed in on:

00.01 – A white male casually dressed and in his early 20s is noted running down the High Street. Because of this behaviour he is zoomed in on and followed. Moments later he reduces speed to a jog then eventually walks. The operator sees that he is not being pursued and that he is not apparently carrying anything upon him and leaves him to walk in peace. (2 minutes, 2 cameras)

09.15 – The operator notices a black male in his late 20s and casually dressed running down the street towards a black woman. Unsure as to whether his intentions are hostile, the operator zooms in, but sees that as the two come into proximity they laugh. The pair stand chatting and a few minutes later go their separate ways. (4 minutes, 1 camera)

18.12 – A white male casually dressed and aged in his mid-30s is surveilled because he is running down the High Street. He catches up with two females in their 30s, has a chat with them which ends in smiles all round, and then runs back in the direction he came. (3 minutes, 1 camera)

10.42 – Another male zoomed in on because he is running. In his late 20s this casually dressed white male is immediately followed as the operator murmurs, 'does he know something we don't?' His run ends when he climbs into a car as a passenger and the vehicle drives away at a regular speed. As it does the operator zooms in on it and takes down the registration number. The car stops at a traffic light and it is here, looking into the car, that the fruits of the sprint are revealed – two burgers from a fast-food outlet. (2 minutes, 1 camera)

00.37 – A female (mid-20s, smartly dressed) is seen running. The operator fixes a camera on her curious as to why she is running. Zooming in his aim is to see if she is in any way upset or distressed. Whilst not obviously distressed she stops running and begins talking to herself! With that the operator laughs and leaves her. (1 minute, 1 camera)

As the preceding examples illustrate, running is seen as indicative of three possibilities, first, a 'fear and flight' response, in which the operators work to locate who or what provoked such a reaction; second, flight from lawful authority such as a shoplifter being pursued by a store detective and finally as a prelude to an attack. The fact that running turns out to be almost always innocent does not seem to deter the operators. This is perhaps because running provides something concrete to look at which is more interesting than just scanning faces in the crowd. Moreover, it invites an answer to the question 'Why?' and, like all of us, operators like to know the end of the story – even if it has a happy ending. But on one occasion during the research, the targeting of someone running did reveal criminal activity, and operators take solace from these rare successes and use them to temper their experience that, in ninety-nine out of hundred times, it will indicate nothing more significant than trying to catch a bus.

Loitering with Intent as we have already noted, youths are particularly prone to targeted surveillance especially if they are hanging around in groups on street corners, here it is the 'youth' and 'group' rather than the 'loitering' which provokes operator interest. However when loitering is compounded by place, it become indicative of 'loitering with intent' as the following examples show:

10.44 – The operator notices two males standing outside looking into the window display of a jewellers. Both are white and in their late teens wearing casual but stylish clothing. One has a shoulder bag which taken together produce the identikit shop thief in the eyes of the operators. Doing an intensive scrutiny of the display the pair then indulge in horseplay and ridicule and after looking in the window again enter the store.

Upon entering the store the operator switches on the real-time recording facility and waits. They come out after three minutes and walk around the town. As they do so they are watched, the operator looking for evidence of gems appearing out of pockets or bags, but nothing seems untoward. After five minutes they return to the jewellers – a state of alert is provoked in the operators, but this time the pair come out within a minute – their return provoked by the fact that one had left a small parcel in the shop from his first visit. Having retrieved it the two walk away smiling. The operator now sees the pair as not worthy of surveillance. (8 minutes, 4 cameras)

11.45 – Another black male is surveilled due to a combination of clothing and location. In his early 20's and wearing a woolly hat and jeans and trainers, he is waiting across the road from a building society. The suspect compounds the operator's suspicion when he is seen to look up and down the street. This elicits the comment 'He might have accomplices'. Zooming in closer the operator looks carefully at the leather jacket the suspect is wearing – it is loose fitting and therefore, in the operator's eyes, ideal for concealing a gun. Whilst awaiting this armed robbery the operator pans the camera up and down the street in search of accomplices and getaway cars. Nothing obvious or untoward is noted so surveillance is resumed on the suspect who at that moment crouches on his hind legs and does a little dance accompanied by a grin. The operator believes this is an attempt to hide from the cameras until seconds later another black male walks towards the suspect and shakes his hand. The two then walk towards two bicycles secured nearby and after unlocking them ride away together. Zooming in the operator can see that the suspect is showing his mate his building society passbook. Far from robbing the bank the suspect was withdrawing or depositing money in it. (15 minutes, 2 cameras).

While running generates suspicion through activity, loitering does so through passivity, but like running it is noteworthy partly because people who loiter stand out from the generally mobile street scene around them, but also because it invites the question: What are they waiting for? When loitering occurs near premises which are thought to be at high risk of robbery (in the examples above, building societies and jewellers) a question is raised as to the moral intentions of the person who thus warrants further surveillance. It is not just places which provide added significance to loitering, so too do cars, or at least certain types of car. The following field notes illustrates the point:

> Whether or not a vehicle was brought to the attention of police depended on the personality and prejudices of the operator. The night shift operator held his own dossier on 'boy racers'; this 19-strong list (with a couple of print-outs of vehicles) included six BMWs, four Mercedes, and three Escorts and half the drivers were black. For him these were 'suspect vehicles' and when seen would be followed. Thus categorical suspicion extended from the person to technology and in many cases the car a person drives was also seen as an indication of criminal intent.

> 02.24 – The operator zooms in on the unforgivable – two white males in their early 20s in a flash car. This XR2i with white-walled tyres and spoilers is parked near a disco. Zooming in the operator explains that such 'boy racers have in the past been caught passing drugs to one another', however, no transactions take place and the car eventually drives out of sight. (2 minutes, 1 camera)

> 03.01 – Two black males and two white males all in their early 20s are standing by a car talking. But, to the operator this is not as innocent as it would seem. The car is stylish and expensive and in his opinion not affordable by males so young. Thus it is a product of ill-gotten gains and being black drug dealing is presumed to be involved. Furthermore the operator presumes the group have left a wine-bar which he tells me from his local knowledge is tolerant towards the smoking of drugs. With this assemblage of guilt the four are surveilled and the police controller contacted and the surveillance put onto the police monitor. Whilst the operator merely tells him how he thinks 'this lot are not up to any good', the Controller does not reply or deploy any officers. Eventually the situation sorts itself out when the four depart – two in the car and two on foot. The operator takes down the car registration number and puts it in his 'Little Black Book' of 'boy racers and suspected drug dealers'. (8 minutes, 1 camera)

> 20.40 – Four white males casually dressed and in their mid-20s and standing around a high-powered car in one of the car parks results in the operator zooming in on them to check their faces to see if they are 'known'. None are but they provoke the operator to ask the police controller to do a PNC check on the vehicle they are standing around. This is done but according to police records it is not stolen and the address is local. These two facts seem to negate the suspicious nature of their appearance and clothing

and whilst surveilling them for a few minutes more the operator eventually looks elsewhere. (6 minutes, 2 cameras)

13.43 – The operator notices three white males in their 20s standing around a vehicle in the car park. Whilst this is not an uncommon occurrence what provokes suspicion are a variety of factors – material and human. Firstly, whilst the vehicle has two registration plates it has another (exactly the same) resting on the dashboard visible through the windscreen. Secondly, according to the operator 'They looked at the cameras as they got out'. Because of this combination they are zoomed in on and contacting the police controller, the operator asks the police to look at them on their monitor and do a PNC check. Within a minute police inform him that the vehicle is not recorded as stolen, but all the same a police mobile unit is deployed to check them out. The three suspects meanwhile pool their money and purchase a parking ticket moments before they are approached by two mobile police officers who question them before driving away. (5 minutes, 1 camera)

Rule Three – *Certain people are immediately worthy of surveillance because they are known by operators to have engaged in criminal or troublesome behaviour in the past.*

It is notable that operators, in the main, did not target people on the basis of personalised knowledge of their past criminality, only thirty cases of targeted surveillance could be directly attributable to personalised knowledge, representing just 3 per cent of the total. There are a number of reasons for this. First, in County Town and Inner City, there were few ways of learning a person's criminal history. As the systems were not located in police stations, the formal and informal mechanisms which would have enabled them to acquire such knowledge, generally by chatting to police officers, were largely absent. Second, none of the sites had an official 'rogues gallery' (a noticeboard with pictures of suspects attached) which would facilitate identification. Finally the sheer volume of people meant that casual identification when 'cruising' with the cameras would be difficult, the faces are too distant unless they are zoomed in on.

Operators would, however, regularly zoom in on a person or group to see if a person was known, and thus warrant more prolonged surveillance but these attempts were rather hit and miss and generally unsuccessful. For example:

10.07 – A white female in her early 20s is sighted walking in the town. Unsure as to whether she is a known drug-user and shoplifter the operator zooms in and realises she is not whom he thought she was and so leaves her. (1 minute, 1 camera)

10.30 – A group of six teenagers (white, male, 12–16) are standing in a group in a pedestrian shopping precinct. They are talking and appear calm, but the operator zooms in to see if they include 'known toe-rags'. None of the group are familiar to him but he leaves the camera on them until they walk elsewhere and he does not bother to follow them. (3 minutes, 1 camera)

When known offenders do come into view they are targeted but, while operators may believe in the adage, 'once a villain always a villain', they know it does not mean that a person is up to villainy today or, if they are, that it will be in view of the cameras. So, unless there are other features which indicate immediate dubious intent the surveillances tend to be short.

17.02 – The operator notices two white males (18–20, casually dressed) who are known shoplifters. Informing his colleague of their whereabouts he adds for my benefit that these two are 'general arseholes' who will probably be using tonight's public gathering for pick-pocketing. (2 minutes, 1 camera)

19.25 – Surveilling the crowds the operator stops upon a recognised face, a derisory comment is made to the other operator about the vision. The male (26, scruffily dressed) is a known drug-user and shoplifter and is followed as he walks through the crowd. (1 minute, 1 camera)

The preceding examples are based solely upon on operator's personalised suspicions and therefore obscures the importance of personalised knowledge which is transmitted from others, external to the system, which also triggers surveillance. This was of marginal relevance in both Inner and Metro City but in County Town, the requests for surveillance dominated the daytime use of the system and this was aided by the 'retail radio' system which linked the twenty or so store detectives to the CCTV system and each other. Many requests from store detectives were for continued surveillance when a person had left their store, after their behaviour, or mere presence had provoked suspicion. However, literally dozens of requests were to track people who were known shoplifters in their passage through the town centre, irrespective of their behaviour. Operators could then alert other store detectives of their impending approach. For instance:

11.50 – A department store security guard has recognised two well-known shoplifters (one white female in her late 20s and her black boyfriend of similar age) who are walking in the town with their two children. The family is found on the camera within 30 seconds and followed and when they enter a shop the operator contacts the store detective to warn him of the guests. The first caller (the security guard) then requests talk-through and warns all the town centre store detectives of this family adding that in his opinion 'it's the kids that do the nicking'. Keeping an eye on the store they are in the operator waits for them to come out which they do at 12.03 and then surveilles them again as they walk to another store at 12.08 and upon entering he warns the store detective of their presence. Leaving the camera on the door of the shop the operator intends to wait for them to leave, but is called upon to look elsewhere. (20 minutes, 3 cameras)

11.37 – Another store detective calls up to inform the operator that a well-known shoplifter has just entered a shopping centre accompanied by a friend. This information is then re-told to all Store Detectives by the operator who further obliges by putting a camera on the shopping centre entrance/exit doors. The two reappear after five minutes and are then followed for the next 25 minutes as they (white casually dressed males in their teens) walk around the town.

Rule Four – *Operators must learn to treat locales as territories of normal appearances and against this background variation can be noticed. This involves utilising the temporal and spatial variation of activities within a locale to judge what is both 'out of place' and 'out of time'.*

The operation of this rule creates within CCTV systems a surveillance clock which patterns operators' activities temporally and spatially. To illustrate how it operates we will describe the surveillance clocks in Metro City and County Town.

In Metro City no operator ever spent a full shift engrossed in the task of surveillance. The discomfort of watching so many monitors combined with the mind-numbing monotony the job offered meant that operators 'drifted' in their concentration. Moments of intense scrutiny competed with minutes of doing nothing with the mind miles away. Because of this, at times, trying to explain rationally the methods of the operators was at times a futile exercise – even they could not explain why they were moving the cameras the way they were! However there were patterns across the hours of the day, and days of the week which suggested a set of shared assumptions about the spatial and temporal distribution of activities.

The different shifts produced varied modus operandi. The 7.00 a.m.–2.00 p.m. would always see operators spend the first twenty minutes busying themselves with the cameras only to lapse into chat and tea-drinking. As the city centre got busy from 8.30 a.m., cameras would focus on the railway stations and from 10.00 a.m. would generally look for 'suspects' in the pedestrian shopping mall, invariably young males who, by virtue of being that category were considered potential thieves. Such a category was the main concern until the shift ended. The other regular targets were the homeless and habitual street drinkers.

Arriving fresh the afternoon shift would cruise the cameras for half an hour and then relax and go into a routine. This would see the different operators choose their particular 'favourite' camera view and put it on their dedicated monitor. As the city emptied between 5.00–6.00 p.m., the operators would take breaks and wind down their state of alertness until the young and dressed-up arrived post-8.00 p.m. for nights out in pubs and clubs. The only early evening 'high alert' occurred on Saturdays when four venues held 'Teen-discos' from 8.00–10.30 p.m. before the real thing for adults began at 11.00 p.m. At such times male youths aged between 12–16 were particular targets for surveillance, be they standing outside the disco, or a fast-food outlet or around transport termini.

Night shift offered the operators better opportunities to generate an arrest. The obvious targets for surveillance were pubs and nightclubs, particularly those known as being 'trouble' hot spots. Meanwhile awaiting a fight the cameras would watch anyone seen in a phone box on suspicion they were robbing it and fast-food outlets wherein the operators believed were drunks who having left pubs would seek sustenance and a fight. Post-02.00 a.m. surveillance was usually centred on the 'red light' area of the city centre – a series of six streets which saw street-walkers and kerb-crawlers and other associated entrepreneurs believed to be pimps and drug-sellers. Interestingly for all the hours of surveillance in this area no prostitute was ever arrested for soliciting on the evidence of the cameras and the cars that were stopped by mobile police patrols deployed by the Controller based on camera evidence were not targeted for kerb-crawling, but for a presence which did not accord with 'normal' approaches to women.

From 04.00–07.00 a.m. surveillance focused on anyone seen on cameras. Thus whatever business the person was going about – be it walking home from work or from a disco or a vagrant raking through bins – the cameras followed them. In these tedious hours operators when not snoozing could only articulate their task as one of watching for thefts of newspapers and bread and milk delivered sometimes hours before the small stores opened. This produced one arrest when a vagrant was seen stealing eight copies of a Sunday tabloid. Not all surveillance had an aim or rationale as many an operator explained, the 'cruising' was done out of boredom and 'just because there's someone to look at'. When not wanting to move the cameras, operators could construct a sequence on their monitors; this way sixteen or eight or four set locations would flick around every thirty seconds in front of their eyes.

Such 'cruising' would be interspersed with 'resting' the camera on sites which were believed to be sites of danger. Thus, bus stops were an hourly zoom-in because operators believed that the queues provided opportunities for pick-pockets and bag-snatchers. The system had never caught such a crime but, the operators stated, such crimes no longer occurred because of the cameras. Another set of locations were cash machines outside banks and building societies; again the suspicion was that waiting nearby were robbers and so the pastoral duty of CCTV was to surveille those obtaining money. However if those withdrawing cash were male, under thirty and looked like 'scrotes' or in other ways deviant they were surveilled because, in the operators' eyes, they may be card thieves. If a clear picture of their faces could be recorded, so much the better, since if their suspicions turned out to be correct it would make subsequent identification easier.

Car parks were cruised for thieves, and this intensified in the early hours of the morning so that any young man would become the object of suspicion. Additionally, groups of young men around a car would almost inevitably produce a zoom-in and cars with a door or boot open and young men standing around were considered particularly noteworthy because the operators saw possible criminal exchange ensuing.

Significantly, whilst paid for in part by department stores the Metro City's scheme played little role in the apprehension of shoplifters. Whilst a file at the operator's console contained a contact number for thirty stores, such communication was extremely rare. The system was rarely called upon to track shoplifters and, with such a vast population entering its numerous shops, the operators had no idea who the town's notorious shoplifters were.

In County Town the daily procedures were also very routine. Arriving at 8.00 a.m., the early shift operators would spend the first twenty minutes perusing the streets to familiarise themselves with anything unusual. After a mug of tea they would then settle down to nothing in particular as the town slowly came to life with workers, only to return to quiet by 10.00 a.m. with everyone now in their place of work. At such time the only surveillance of note was upon cash-transit vans and shop delivery vehicles. From 10.30 onwards with nothing eventful happening in the town except shopping six days a week the system would be virtually redundant were it not for the Retail Radio. The majority of surveillance on the day shift was not initiated by the operators but in response to messages from store detectives and involved following known and suspected shoplifters and known and suspected offenders. The only other category to receive repeated observation was well-known vagrants and alcoholics numbering around a dozen who were found daily in two rendezvous.

The four till midnight shift would see a repeat procedure of familiarisation, refreshment, and lull as the town emptied from 5.00 p.m. hours onwards until around 8.00 p.m. when the night revellers entered for the entertainment offered by pubs, clubs, restaurants and theatres. But, between Monday and Thursday the town centre was often empty. To the operators, relief came on Friday and Saturday nights which would see thousands out, but this was not a 'rocking' town and the streets were never awash with drunks or the carnivalesque. It was all rather sedate. The system did not have much use until 9.00 p.m. when the occasional disturbance around licensed premises would result in police via their Controller requesting the operator put a camera on the situation. Apart from such requests pub-closing time was 'high-alert' as operators watched for drunken transgressions around pubs and food outlets even though uniformed police were available in numbers on foot and in vehicles. In former years, we were told by police, managers and operators, the town had been far busier but the number of users had declined and many had shifted their pub crawling to venues on the High Road a mile outside the town and not covered by CCTV during the research.

Beginning at midnight, the night shift, six nights a week unofficially ended about 2.00 a.m. That was when the operator decided to sleep! Having looked around usually in vain for drunken fights and then amused himself and police officers with copulating couples in cars he would make himself comfortable and drift off. In truth he missed little, five nights a week after midnight the town did not even have cats moving. As a consequence, when the operator was awake anybody and any vehicle that appeared on camera was surveilled mainly out of boredom. The one night the operator stayed awake until 3.00 a.m. was Friday, hoping to capture a fight. The task would be futile beyond this time and so he relaxed. The Saturday night operator, however, remained awake and alert all night, but between 4.00–8.00 a.m. there was barely a soul to be seen.

Sundays were similarly devoid of activities. No operator could remember any significant event being captured on camera on a Sunday, and as the field notes show, there was little to watch and, with store detectives rarely at work beyond the run-up to Christmas, there were hardly any messages passed to the system.

The daily and hourly rhythm of the streets provides the backdrop against which people and their associated activities can be judged. While large groups of youths always warrant targeting, the significance this is accorded will depend on how it relates to the locally established patterns of congregation and dispersal. Thus the queues for the 'teen discos' were always targeted, not because they were temporally or spatially unusual but because the operators generally viewed youth as indicative of trouble – particularly when found in large numbers. On the other hand, where groups of youths were congregated in areas that were not recognised as established meeting places, they would be subject to target surveillance because they were 'out of place' as the following extract makes clear:

21.54 – A group of young people sitting around a town centre statue catch the attention of the operator. Numbering ten, all are white and in their late teens/early 20s and two are female. Whilst sitting in an unusual location they are laughing and chatting without evidence of alcohol or smoke. Zooming in, but not on anyone specifically the operator explains 'I'll get a few faces in case they start anything, then I'll keep on them from a distance'. His suspicion that one male amongst them was 'well-known' were unfounded and minutes later the two operators agree that by their appearance and manner the group is a bunch of students, and warrant no more attention. (3 minutes, 1 camera)

For operators the most important element of the space-time relationship is that it determines the availability of potential targets. As we have noted, during the day in County Town, the system was, to a large extent, an adjunct of the City Centre store detectives and operators initiated little work themselves. In part, this is because there was little to distinguish one group of shoppers from the next, particularly on school days when few youths were available for targeting. They were, in a sense, overwhelmed by the sheer volume of normality. However, as day turned into evening and evening into night in all the sites the numbers available for potential surveillance fell, thus making any selection easier. By the early hours of the morning, when there were few people on the streets, selection was not really an issue, and any person sighted was deemed to be out of place and out of time and thus worthy of targeting.

Rule Five – *For operators the normal ecology of an area is also a 'normative ecology' and thus people who don't belong are treated as 'other' and subject to treatment as such.*

This normative ecology goes further than merely signalling 'otherness' as a statistical property but also as a moral property related to conception of the legitimate and illegitimate use of social space. From the operators' perspectives, if a person was defined as 'other', either their moral propensities were unknown, and therefore worthy of surveillance in case they turned out to be malign, or they were already 'known', by reference to stereotypical assumptions contained in media, political and everyday discourses. Operators, of course had their own common-sense understandings, informed by their localised knowledge, as to which people fall into the category of 'other':

12.10 – Seeing two white males in their early 40s walk into a department store, one carrying a suitcase, the operator suspects they could be up to no good. Via retail radio he warns the store detective of their presence. However, the camera which is trained on the shop door shows them leaving the store in less than a minute, the store detective has noticed them in the short time they were in the store and by his reckoning they are two foreigners who are searching for an address. The two are out of place on the Inner City high street, their garments are a long fur coat and long leather coat, respectively, and their suitcases are of the battered leather variety. Followed as they walk down the road they approach no one, but look bewildered as they trudge around. (10 minutes, 3 cameras)

As we have already noted, the surveillance of black people in both County Town and Metro City can in part be explained by the fact that they were seen in the context of a predominately white community, which immediately singled them out as a 'not the norm' but also in part because of the moral properties that operators ascribed to being black. But it was not just blacks who were treated as 'other', as the following illustrates:

A couple of operators were particularly keen on surveilling the homeless. In Paul's case this was accompanied by verbal abuse towards those standing on the monitors in front of him, and he made clear he did not have much time for: 'Big Issue scum', 'Homeless low-life' and 'drug-dealing scrotes'. And he would cruise the town, in search of these 'undesirables' and when found he would become agitated and animated in his revulsion. The other operator who did not care for the homeless was Martin who considered most sellers of 'The Big Issue' as drug-dealers concealing their true motives behind the facade of poverty. In the Shift Diary he had written for the benefit of other shifts that they were to surveille one seller whom he considered a drug dealer and 'check all weekend and report on Monday'. Underneath this instruction another operator from a different shift wrote that the suspect had been checked by police 'and he is clean'. Further to this the System Manager wrote 'surveillance no longer required'.

The concept of 'otherness' is intimately bound up with views as to the appropriate use of social space and who has a right to do what in the city centre. In County Town, for instance, one group that was continuously surveilled was the town centre drunks – not because they caused any trouble but because their activities did not accord with the appropriate use of town centre space.

A dozen drunks were surveilled on a daily basis in two favoured haunts – the bus station and an alleyway off the market square. Such places were shelter from the elements and a place to exchange bottles and chat away the hours. Whilst unsightly, no offences were committed by them during the observational research and although the operators looked at them regularly they did not see them as a particular problem. The more recent homeless, however, were not tolerated, but this could not be attributed to the operators. As a police visitor to the control room explained because all such people had mortgages and cars and were a fraud, they were not allowed to sell their magazine in the town and operators were requested to bring to police attention any that they found in the centre.

As the above extracts illustrate the targeting of the homeless, the vagrant and alcoholic was a regular feature of both Metro City and County Town. But this was also differentiated by the degree of 'otherness', with Big Issue sellers considered as the nadir of the undeserving poor while the ordinary vagrants were merely 'other'.

The targeting of such groups, however, had less to do with their criminogenic potential but more to do with the capacity to convey a negative image of the city. In this sense targeting is as much about the commercial image of the city than crime and reflects the values contained by the movement towards formal Town Centre Management programmes. As Reeve has illustrated, the concept of Town Centre Management (TCM) was developed by Peter Spindal of Marks and Spencer 'in order to give coherence to the principle of managing any urban centre with a retail focus as a single entity' (Reeve 1996: 7). In essence the principle of TCM is to coordinate the activities of various parties, both public and private sector, with an interest in the city centre, in order to promote competitive advantage. Reeve identifies three pressures which have encouraged this development. First, the economic decline of the town centre as the primary site for consumer spending: the development of out-of-town shopping centres, led during the late 1980s and early 1990s to a 40 per cent decline in High Street spending. Second, one of the factors identified in this decline was the 'environmental competitiveness of the out of town retail centres and in town malls' which resulted on them being seen by consumers as convenient, comfortable, safe and ascetically pleasing places to visit. The final factor that Reeve identified is a defensive response by a number of large retailers to 'the decline value of their town centre assets'. Companies like Boots, M&S, WH Smiths and McDonalds have increasingly felt that, unless the town centre as a whole is made more attractive to the spending public, then their continued investment in such locations would no longer be profitable' (Reeve 1996: 9).

With these pressures it is hardly surprising that TCM has developed as 'an explicit strategy involving a manager or management team treating the town centre as a (commercially) coherent (consumer) environment' (Reeve 1996: 12). Importantly, the number of towns operating TCM schemes has risen from fewer than six in 1986 to over a hundred in 1995 (Reeve 1996: 13). From our point of view, TCM is significant because it has provided one impetus for CCTV, and created a platform for joint, public-private, funding of CCTV schemes which prioritise commercial concerns in the management of city centre space. This prioritisation brings with it a number of dimensions which are directly related to the 'normative ecology' of the town centre. As the town centre managers in Reeve's study revealed, they wanted to discourage certain people and activities within the city centre which were seen as non-conducive to their consumer-led vision of the desirable: a quarter wanted to discourage political gatherings, half discouraged youths from 'hanging out', and half prohibited begging in the streets (1996: 22)

In County Town and Metro City similar values were present. In Metro City, the promotional video of the system emphasised not the detection of crime but the role CCTV was to play in revitalising the city centre's flagging fortunes by contributing to the 'feel good factor' and encouraging the shopper back to the centre. In County Town the impetus for CCTV was the threat posed by a number of out-of-town developments. The initial response was a complete refit of the town centre car parks which had fallen into a state of disrepair, were theft prone and seen to be discouraging consumers from coming to the city centre. This refit included the installation of CCTV and the town centre system followed shortly after. In Inner City, the manager of the scheme was less optimistic about attracting business but was concerned to prevent any further losses. As he stated: 'attempts at regeneration are futile. The best we can hope for is that it does not degenerate any further.'

In both County Town and Metro City, the issue of image was made explicit by those with a management role over the systems. In the first example the manager is concerned with the image of the town during the annual show, in the second with the general image of the city.

19.00 – The system manager entered the control room early one evening to watch the system at work and brought his wife to watch proceedings around the town centre annual show. Assuming control he directed the operators to have a look at one area where 'the bloody gyppos' had been residing. They had gone but he had ordered a body count days before as to how many more were down there (answer 61). Then he recognised a couple of 'toe-rags' who were 'up to no good', he knew this instinctively. Likewise when a group of eight black youths were noticed at the show he commanded the operator to 'watch that lot . . . our ethnic problem'. Later, discussing the proposed building of a rehabilitation centre for young offenders a few hundred yards from the control room and in the town centre he opines that such a scheme should not have been given planning permission or, if necessary, be out on the edge of town near the Council estates such people come from anyway.

11.20 – The surveillance of two operators is interrupted by the arrival of the Inspector (Community Involvement) who calls to have a chat and kill a few minutes. Standing at the side of one operator the chat is banal as the cameras do not show much out of the ordinary. Minutes later the Chief Superintendent arrives and without saying a word of greeting to anyone stands behind the operators and intently watches the bank of monitors.

After two minutes of silence the Chief says to no one in particular that there are too many alcoholics sitting on the benches by the river. A brief silence provokes the Inspector to reply that they are always there which is just the answer the Chief needs, not altering his stare or location he barks 'shouldn't be. They're giving the wrong image to the city'. Nobody contradict's him.

All concerned now stare intently at any camera in this embarrassing stand-off. After a minute and a half the Chief having proved his power and made his point turns and leaves without a word to anyone he has just shared the past few minutes with.

In Metro City the system was used to surveille two other groups who posed a threat to the 'good image' of the city: those involved in fly-posting and street-trading. The latter were one of the first groups to be specifically targeted by the operators and then arrested by the police. As the operators explained, in the first few months of the system (before the research began) around a dozen individuals selling everything from tea cloths to perfume of a dubious origin were arrested in joint operations between police and trading standards officers. Six months after the scheme had begun no street traders were visible within the parameters of CCTV.

Those fly-posting, mainly to advertise up and coming musical events, were also actively targeted, on the grounds that they were formally guilty of criminal damage as they attached posters to, amongst other things, council rubbish bins. During training all operators were told to watch out for fly-posting because, according to one operator it 'defaced the City's structures' and 'made the City look dirty'. During the observational research the cameras were responsible for providing evidence against two people charged with the offence.

Rule Six – *There is an expectation that just as operators treat territories as a set of normal appearances, so others are expected to treat them as such. And thus if a person appears lost, disorientated, or in other ways at unease with the locale, this will indicate suspiciousness.*

In practice the operation of this rule is often bound up with the other rules of the incongruity procedure. However, what it draws attention to is those whose orientation to the locale through their interaction with both the social and physical environment is 'out of place'. Thus, those who suddenly change direction, or appear to be wandering aimlessly will become targets or have the suspicion intensified if they are already selected. In the following example, the group has already been selected as warranting surveillance, on the basis of age, number, dress and location. What turns this from a routine targeted surveillance to an extended twenty-five minutes is the youths have not continued in the predicted direction but retraced their original path. It is almost as though operators construct a map of moral progress through the streets which is unidirectional. People of good moral character know where they are going and proceeded to their destination without signs of deviation.

16.35 – A group of five black teenagers are noticed walking in the rain down the High Street. The operator immediately zooms in on the three males and two females, all casually dressed, three of them wearing baseball caps. As they walk they look in shop windows then they enter a shop which specialises in records and stereos, this provokes the operator to shout at the screen 'Get out of there you little devils!'

They come out minutes later and saunter down the street in the rain and after four minutes of this all turn round and retrace their steps. This provokes analysis from the operator who states to me: 'This is how they draw suspicion to themselves . . . when they turn round for no reason . . . they've been to a few shops and now they're going back'.

They had in fact entered only one shop. They were to head towards a grocery store where one entered and bought a can of drink whilst the rest waited outside. Still they are followed as they window shop in the rain until after using four cameras on them over a 25-minute period the operator leaves them alone.

In the next example the implicit rules governing street behaviour (Goffman; 1971) are broken. Normal orientation to the street relies on minimal interaction with strangers and treating the environmental features of the locale as routine.

17.18 – A summer's Saturday afternoon, the city centre is still very busy but not as full as an hour earlier. A quiet, uneventful shift has seen one operator depart for a meal break allowing Eddie and myself to stare at the screens. Whilst still talking to me Eddie notices a boy aged about ten outside McDonalds. Whilst this was not an unusual sight what alerts the operator is the fact that this child is approaching adults asking them something then, as they depart, going up to others.

To ascertain that he is alone the operator watches more carefully. No adult or juvenile approaches the child for four minutes. Eventually the child confirms the operator's suspicion when he looks into a bin and pulls out a discarded McDonalds' carton. Without drawing the Controller's attention to the image Eddie asks if there has been any reports of missing children. The answer is 'No'. Seconds later, alerted by the question, the two police controllers look at the same camera Eddie is on and see his object of suspicion. Tim, ever the expert, says 'sign of the times' adding that the child must be from an estate where the parents don't care. Ignoring this the operator watches and sees the child ask a woman for directions which, we can see, she directs him to. As he is followed he does something which confirms to the operator that this child is unusual; he takes the few remaining French fries from the McDonalds' carton, throws the carton away and puts the fries in his pocket! He then enters Woolworths. The controllers have seen this and they decide he could be going shoplifting and deploy a patrol officer to question the child. Tim elaborates over the air saying that the child had been seen begging (he had not, although he could have been outside McDonalds) and that he is 'wandering and confused'. This is debatable too. Inside two minutes we can see two officers standing with the child outside the store. Eventually it is ascertained he is from a children's home on the outskirts of the city, but has not been reported missing. He is taken to the police station to await collection. This incident required an observation via three cameras lasting seven minutes. The incident book now records that the cameras located a missing person.

The child's interaction with people is inappropriate, in general people do not repeatedly approach strangers, and children certainly do not. Similarly litter bins are dirty and unclean, and are generally avoided except when they are used for discarding rubbish. Lingering over them and removing objects not only signals a breach of a general social taboo but inappropriate orientation to place.

Rule Seven – *Operators learn to see those who treat the presence of the cameras as other than normal as other than normal themselves.*

Operators work with the absolute assumption that they have the right to surveille anyone on the street. Anyone who by gesture or behaviour challenges this assumption immediately places themselves in the category of morally suspect and therefore worthy of surveillance. For example:

17.11 – The operator resumes his surveillance of Santana's and sees half a dozen of the group board a bus and disappear leaving only four black males who walk across the road and down the High Street eventually disappearing from view. Before they are out of range, however, all four gesture abusively to the camera which angers the operator who says to his colleagues 'I'd love to go down there and run them all over'. (10 minutes, 3 cameras).

Such overt and theatrical resistance to the camera's gaze was not uncommon, especially in Inner City, and token gestures of defiance often accompanied departure from the area. As such, however, they could not be used as the basis of extended surveillance except where the faces were remembered as in the following example:

16.00 – The youths outside Santana's provide some entertainment for the operators. Eight casually dressed black males are zoomed in on and one elicits a venomous reaction in the operator 'That one's a right little shit . . . he knows where all the cameras are'. Whether he does or not the operator has no way of knowing, but he is certain in his dislike of this diminutive 14 year old who is regularly standing with the various gatherings. Others come and go over the next 30 minutes providing a form of intelligence report between the operators 'He's one of the new ones' 'He's usually got a mobile phone'. The youths stand and chat occasionally larking about in the pouring rain as they are discussed at a distance. (30 minutes, 1 camera).

If a person is, in the view of the operator, orientating their behaviour to the presence of the cameras this provides a strong warrant for initiating or prolonging surveillance. It is not just overt resistance to the cameras which promotes suspicion but a belief that if a person is demonstrating an awareness of the cameras this may be because they have an immediate criminal intent:

11.23 – A black male becomes the object of suspicion because of his appearance and location. In his early 20s and wearing trainers, jeans, leather jacket and baseball cap he is a prime target for surveillance anyway, but to add to his woes he is standing outside the door of the Building Society. The operator tells me that the chap could be waiting for someone, but he is suspicious about his motives because 'he's been looking at the camera'. I watch carefully but do not see him looking at the camera, but still the camera remains on him. Four minutes later a white female in her 40s appears, speaks to the suspect and the pair walk away together crossing the road and joining two other black males, both with baseball caps and casual attire. The four are followed until they go out of range of the camera. (6 minutes, 2 cameras).

While in the previous example merely looking at the camera compounded suspicion, if activities are seen as deliberately aimed at avoiding surveillance, suspicion is further intensified as the following illustrates:

13.24 – A group of five black males are now surveilled. All are casually dressed and aged around 15, two wear baseball caps another has a woolly hat. They walk orderly and quietly through the streets, but are followed as they do so and the operator asks for confirmation from his colleague as to whether they are known to him as part of the 'Three O'clock Gang' (Those who hang around Santana's after school). The co-operator says they are. The operator continues his surveillance until all five jump onto the back of an open-door bus and disappear up the road. Knowing the direction the bus is going the operator moves his surveillance to a camera opposite the bus stop the bus will next call at. At this stop all five jump off and walk back towards where they had come from. The other operator sees this and tells his new colleague 'This is what they do all the time to avoid surveillance'.

The five then cross the road and stand in a bus shelter. Then, changing their mind they walk to McDonalds so the cameras follow them then await their departure and further journeys. What happens in effect is that having found a group of suspects the operator becomes fixed on following them and so ignores other people and places. The necessity of keeping watch on them is periodically confirmed when one of the suspects is noted to be watching the cameras' movements. The mutual watching has required 5 cameras and taken up 66 minutes.

As the previous examples reveal, operators believe that if those they have already selected as targets change direction, back-track, split up, or move out of camera view this is treated as further evidence of malign intent. But what is apparent from these examples is that rather than trying to avoid surveillance the youths are actually trying to provoke it. Moreover, by demonstrating those behaviours they know will provoke surveillance, they indicate that they are not merely passive objects of a disciplinary gaze. They too can have power, if merely by wasting the operator's time or by subverting the intentions of the system for their own entertainment. Of course, for the operators this merely compounds their belief that people are up to no good. Displaying a knowledge of the modus operandi of the system implies knowing what a person should not be interested in knowing and this knowledge could then be used to 'hoodwink the operators and to neutralise the system'. Indeed a couple of system mangers spoke of how people have created a diversion to concentrate the attention of the cameras in one area while 'something was happening in another'.

In this way the rule that states people who treat the cameras as other than normal are treated as other than normal themselves extends to the prospect that people may deliberately through their actions be able to conceal their identity or true intentions from the cameras.

This is most obviously manifest in the manner in which operators respond to those wearing hats. As we have already noted this is, in part, explained by the association of hats with sub-cultural affiliations. But more importantly, operators know that hats can potentially deprive them of recording a clear image of a person's face. As operators know this, they also act on the assumption that citizens do as well. Operators believe they have a right to surveille any person's face who appears in their territory. Anyone who supports a visible means of denying them the opportunity, immediately places themselves in the category of persons of question-able intent and worthy of extended surveillance. Moreover, in the eyes of the operator, if the headgear is moved to deliberately obscure the face this merely compounds suspicion as the following incidents reveal:

13.13 – Three youths are zoomed in on outside Santana's. One has a baseball cap on and elicits suspicion when in the interpretation of the operator he adjusts it so as to conceal his identity from the cameras. Whilst standing talking they are zoomed in on and when the three walk down the street they are followed until out of sight. (3 minutes, 2 cameras).

15.54 – Three black males are noticed. Two were noticed earlier in the shift and once again they are followed as they walk. Surveillance begins as they walk down the High Street towards the bus stop and intensifies as one of them places a hood over his head to the obvious annoyance of the operator who zooms in on his face. Then as one remains at the bus stop his two companions continue to walk down the street and as the latter are followed the former runs to rejoin them. The three then make an abrupt left turn and hide behind a wall obscuring the view of the camera. Realising he is being tormented the operator states to his colleague 'They think I can't see them' and with that uses a different camera to get a side-on view of the three. Moments later one of the three recognises the movement of the second camera and gives it the middle finger gesture before resuming their walk. As they do so they occasionally glance at the camera and give it an occasional gesture, making the operator more determined to follow them until they go out of sight. (7 minutes, 3 cameras).

Operators of course have few means of responding to such challenges to their right to surveille people. In contrast the literature on policing is replete with examples of people who failed the 'reasonable person test' or were in 'contempt of cop' and thus provoked an extended stop and search or even arrest as a means of summary punishment (Reiner 1992). What operators can do is keep a mental or physical record (by taking a printout of their faces) of 'challengers' and ensure they are subject to intense surveillance whenever they enter the area. However in the next example the operators, displaying a remarkable degree of creativity as well as a complete disregard for their own code of conduct, found a novel means of 'punishing' the recalcitrant.

14.00 – A store detective contacts the system to request they look at two males who have just left the store's car park. The two are known to the store detectives as thieves who also steal from cars and suspicious because they might have stolen from or damaged customers' vehicles. The store detective requests that they be recorded leaving the area. Complying with this request the operator sees one well-known character (white, male, 17, casually dressed) with another male not recognised (white, male, mid-20s, casually dressed) and they are surveilled for the next ten minutes as they walk around the town.

The pair soon become aware of being watched and begin tormenting their observers by splitting in two or suddenly changing direction or stopping then running a few yards then stopping again. This only annoys the operators and makes them determined to keep tabs on the two 'toe-rags'. Whilst this is going on the store detective contacts the operators to inform them that having checked the car park there is no evidence of any theft or damage. But the operators are now drawn into a game with these two. Determined not to let them out of their sight and responding to 'V' signs with abuse the suspects cannot hear the operators plot their revenge.

Amidst the mutual abuse there is fun to be had in the Control Room. The two under surveillance meet up with a couple of mates and at one point stand near two public phones. The Control Room has a list of these numbers so Stewart phones and we watch as the suspects look at the ringing phone before one picks it up. The operator using an affected accent suggests to the suspect that Nextborough is a good place to shop before putting the phone down. Moments later the operator phones again, confuses the suspect with a request for a direction claiming to be lost then moments later calls again and abuses him ridiculing what he is wearing. The suspect and his three mates all laugh at this scenario, but do not look at the cameras and in all probability have no idea that those watching him are also speaking to him. In total the operators spend 30 minutes using ten cameras to watch over these two before being forced to leave them when contacted by another store detective wanting cameras on other people.

We have described in some detail how the working rules developed by CCTV operators first preselect targets of surveillance on the basis of their common-sense assumptions as to who is responsible for the crime problem and how this is then further refined by a set of behavioural and visual clues that narrow down the target population. We have also indicated that it is not just selection for targeting that is influenced by such rules but the intensity of surveillance, and we now want to consider this more systematically in relation to the quantitative data.

The Intensity of Surveillance

We have seen how the frequency of surveillance is centrally related to the social characteristics of the surveilled. The next question we wish to address is whether the intensity of surveillance is also patterned in a similar way. We have three indices which are related to the intensity of surveillance: whether the police took control of the system; the number of cameras used to track a person and finally, the duration of the surveillance.

Police Control of the System

In Inner City, police regularly took control of the system almost on a daily basis. However, these incidents do not feature in the 888 incidents of targeted surveillance, because what initiated the surveillance was not known. Of the 888 targeted surveillances, the police took control of the system on only 22 occasions after being informed of an incident by the operators. This was unrelated to either the appearance, age, race or gender of the targets.

The Number of Cameras Used

The majority of targeted surveillances only involved the use of one camera (60 per cent), two camera surveillances accounted for a further quarter (25 per cent) and three or more camera surveillances comprised one sixth (16 per cent) of the total. While the number of cameras used to track a suspect was not related to either their appearance, sex or race, age was important. Teenagers were nearly twice as likely (18 per cent) than those in their twenties (11 per cent), or thirty-plus year olds (11 per cent), to be tracked by three or more cameras.

Duration of Surveillance

The majority of targeted surveillances were short, four out of ten (40 per cent) lasting two minutes or less and three quarters (77 per cent) lasting six minutes or less. A person's gender and appearance played no part in influencing how long a targeted surveillance lasted. However, both race and age did have an influence – 30 per cent of targeted surveillances on black people, compared with 13 per cent surveillances on whites, lasted nine minutes or more. Similarly 26 per cent of targeted surveillances on teenagers lasted nine or more minutes. In contrast, only 14 per cent of surveillances of twenty-year-olds and 12 per cent of those aged thirty years or more lasted for nine minutes or longer.

Discretion, Differentiation and Discrimination.

The power of CCTV operators is highly discretionary as they have extraordinary latitude in determining who will be watched, for how long, and whether to initiate deployment. The sum total of these individual discretionary judgments produces, as we have shown, a highly differentiated pattern of surveillance leading to a massively disproportionate targeting of young males particularly, if they are black or visibly identifiable as having subcultural affiliations. As this differentiation is not based on objective behavioural and individualised criteria, but merely on being categorised as part of a particular social group, such practices are discriminatory.

Of course, it may be argued that since those officially recorded as deviant, are disproportionately young, male, black, and working class, targeting such groups merely reflects the underlying reality of the distribution of criminality. Such an argument is, however, circular: the production of the official statistics is also based on pre-given assumptions as to the distribution of criminality, which itself leads to the particular configuration of formal and informal operational police practice. As self-report studies of crime reveal, offending is in fact, far more evenly distributed throughout the population than reflected in the official statistics (Coleman and Moynihan 1996). Indeed, the race and class differentials, so marked in the official statistics, disappear when self-reported offending behaviour of juveniles is examined. (Bowling et al. 1994). Thus, McConville et al. argue the convicted population:

> is a subset of the official suspect population. Whilst convicted criminals may be broadly representative of suspects, there is good reason to believe that they are very dissimilar to the 'real criminal population'. The make up of the convicted population is, therefore, like the make up of the suspect population: a police construction'. (1991: 35)

Another argument is that even if there is differentiation in target selection it is irrelevant because it does not result in actual intervention and therefore no 'real' discrimination occurs. As our own results clearly show even though teenagers make up 39 per cent of those targeted they constitute only 23 per cent of those deployed against and 18 per cent of the arrested population. In which case we would respond that, on effectiveness measures alone such targeting is inefficient, but would also challenge the notion that it is irrelevant. Just because no intervention or arrest results does not mean that a significant social interaction, albeit remote and technologically mediated, has not taken place. Imagine two youths, who on entering city centre space are immediately picked up by the cameras. They notice the first camera moving to track them, as they move through the streets and go out of range of one camera, another is seen altering its position to bring them into view; in fact wherever they go they can see cameras being repositioned to monitor their every movement. How do these youths feel? They have done nothing wrong, they have not drawn attention to themselves by their behaviour, and they are not 'known offenders'. But they are being treated as a threat, as people who cannot be trusted, as persons who do not belong, as unwanted outsiders. The guarantees that such systems will show no interest or 'deliberate monitoring of people going about their daily business' is an empty rhetoric.

This technologically mediated and distanced social interaction is, then, loaded with meaning and for literally thousands of black and working-class youth, however law-abiding, it transmits a wholly negative message about their position in society. But it has wider consequences than just its impact on individual psychology. The central tenet of policing by consent, that policing is viewed as legitimate by those who experience it, is undermined. If social groups experience CCTV surveillance as an extension of discriminatory and unjust policing, the consequential loss of legitimacy may have serious consequences for social order. As Brogden, Jefferson and Walklate have argued it was precisely this experience of unjust policing which was both the 'underlying cause and the trigger of all the urban riots of the 1980s' (1988: 90).

—8—

Communications and Consequences

So far we have concentrated on the manner in which operators construct suspicion on their own account. However we now want to consider how they interact with the external environment, both in responding to requests for surveillance from others bodies, and by making requests themselves for deployment. It is our contention that there is no simple correspondence between operators receiving requests for surveillance and the action that will result, and neither is there a simple correspondence between what is seen on the screen and requests for authoritative interventions from others, particularly the police. Both are filtered through a personally inscribed local reading of occupational and organisational norms and mediated by the nature of the communications infrastructure. From an organisational perspective the interactions between the CCTV control room and the external environment are governed, at least in part, by the codes of practice found in the respective sites. The codes sought to regulate interactions through three primary mechanisms: prohibitions, documentation, and authorisation.

Regulating Communications

Prohibitions

Communications: One of the codes contained explicit reference to communication with unauthorised personnel:

> Unless specifically authorised at no time should the operators or contractors discuss any aspect of the system with, or make any comment to, the media or any person not directly involved in the CCTV system.

Another touched on the subject more tangentially stating:

> Any misuse of information obtained from a video recording will be considered a disciplinary offence and dealt with accordingly.

The third was silent on the issue.

Access: All three of the codes sought to regulate access to the control room and prohibit unauthorised personnel from viewing the screens:

> No unauthorised persons shall be allowed into the lodge expect in the event of an emergency. In such cases, the person allowed in must be escorted at all times. Under no circumstance would they be allowed in the monitoring room.

> Access to the general area (the control room) will be restricted to authorised personnel.

> Access to the CCTV control room will be strictly limited to the duty controllers, authorised management from .... (the council and security company).

In two of the schemes these general prohibitions also applied to police officers unless specific authorisations were given, while in the other scheme, since the system was housed in the operations room of the local police station, police had free access to the monitors.

Documentation

The main form of regulation was through documentation and through these procedures accountability could be claimed as it would enable a review of how the system had been used. Thus, operators variously had to maintain a log and, in some cases obtain the signatures, in respect of: visitors to the system; requests for surveillance; requests for the police control of the system; requests to view, copy and take possession of tapes; and requests for hard copy printout. Many of these procedures were primarily concerned at securing 'a chain of custody' of a tape so that if it were used in court proceedings its provenance could be accounted for. However, by default, they also provided an 'audit trail' which could establish use and possible misuse of the system. For example, the codes variously state:

> Police officers visiting the site are required to complete the Log Book indicating time, place and purpose of visit.

> The register for the use and reviewing of tapes will be completed on each shift. Continuity must be maintained especially for evidential purposes.

> When incidents arise, information will be relayed to the police and any formal request for them to assume control will be accepted. Details and response should be noted in the log

> The Record of Use log will be maintained at all times. In it will be recorded dates of erase and who performed the task. Records of who inserted or removed masters will

also be recorded in the log, as well as details if and when, and by whom, the tape was viewed.

Authorisation

The final manner is which control was exercised was through authorisation by a higher authority for specific courses of action, although what required authorisation varied considerably between sites. This included access to the control room, the generation of hard copy printouts from the tapes, copying of the tapes, and, perhaps most importantly the level of authorisation necessary for the police to take control of the system.

In all three sites there was the potential for the police to remotely take control of the system and to be able to operate the cameras themselves, from their own command and control console. In all three of the systems, the authority for this rested with the duty officer at the local police station. One of the codes stated that 'with the agreement of the respective control room supervisor' and in another that 'control will normally be given to the police on request'. The final code is silent on this matter. There are no indications of what would constitute grounds for refusal and in, practice, when police asked for control it was granted.

More contentiously, in the two sites which were not on police premises, procedures were also laid down for the police to take command of the control room, both with the operators present and, in extreme cases, enjoying the right of sole occupancy. Both of these courses of action required high-level authorisation between senior police officers (superintendent level) and senior council officers (deputy director level).

The efficacy of the codes in regulating the use of CCTV is of course an empirical question, however three points must be noted. First, although none of the systems are owned or formally controlled by the police it is clear that the police have a privileged status over the operators since the codes make clear the controls of the system will be handed over to them on request or demand.

Second, the codes do not have the force of law, although in all three cases they are backed up by the threat of disciplinary sanction should they be breached.

Third, for codes to be effective there needs to be a mechanism by which compliance with them is monitored and enforced. In this regard all three systems were weak. There are a number of reasons for this:

1 The direct supervision of any 24-hour-a-day operation is resource intensive. In reality, during out-of-office hours, there tends to be little managerial presence.
2 Compliance with the codes requires at the very least operator and police awareness of their provisions. However this was patchy. As one internal review found 'Operators were unfamiliar with the Code of Practice' and 'The Log Book was

illegible in places and not properly maintained,' or, as another internal memo stated, 'It is sometimes the case that officers appear to think they can do what they want and speak to the control room staff in any manner they want in order to get video tapes. Until such time as there is a national or at least Force wide standard Code of Practice, there will remain confusion. I have improved the written instructions for police at the viewing room in the hope that they'll start doing things properly.'

3 The low status of the civilian operators vis-a-vis police officers makes it difficult to resist police demands even if they appear to breach the codes.

4 In only one system was there any review process to ensure that the codes were being complied with.

As a result, in all sites, we witnessed, or operators reported, a whole range of breaches of their respective codes: hard-copy printouts were made and given to police and store detectives with no documentation being completed; tapes were taken without the necessary documentation being completed; police took over control of the cameras with no explanation to justify the necessity, and no entry in the log book of its occurrence; access to the control room was granted to police officers with no note in the visitors' book or operational log; requests for targeted surveillance went unlogged and so forth.

However, we would not argue that the codes were irrelevant in regulating interactions with outside bodies. As our observations revealed, while the codes were breached on some occasions by some operators, on other occasions the same or different operators would comply with them. Our point is that in the absence of managerial control and established procedures for ensuring compliance, claims of the efficacy of the code in regulating CCTV are based on faith and trust. And faith and trust are poor guarantors of the integrity of a system.

Communication Links

All three systems had direct communications links with the police, and these requests were afforded the highest status and priority. However, the different systems had different mechanisms both for receiving and acting on requests for surveillance from other external sources. In Metro City, where the CCTV control room was located in the police communications room, practically all requests emanated directly or indirectly from the police control room personnel, or occasionally via the 'request for surveillance book' which enabled other officers, particularly the CID, to ask for specific attention to be paid to a person or locale. There was one external channel of communication, the direct telephone line to the operators, but this was rarely used as a means to request surveillance. And requests were not encouraged, since the legitimacy of the system was defined in terms of it being used solely for policing purposes.

This was illustrated forcefully in the early days of the system when an operator received a call on the dedicated telephone line from the Council's Cleansing Department who requested the operators surveille a public toilet to record a toilet attendant believed to leave work early each day. This was initially undertaken (even though the operators did not really know what he looked like), but after a few days the surveillance was ended when a number of operatives grew uneasy about the situation and raised it with the System Manager. He informed the operators to refuse such requests in future and to direct people to him for an explanation.

Moreover, the operatives had no direct communications link with other private store security personnel, either in the form of store detectives or private patrol guards. In short, despite the system being run by an independent trust, it was, for all intents and purposes, a police system. This was in direct contrast to County Town and Inner City which both had police-independent communications networks. In Inner City this consisted of a retail radio link, which connected the CCTV operatives to the twelve store detectives and security guards who worked in the high street. However, despite the existence of the link it was rarely used. Occasionally a request would come from a store detective but, on average there were fewer than one a day. Conversely, on occasions the operatives would alert a security guard to the approach of potential shoplifters or 'trouble-makers' but again this was rare.

In County Town there was a Council-operated town-wide radio network which linked a variety of Council employees to each other and to the CCTV control room. These included maintenance workers as well as car-park attendants. Again, this was rarely used in practice, but in theory, a variety of Council workers could liaise with the CCTV system should the need arise. There was also a retail radio link and, in contrast to Inner City, this played a central role in generating surveillance requests during shopping hours.

It is important, therefore, to understand that, although on the face of it, we have three broadly similar CCTV systems – they all have 24-hour monitoring, they all have PTZ cameras, and they are all monitored by non-police personnel – their day-to-day operation is structured by the technological and social organisation of the communications system. In effect, this means that Metro City is a police-led system, Inner City is an operator-led system and County Town a hybrid system. But, as we shall see from the operation of County Town's retail radio network the impact of the communications system is not only mediated by organisation and technology but by the personal values and attitudes of the operators.

Mediating the Message: the Retail Radio Link

The initial cost of setting up the retail radio system was financed by one of the major town centre stores, and all participating stores had to pay a £150 annual fee to be connected. The CCTV operators, however, were not just passive conduits of information; they actively controlled it and were brokers of the entire system. The store detectives, or 'romeos' as they are hailed by their on-air call sign, could not talk to each other directly but only through the mediation of the CCTV operatives, who could either pass the message on or, if they felt it necessary, grant the 'romeos' the talk-through facility which enabled a caller to contact all 'romeos' simultaneously. Originally, talk-through was an automatic facility controlled by the 'romeos' themselves. However, it was felt by some, including the CCTV manager, that the system was poorly used and even abused with the store detectives collectively overreacting to pursuit incidents and all rushing out of their stores to join in the chase or, in other instances, engaging in wild goose chases on the basis of spurious and overzealous suspicion raised by one of their number. To avoid such scenarios the CCTV manager decided to give the operators the sole authority for talk-through.

Thus, through their role as custodians of the radio network the control room staff are also formally integrated into the private security apparatus of the town centre and CCTV plays a central part of the system in two ways. First, by allowing the operators to alert store detectives of the approach of known shoplifters or others deemed suspicious, and second, enabling stores to extend their internal surveillance systems onto the public streets through the tracking facilities of the CCTV system. This enables store detectives to warn other stores of the presence of 'trouble' in the town and request that the CCTV operators track a suspect's departure from their store so as to alert the store detectives at their next port of call. During the day the system is dominated by these transactions, but how they are responded to depends on which operators are working the shift. Below we illustrate how three different pairs of operators employ a very different working style with their interactions with the town centre 'romeos' ranging from cooperative to reserved to hostile.

Marcus and Darren: the Courtship of Youth

This following shift involves two young and inexperienced operators. Marcus is twenty-five years old and has only worked as an operator for six months. Darren, his colleague, is twenty-three with only one previous shift to his name. They were both keen to make the cameras busy and were eager to be of help to the guardians of corporate profitability:

11.02 – A store detective contacts the operator to inform him of 'suspicious behaviour' in his store manifested in four people about to leave. What the operator has to look out for is a white male and female and a black male and female all in their late 20s. Putting a camera onto the shop doors the operator asks the store detective to tell him when they are about to leave – which he does about 30 seconds later. Informing him that they are in his vision the operator *now* asks whether they have actually done anything. The answer is no! Ever keen to oblige one operator asks the store detective would she like 'talk-through' so as to warn all other 'Romeos' about them. Accepting this all 15 other store detectives are told of these 'suspicious' people and how they came to her attention 'acting suspicious in the obvious thieving area of the store'. The operator does not recognise them as 'regulars', but follows them as they walk in the town until they enter another store whereupon the operator contacts the shop's store detective via the retail radio and informs him of their presence, adding 'They've not done anything, they're just actin' suspicious'. The operator follows the suspects through the town without any further conversation with the store detective. (6 minutes, 2 cameras)

11.20 – A mall security guard contacts the operator. A white male in his late teens has come to his attention because whilst leaning against a wall in the shopping mall 'he put something in his pocket'. The caller did not see this incriminating action first-hand, rather a member of the public reported it to him. The suspect has just left the mall, the operator follows him zooming in close to see if he pulls anything out of his pocket believing perhaps that he is safe to do so having left the site of surveillance. He doesn't, but the operator reassures the guard that he will tell him if anything appears in his hand from nowhere. The suspect is followed for a few minutes, but pulls nothing out of any garment and so the operator tires of following him. (3 minutes, 2 cameras)

11.37 – Another store detective calls up to inform the operator that a well-known shoplifter has just entered a shopping mall accompanied by a friend. This information is then re-told to all 'Romeos' by the operator on talk-through and he further obliges the caller by putting cameras on the shopping mall entrance/exit doors. The two white males, late teens, casually dressed reappear after five minutes and are then followed for the next *25 minutes* as they walk around the town. They reveal no criminal actions or stolen items. They are followed because they are known offenders.

12.04 – Another sighting of a well-known shoplifter provokes another call to the operator from another store detective. Accompanied by a mate the two white males, in their 20s, and casually dressed are not picked out of the crowd by the operator. So to assist surveillance the operator tells all Romeos on talk-through of their lurking presence. (4 minutes, 1 camera)

12.14 – Two suspects have come to the notice of a store detective who now informs the operator that they have just left his store. A display unit they were seen near has items missing, but he has no evidence if they took anything. The operator meanwhile has located the suspects on camera and tells the store detective as much and which other shop premise they are about to enter. Minutes later when the suspects leave this shop it is noted by the operator that the pair have swapped department store plastic bags they each carried. This information is relayed to the store detective who initiated the surveillance. The latter is now mobile seeking to follow the two, but admits that he cannot find them in the crowd. After ten minutes of a futile search by both cameras and store detective the latter informs the operator that he is now 'standing down' from the pursuit and the operator happily looks elsewhere. (14 minutes, 5 cameras)

14.29 – A store detective's suspicion has been aroused sufficiently for him to call the operator. Noticing in his store two white males in their late teens and with one wearing a baseball cap he considers that the box one is carrying under his arm is empty and furthermore thinks they may have tried to put jewellery from a display into it. Additionally, as he followed them he saw them enter a newsagent and steal two cans of soft drinks. They are now on their way towards the shopping mall.

The operator finds the two suspects, but in so doing realises that they are aware of the cameras on them. Suddenly changing direction and furtively glancing at the cameras the two then run into the mall. The operator immediately contacts the security guard there saying 'I'll leave it with you . . . you know where we are if you need us'. Meanwhile a camera is left trained on the mall doors. About two minutes later the suspects reappear and walk towards another store and the operator dutifully warns the store detective there about them. Moments later they walk out, the one wearing the baseball cap having taken his head-gear off and as they continue their walk they aim a few choice gestures towards those watching them. (8 minutes, 1 camera)

14.35 – Noticing what he describes as a 'suspicious character in the store' a store detective tells the operator of his find over the retail radio. Suspicion centres around this white male's attempt to claim a refund on items which are believed to be faulty goods thrown away by management into the store's bins. This bewilders the operator; firstly the suspect is still in the store and secondly he has, as yet, done nothing wrong. Before he can ask for clarification as to what it is the store detective wants him to do the latter tells the operator that the store will proceed with the refund because she only has *suspicions* about him. Unsure about what to do the operator finds a way out – by lying – he tells her that the cameras are tied up on another job at the moment, and that he cannot surveille anyone leaving the store.

Eight minutes later the store detective gets in touch again informing him that the suspicious person is now persons (a white male in his 40s with a white female in her 40s) and they were in fact not given money, but promised a refund if their complaint was authorised via head office. The store detective's request is specific – as they leave the store she wants a camera on them 'so they're captured on video and we can do a print-out of them'. The operator is unsure of the morality of this. On this he is alone, the new man has no opinions either way and has little confidence to say anything. He gets round this dilemma by lying when informing the store detective that he is unable to see the suspect couple, but he would 'keep an eye out'. Off the air he tells his co-operator that not only was the description given of the suspects poor in detail, but that the two suspects had been given 'half a refund' so the store 'was wanting it both ways'. (10 minutes, 1 camera)

15.20 – A 14 year old white female disturbs a store detective. Whilst she has just left the store, shop staff have found a security tag which could have belonged to an item she has taken and now has upon her. Given a description the operator searches the busy streets but cannot find her and out of curiosity then asks the store detective that if she is found what is his intended course of action? This provokes silence. The store detective responds two minutes later requesting the operator stop his search for the female as 'she is not worth following as the tag is for less than £2 worth of goods'.

15.40 – A store detective has three women outside his store who were, in his opinion, 'acting suspicious in the store earlier'. All are black and aged between 30-40 and are standing talking in the doorway of the store. The operator zooms the camera in close to pick up their faces then leaves the camera on them until they are forgotten as the next shift personnel arrive. (5 minutes, 1 camera)

It is clear, that at times Darren and Marcus are uneasy with the requests made by the store detectives and resist what they see as the more excessive and even improper demands. However, in the main, under their guardianship the CCTV system becomes almost entirely co-opted by and subservient to the demands of the private security nexus of the town centre store detectives.

John and Marcus: Chaperoned Flirtations

In contrast to the above another day shift illustrated how an older and more cynical operator could restrain the enthusiasm of the youthful and inexperienced Marcus who seemed prepared to willingly accede to any demands made of him by store detectives.

11.47 – A store detective has noticed a known shoplifter and has decided to tell the operators. The suspect is a mixed-race female aged 18 currently out shopping with a woman the store detective presumes is her mother. The pair are found on camera standing talking to two white women in their 40s. The operator assures the store detective saying 'I've got her in my sights' and the suspect and her mother are surveilled as they walk through the town occasionally looking in shop window displays. At this point the operator's elder colleague points out that the women are not actually doing anything criminal and even if she is a shoplifter she looks at this point to be out with her mother and, implicitly, chaperoned from temptation. This seems to have an effect on the younger of the two operators, who agrees with his colleague's reasoning and stops following them, but does not inform the store detective. (3 minutes, 1 camera)

13.00 – Three people have alerted a store detective sufficiently for him to call the operator. The three white females who are in his store range in age from mid-20s to 50 and according to the store detective, 'their eyes are all over the place looking out for staff'. Giving brief descriptions of them he further claims they are about to leave the store. Whilst putting a camera on the doors the operator is unsure of whom precisely to look at and the fact that dozens of people per minute enter and leave the store's 12 doors only confuses the issue. Reasoning that the women have not done anything the elder operator tells his colleague that he is not going to bother looking for them, and after a half-hearted attempt at locating the 'suspects' the younger operator looks elsewhere. No message is passed to the store detective. (1 minute, 1 camera)

14.20 – A handbag snatch in a department store provokes the store's security guard into contacting the operator to both tell him of the event and request that he contact the police on his behalf. Whilst the younger operator is willing to do this his older colleague interrupts him on the radio to ask the security guard 'Are you currently chasing the suspects?' Answering in the negative the operator suggests that he call police himself from the telephone in the office! This provokes a silence at the other end and a realisation (and giggle) at the operators' end that the guard will be annoyed that they will not do his job for him. There is, consequently, no dialogue for the next minute until the operator who first took the message contacts the guard to ask for a description of the suspect. The terse reply is that she is black and in her mid-30s. No clothing is described and no indication is given of which direction she was going is given. Both operators move a couple of cameras in the rather futile hope of seeing the culprit and whilst doing so three minutes later receive a phone call from the same security guard informing them that the bag and its contents have been found in the store. The operators whilst polite to thank her for this information are somewhat annoyed that they have been informed of what in hindsight was not a theft, but a misplaced bag and bewildered at how a 'suspect' can be so willingly identified by somebody, and their identity promoted by the security guard. (9 minutes, 4 cameras)

Having been the one to control the enthusiasm of his younger colleague, I ask the older operator how the system would handle this circumstance, i.e. if a female fitting that description had indeed been seen walking around. His reply was: 'If found I would inform him (the guard) where she is and tell him to go and have a look at her. If he thought she was the suspect then *he* could call the police, that way it's his job not ours and if the wheel comes off it's not down to us.'

15.35 – Two white teenage males have aroused the suspicion of a store detective. Contacting the operator over the retail radio she tells him how 'our cosmetics store were worried about them', adding that the suspects have just left the store. Locating them the younger operator follows their movements until they enter the shopping mall but then loses interest, and neither contacts the store detective nor warns others in the mall of such suspects. How much this is due to the paternalistic advice given earlier by the older operator is difficult to say. (3 minutes, 3 cameras)

Danny and Jerry: the Affair Turns Sour

Some operators' toleration with store detectives was stretched so far that the communications were more like a war than an exchange. For Danny and Jerry, the two longest-serving operators on one shift, an accumulation of what they saw as ridiculous messages, combined with hot pursuits for which they could see no real rationale, led to a policy of almost total non-cooperation.

09.39 – A store detective contacts the operator via the retail radio. A white male aged 16 has just left her store and she suspects he might 'have taken something' and, with this vague suspicion, not only follows him through the streets but requests of the operators that they contact police to deploy an officer to apprehend the suspect and do a 'stop and search'. The two operators (off the air) abuse and ridicule her for this suggestion when all she has to go on is 'suspicion'. Whilst following the suspect on camera the operator asks the store detective to find out what it is he has stolen, her reply (somewhat peeved) is that she will, in a few minutes, when she returns to the shop.

Meanwhile the suspect is followed on camera into public toilets and remains in there. The operator wishing to maintain a good rapport with the store detective tells her of his location. In reply she tells the operator that she is making her way to the toilets accompanied by a PC she happened to see on his beat and whom she is now pursuing the suspect with. A minute later the operator watches as the PC enters the toilets and over his personal radio (which can be heard on the 'unofficial' radio frequency on the radio on the console) that the suspect does indeed have stolen items upon him. The operator can then only watch as a police vehicle arrives as the suspect is arrested. (8 minutes, 2 cameras)

09.50 – Another store detective contacts the operator. The message is vague: 'I just want to bring it to your attention that I've just walked past a group of four males and they're really moody'. Allowing a pause to see if this suspicion has anything to be elaborated on the operators look at each other in amazement and shake their heads slowly in disgust at such a vague and trivial request. After a break of 60 seconds Jerry takes the initiative and replies with a lie: 'Yes, thanks for that . . . we've searched the area but no trace'. Neither operator has attempted to look for the four, but wish to placate the store detective and, on giving their reply, Danny compliments Jerry stating 'That'll fuck him off'. Jerry replies 'We don't look at all and sundry on their whim . . . bollocks to 'em' and leaves the incident to look elsewhere.

10.19 – A security guard employed to patrol the bus station contacts his colleagues in the Control Room via their radio link. The guard is with a store detective and the pair wish to pass on a description of a white male aged around 18 and casually dressed who had 'earlier caused trouble in a department store'. Again the operators raise their eyes at such a vague criteria of suspicion and Jerry requests of the guard to ascertain from the detective what it is precisely that this suspect has done. The answer given 40 seconds later is that he was 'acting suspiciously' which provokes further ridicule and abuse from the two operators for the benefit of each other. Agreeing that he has in fact done nothing criminal the operators are then relieved of further dilemmas when the guard tells them that the suspect has entered the library. Promising to keep an eye out for him the operators wilfully forget the suspect immediately and look at other cameras. (2 minutes, 2 cameras)

10.41 – A store detective contacts the operator via the retail radio. Informing the operators that 'an attempted snatch' has taken place earlier and the culprits are described. Neither operator knows anything about this attempted theft, but by now are at the end of their tether with store detectives. Feigning interest Jerry listens to the name given (neither of them have heard of him) and lies when replying that he suspects that the culprit is 'well known'. Off the air the two abuse store detectives and do not look for any such culprit!

11.33 – A store detective (the same one as in the incident at 09.50) contacts the operators via the retail radio to inform them that she is following two white males who, moments earlier, had tried to return a garment to her store claiming cash back. The basis of the suspicion of criminal activities was that whilst they had a receipt for a purchase made by Switch card they did not have a Switch card on them. Now following them the store detective is requesting assistance both from the cameras and any other store detective by asking for 'talk-through'.

By now the word store detective has a Pavlovian effect on the two operators. Jerry rages at the speaker (not on air) that she has no grounds for arrest and very few grounds for suspicion and besides which if they were so suspicious why did they give them cash back on their goods or better still arrest them whilst in the store? Of course there is no answer but before Jerry becomes apoplectic the same store detective radios in saying that she has lost the two suspects. When the derisive cheers and abuse die down Danny, in sweet moderation, informs her this was unfortunate but on seeing her the culprits 'must have done a runner'. Her reply is to request that the operators 'sweep the area' with the cameras which they reply they 'will do' and then seconds later off the air add 'like fuck'. With that the pair forget the request.

Ten minutes later the store detective contacts the operator to inform him that the store did not give a refund and in fact kept the item of clothing he was attempting to return for cash. Thanking her for imparting this knowledge to them the operators agree that the whole scenario was 'ten minutes of crap which had no criminal justification'. (6 minutes, 4 cameras)

13.30 – A store detective phones the operator to tell him that he has sighted someone suspected of a theft earlier in the day. A story unfolds that this chap had been overheard 'by someone' saying that he 'had nicked these jeans 10 minutes ago' and was now asking for a refund on the garments. Having listened to this and looked at his colleague with raised eyebrows the operator is unsure of why the store detective has called him: the suspect is still in the store, he does not know whether he is to be given a refund, he does not know if he is innocent and what information the store detective has is in his opinion 'fourth hand'. After a one-minute silence the operator eventually speaks to the store detective and asks of the suspect's whereabouts. The operator is told that he has left the store, but is still in the shopping centre and so the store detective now asks the operator to inform the centre's security guard of this suspect. The operator politely refuses to do this explaining that the intelligence he has is not first-hand and the man could be innocent and it was not his job in the circumstance to add to the suspicion. The silence from the store detective is an indication of his anger. No message is forthcoming and the two operators laugh enjoying the power they hold over such people. (1 minute, 1 camera)

12.07 – The operators receive another daft message from another store detective. This time the operators learn that two white males were 'very worried' when they realised the cameras were surveilling them as they stood in the market square. The description given is not that of the above two. In fact the operators have no idea who these two worried men are. A description is given (early 20s, casually dressed) but the operators do not bother to look for people who are exhibiting 'worry'.

12.33 – Another store detective calls over the retail radio. The request is very specific – could a camera surveille the store's front door because a white man aged around 20 and scruffily dressed is shortly to leave who has just had a credit card retained by a cashier. This causes exasperation from the operators who agree that if the suspect has done something criminal the store detective should have apprehended him there and then and what's more even if his card has been retained, so what? The store detective moments later asks whether the suspect is on camera, the reply from Jerry is to inquire whether he is about to be stopped or arrested (without revealing that he has no one of the description on camera and is not even looking for him!). The store detective explains that she was wondering if the operators might be able to put a name to his identity and volunteers that their store's surveillance system has footage of him from earlier in the day. This does not placate the operators who after an off-air discussion agree to reply that until told that this suspect will be arrested they will not be following him.

13.00 – A store detective contacts the operator via retail radio. The request is for a camera to be put onto the exit of the department store wherein are located three people who have been 'thrown out for being a pain . . . you might want to look at them'. With a groan one operator briefly surveilles the shop to see the three suspects – two white males and a white female all in their early 20s and all casually dressed. Wanting no further part in such a vague notion of suspicion and surveillance and not prepared to ask for greater details as to what constitutes 'a pain' the operator claims via a lie that his priority is elsewhere at the moment in dealing with 'a retard harassing woman' which stops any further requests to surveille. (1 minute, 1 camera)

13.47 – Yet another vague message from a store detective. This time the objects of suspicion are two white males who have just left the store but who 'looked a bit suspicious'. Informing the operators as to which direction they were walking the operator politely replies that they will look in that vicinity and get back to her should any further suspicion become manifest. By now exasperated the two operators cannot articulate their rage and sit staring into the middle-distance smirking!

13.55 – The manager of the 'Double D' sports shop phones the operator with the following message: 'There's a black female stood outside my store . . . is she known to you?' Moving a camera to the store and zooming in to the display window the cameras reveal a black girl aged 14 standing with a white female of similar age. The operator has no idea who they are and tells the store manager as much. The latter expands on his suspicion: 'They were acting funny in the store a while ago and you never know . . .' Off the air the operator swears in desperation at what he considers the stupidity of the shop manager; then tells me that he calls the Control Room regularly on the slightest suspicions requesting cameras front and back of his store whilst giving stupid messages like 'someone left ten minutes ago with a check shirt who might have stolen something'. Whilst considered a constant source of annoyance the operator feels helpless to do or say anything reasoning 'We just keep polite and hope he'll go away'. (1 minute, 1 camera)

14.10 – To end the day as it began the operators receive a message from a store detective informing them that three white females 'known shoplifters' have just left his store. To the operators' inquiry as to what they have stolen he can only reply 'nothing – but they are well-known'. By now with the shift nearing the end the operators could not even bother to continue the conversation and do not bother to search for these suspicious characters.

In County Town the technology of the communications network facilitates the integration of the public CCTV system with the interests of the commercial sector's private security apparatus. However, as is clear, such integration rests on more than just the existence of technological links, it is fundamentally influenced by the practices of the CCTV operatives in filtering requests for both surveillance and information exchange. Thus, there is variation both between sites, as to how CCTV is used, due to the nature and organisation of communications technology, but also within the same site depending on distinctive practices of the operatives. This interaction between technological, organisational and personal features alerts us to the need to pay attention to the technology, without falling into the trap of technological determinism, while at the same time being aware of how the impact of technology is socially constructed without ignoring the importance of the technology in setting the parameters as to what a system can be used for. As we have said before, it is simply not possible to know in advance what the effect of a CCTV system will be, merely from the existence of the cameras. These are empirical matters which are situationally specific and, as we shall see, these become even more salient when we examine the manner in which CCTV systems mobilise deployments.

Table 8.1 Nature of Surveillance which Resulted in a
Deployment

Nature of surveillance	No.	%
Property Crime	11	24
Violence	17	38
Order	12	27
Other	5	11
Total	45	100

Deployments

One of the central claims for the effectiveness of CCTV systems is that they deter potential offenders and enable a rapid authoritative response to the recalcitrant whose behaviour is not modified by the presence of the cameras. However, our data suggests that such interventions are relatively rare. In total, nearly 600 hours of observation resulted in only forty-five deployments, on average then, one would expect no more than two deployments to result from a system in twenty-four hours. In all but one case in our study, this deployment was of police officers.

The most important point to note from Table 8.1 is that crimes involving violence constitute the largest single category of surveillance incidents which led to deployment and this is closely followed by order-related crimes. These two categories between them constitute two-thirds of deployments (65 per cent). National crime statistics, (Home Office 1996) supported by the British Crime Survey, (Home Office 1996) suggest that property crime constitutes 94 per cent of crimes and crimes involving violence only 6 per cent. In terms of deployment, then, the three CCTV systems are heavily skewed towards violent crime. This is not surprising. Property crimes are far more likely to be committed by stealth and in shops or residential areas which are out of the gaze of the cameras. In the case of theft of and from cars (which may be in the gaze of the camera) these offences are the most likely to be deterred (Tilley 1993). Even if a property crime is known to have been committed and the operators are alerted by the public or store detectives, the chance of finding a suspect in a crowded shopping area is not high – in nearly half (44 per cent) of incidents where someone other than the operator initiated the surveillance the suspect was not found. As our observations revealed, this is because location is often imprecise and descriptions are too vague to significantly differentiate a suspect from the crowd. Significantly, only three deployments were initiated by the system in relation to shoplifting. Of the six other property crime deployments initiated by the system operators, four concerned suspected theft of or from cars, and two related to criminal damage.

Table 8.2 Characteristics of Primary Persons who were Surveilled, Deployed Against and Arrested

Characteristic	Deployment against no.	Deployment against %*	Arrested %	Targeted for surveillance %
Sex				
Male	36	84	91	93
Female	7	16	9	7
Total	43	100	100	100
Age				
Teen	10	23	18	39
Twenties	22	51	82	46
Thirties +	11	26	0	15
Total	43	100	100	100
Race				
White	36	86	91	68
Black	6	14	9	32
Total	42	100	100	100
Appearance				
Smart	3	7	18	10
Uniform	0	0	0	1
Scruffy/sub	10	23	27	17
Casual/ind	30	70	54	72
Total	43	100	99	100

* Percentages may not add up to 100 due to rounding.

Violent and order-related surveillance were far more likely to be the result of system operators' observations, and where deployment resulted were directly related to the observed behaviour of those surveilled. Over half (54 per cent) of all deployments were the result of behavioural suspicion.

The order-related deployments mainly concerned two types of incidents: groups of men loitering or kerb crawling in a street with a reputation for prostitution (3 out of 12) and drunks either collapsed or causing a nuisance (6 out of 12). Of the violence-related deployments, one related to 'mugging', two to the brandishing of knifes, and the other fourteen to fights/assault. Nearly all of the fights that led to deployment were between young men at night, were drink related, and in the main involved much posturing and the occasional fisticuffs. Three were more serious and involved either weapons or sustained and prolonged attack. In none of the incidents observed were injuries, if any had been sustained, serious enough for police or others to call an ambulance to the scene.

The level of seriousness these incidents were accorded can also be gauged by the type, speed and strength of the deployment. On average these were most likely to be a routine response (84 per cent) from a double-crewed (54 per cent) beat car

(40 per cent). In only six incidents (13 per cent) was there an emergency response and, as far as could be judged from the monitors, the police used force to restrain someone involved in the incident in only a quarter (24 per cent) of all deployments.

Table 8.2 shows deployment is still disproportionately skewed towards male youth, and black people are still over-represented, but in a less marked way than at targeting. Thus, while women constituted only 7 per cent of the targeted population, they made up 16 per cent of those whose activities merited deployment and only 9 per cent (one person) of those arrested. Similarly those aged thirty or more accounted for only 15 per cent of targeted surveillances but 26 per cent of deployments, none of which resulted in arrest, while teenagers who made up 39 per cent of targeted surveillances constituted only 23 per cent of deployments and 18 per cent of arrests. Even more dramatically, while black people accounted for 32 per cent of targeted surveillances they only accounted for 14 per cent of the deployments and 9 per cent of the arrests. Conversely the scruffy or distinctively subculturally dressed constituted 17 per cent of the targeted surveillances, 23 per cent of deployments and 27 per cent of arrests.

These figures give credence to the view that operators' initial selection of targets categorically discriminate against certain social groups, particularly the young and the black, but when it comes to both deployment and arrest, objective criteria, such as overt displays of criminal behaviour, become more salient. Further, given that the particular configuration of arrests is premised on the unproductive over-targeting of certain social groups, it invites speculation as to what the arrest statistics would look like if surveillance was more evenly targeted across the whole population.

Outcomes

Of the 45 deployments, two resulted in no suspect/target being identified by police on the ground. Of the remaining 43 incidents, 76 per cent resulted in no more than a warning and those identified were allowed to go on their way. An arrest was made in only 12 incidents, that is in less that one-quarter (24 per cent) of all deployments and less than one in seventy targeted surveillances.

Authoritative intervention is a relatively rare phenomenon, and few incidents result in deployment, fewer still in arrest. Moreover, the number of arrests is a function of the level of targeted surveillances, on average there were only twelve targeted observations per shift, roughly one every forty-five minutes and deployment only resulted from about 5 per cent of target surveillances. It is therefore, important to try and unpack the processes by which surveillance triggers deployments and subsequent arrests. These are not simple matters since there is no necessary relationships between operatives finding an incident worthy of intervention (for instance because it displays clear evidence of criminality), and police deployment. Nor,

Table 8.3 Reason for Arrest from Targeted Surveillances which Resulted in a Deployment

Reason for arrest	no.	%*
Theft	3	25
Assault	4	33
Public order	3	25
Wanted on warrant	1	8
Offensive weapon	1	8
Total	12	99

* Percentages may not add up to 100 due to rounding.

when police are deployed is there a necessary relationship between the evidence held on tape and the subsequent police action.

In trying to account for these processes it is necessary to attend to the personal, organisational and structural features which limit deployment. The most important point is that, as operators mostly target people on the basis of categorical suspicion, this only rarely reveals concrete evidence of a criminal infraction. Even where targeted surveillance is triggered by a person's behaviour, this is most likely to because they are running, not to attack someone but to catch a bus or a taxi.

This issue is compounded by the relationships between CCTV operators and the police and how this is organisationally and technologically mediated. CCTV operatives do not have the power to intervene on their own account when they see something or someone suspicious. This puts them in a very different position to a patrol officer on the street.

The patrol officer on noticing something he or she deems suspicious has both the legal and organisational mandate for intervention. This may involve nothing more than 'having a word' with a group of youths, to a full adversarial stop and search. But in these matters officers are acting as their own agents. Under the Police and Criminal Evidence Act the police have the power of stop and search based on the concept of 'reasonable suspicion'. As various commentators have noted, this concept of reasonable suspicion is remarkably slippery and contestable and as Dixon et al (1989) have convincingly argued, stop and search is a process rather than an event. As such, the police often do not have reasonable suspicion to stop and then search a person before a stop is underway; the justification for a search is generated in the process of the encounter. And if a stop does not result in a search or a search is deemed consensual, then the officer is under no obligation to make an official record of the event. Officers can, therefore, act on their suspicions in the knowledge that they are of low visibility and are unlikely to be called to account for them. Put simply, if the officer, decides to intervene with someone on the street, in the main they do not have to provide any official justificatory account as to what warranted it. When they do have to provide an account these are constructed in the light of what was found during, not before, the interaction.

The CCTV operative is not in such an autonomous position as they do have to involve others, and are therefore always liable to be held to account as to what justified the request for intervention and, unlike the patrol officer, do not have the benefit of hindsight. This very process of accounting serves to limit requests for deployment to only those events which can generate the most concrete and strongest justifications.

Given that operators cannot demand deployment but merely request it and are reluctant to be held to account for their hunches, one solution to this problem is to allow the police to make the decision as to deployment on the basis of the evidence from the screen images. In all our sites this was facilitated by providing a direct feed of the incident on to a police monitor. However the extent to which this option was used in practice was dependent upon the degree the CCTV system was integrated with the formal and informal system of police deployment. This varied substantially between the three sites as did the number of deployments and it is this differentiation that is the subject of the next chapter.

From Images to Action:
From the Control Room to the Street

As we saw in the previous chapter the deployment of police or security guards as a result of what was seen on the monitors was a relatively rare occurrence in the sites we studied. However there was considerable variation between the three sites. Metro City accounted for thirty-two (71 per cent) of the total deployments; County Town, ten (22 per cent) and Inner City produced only three (7 per cent). In this chapter we explore the aspects of formal and informal organisation which lead to different levels of deployment before going on to consider the influences on operator and police decision making regarding deployment and arrest.

System Integration

In Metro City, the CCTV control room was housed in the operational control room of the local police station. The police controller who activated deployment from a variety of sources was in close proximity to the operators, no more than ten feet, with no physical barriers between them. They, therefore, shared the same working space and the police controller could view the bank of monitors from his or her desk independently of any specific request. This close and sustained proximity between operators and police controller/dispatchers facilitated the development of a set of informal understandings as to what may warrant deployment and what would at least warrant a further look. Operators could simply ask the controller to 'take a look at this' either on the banks of monitors or by relaying it to the dedicated monitor on their desk. Similarly on receipt of a call from the public, the controller could relay the information to the CCTV operator to place the cameras at such and such a location. Often, even this was not necessary because the operators could easily overhear the controller's conversation.

This integration was enhanced by the constant flow of visitors into the control room, on average seven per shift, as patrol officers would regularly come in to see if an incident had been captured on tape, or just for a general chat, and at night some would take their meal breaks while watching, and at times playing with, the cameras. If a major incident was captured on screen there would be a stream of visitors requesting to see the highlights. In this way the formal and informal aspects of the system facilitated the development of a set of shared understandings which encouraged the sharing of information and led to a high level of integration with police deployment practice.

The contrast with Inner City could not have been more stark. The system was housed in a purpose-built control room in the grounds of a local authority car park, a few hundred yards from the main area under surveillance. There were few visitors, less than one per twelve-hour shift. If police did try to visit, they had to ring the bell, be formally admitted and were always made to sign the visitors' book, a fact that may have discouraged them from using it as an unofficial 'tea-hole' when out on patrol. Although they could relay the pictures to a dedicated police monitor in the police station some 500 yards away, this would involve a telephone call on a line that was prone to be engaged and, when they did get through they would be talking to an unknown voice at the end of the line. Moreover, police rarely sought CCTV operators' assistance when they had received information. Instead, they would ring up and ask for the system to be turned over to them and would offer no explanation as to what they were looking for. The operators often merely became passive spectators as cameras moved at the hands of the police. This low level of integration is best illustrated by the following, not untypical example:

20.58 – The operator receives a call from the police requesting the system be given over to them. The request is granted without question and the operators can only watch as a police transit van appears alongside a police car and six officers get out and move the group outside Santana's on. The majority of the group vanish within a minute. Two who remain are seen being talked to by police. The operators at this point cannot do anything with the system because all the cameras and the ability to move them are in the control of police. As such the operators are mere spectators awaiting police to give them their job back! Meanwhile by 21.17 we can see how 20 of the group have drifted back to Santana's and minutes later some form of excitement begins when the majority of the group gather around the front door and begin looking into the shop at what is obviously some drama unfolding. A group of six black males then appear from the shop somewhat animatedly gesturing at shop staff who are Asian and words and a couple of punches are exchanged. As the mob remains around the door one youth can be seen to fetch an empty plastic bread crate from a nearby stack, however, whilst he postures with it he does not use it to strike anyone or damage anything. A minute later the group scatter as police in two vehicles arrive and clear the area, but do not arrest anyone nor seemingly do they discuss the nature of the incident with the shop staff.

One hour after taking control of the system the operators are still awaiting to resume their task, but they are reluctant to phone the police because for all they know police are still involved in an operation. By 22.00 there are 15 black males back outside Santana's generally looking about but not hostile and the two operators sit in front of the screen like two plums until exactly two hours after giving the cameras to police, Victor phones them to ask if they have finished. They have and explain they had an hour ago, but forgot to hand control back!

If Metro City was highly integrated and Inner City characterised by low integration, County Town is best seen as lying somewhere between the two. Like Inner City it was housed in local authority premises, in a car park building and therefore shared the same structural isolation. However, there was much more informal contact. The head of the security company which ran the system was himself a former local senior police officer, as was one of the council employees who was directly responsible for managing the scheme. There were daily, unofficial, visits from patrol officers who would enjoy a cup of tea and a respite from plodding the beat. Although they should have signed in they were not required to by the operators and rarely did so. On average they had four visitors per eight-hour shift. These informal contacts were enhanced by access to police communications. The operatives had requested access to a police radio so they could monitor communications in an effort to guide the cameras as to where they would be of most use. This request had been turned down but one enterprising operator had unofficially donated a scanner which at night was tuned into the police frequency with the full knowledge of numerous police officers. The effect of this was to produce a far more cooperative relationship than in Inner City and the cameras were rarely just taken over by the police, rather police would request operators' assistance, leaving them in control of the system and, in the process, brief them as to what the incident was about.

We have explored, in some detail, the processes which shaped deployment practice and argued that the generally low level can be explained by the difficultly operators would experience in providing an account as to what warranted the deployment should they be asked to justify their decision. Furthermore the variation in deployment practices is a direct result of the level of integration that CCTV operators have with the police deployment system. These features are important in influencing whether incidents are drawn to police attention at all and also the manner in which the system is used when deployment does result.

In practice what this means is that it is not possible to explain operator or subsequent police behaviour merely on the basis of what is displayed on the monitors. Even where there is prima facie evidence of an offence having been committed which is seen by operators and captured on tape there is no guarantee of deployment or, if deployment does result, of arrest. The contingent nature of the relationship between evidence and outcome can be illustrated by way of the decision model outlined below.

If CCTV operators see and record activities which, in their view, constitute an offence, whether or not a deployment or arrest follows, and for what reason someone is arrested, depends on the following conditions:

1 whether the operators choose to inform police of the incident
2 whether the police choose to respond, and the speed of that response, on the basis of what the operator says or the evidence on their dedicated monitor

3 if police do respond when they arrive at the scene is there any ongoing behaviour which would justify arrest on its own merits. If this is the case officers may:

(a) simply choose to ignore the existence of the cameras and make their decision on the basis of what is immediately apparent

(b) ask if there is any evidence on tape which may shed light on who to arrest for what reason and take note of any information that is volunteered by the operators

(c) arrest on the available evidence, for instance on a low-level 'resource charge' such as breach of the peace, and then check at a later time whether a more serious charge can be sustained on the basis of the tape recordings

4 if there is no ongoing evidence an arrest will depend, at least in the first instance, on whether the police seek confirmation of taped evidence or operators volunteer this information.

The Operator's Decision to Inform the Police

We have outlined structural constraints that operators have in making requests for deployment. What we need to draw attention to now is the effect of individual operator discretion in making these choices. Just as police discretion has been shown to be influenced by concepts such as seriousness, justice and fairness (Lustgarten 1986) operators too have their own views as to what level of criminality and in what context intervention is warranted. But these differences are also more systematic. While in Metro City, neither street trading nor bill posting were tolerated by the operators; in Inner City, where any entrepreneurial activity was, perhaps, to be welcomed, these activities were systematically ignored by the operators:

10.40 – A white male in his mid-30s is noticed standing on High Street outside a newspaper shop selling light bulbs and batteries from a wooden tray balanced on a Council litter bin. The operators discuss his presence, but do not call the police. As the operator explains to his new colleague, 'he shouldn't really be doing that, but we'll leave it to police to move him on'. (15 minutes, 1 camera)

23.35 – Walking along the High Street are four black males aged in their mid-teens. They are dressed in a smart, casual manner, but not sub-cultural. They have short hair, and none wear any form of headgear. Two have papers rolled up in their hands, another has a paint roller, another has a pot the size of a tin of paint. Walking to a corrugated iron fence which conceals derelict land, the four then set about their mission which is to stick up bill posters. We watch as they paste three up – one on the fence, another on a bus shelter and another on the blank white space of an advertising hoarding.

This task takes about six minutes. Whilst it is clearly visible and obvious what they are up to the operators do not become alarmed about their presence. In fact the only curiosity for the operators is what the posters are advertising. The four climb in a car and depart at 23.42, the operator not interested in the vehicle registration number. Later in the night whilst fetching food I looked at the posters. All were advertising an evangelistic preacher and his next meeting. (8 minutes, 2 cameras).

Although these incidents may seem trivial they do highlight the manner in which different systems are used for different purposes on the basis of operator judgments and how they serve some interests and not others. We suspect that, in Inner City were operators to draw these incidents to police attention, no action would have followed anyway. This alerts us to the interplay between operator decisions and the anticipated police reaction. Operators, on the basis of experience, may choose not to request deployment, or even alert the police to an incident, on their judgment of anticipated response, if in the past such requests have met with no action. In this way the underenforcement of Inner City should not be seen simply as a result of operator discretion. This is important because the decision not to bring matters to police attention extended from the trivial to the serious:

14.48 – The camera zooms in on eight black males standing outside Santana's. and within a minute of finding them the camera sees a fight involving two teenage females. For the moment the pair indulge in mutual pushing and insults before the boys intervene to stop it. But across the bodies of reasonableness the two females continue their war of words and two minutes later breach the line and start thumping and grappling, bouncing off the bus shelter and falling into the road.

The fight comes to the attention of uninvolved older people. Black men and women shout at the pair and when two black women stand protesting the boys intervene again and break it up. The two remain nearby, but in their separate camps doing up their hair and clothing. Eventually one crosses the road and disappears whilst the other goes into Santana's. Both operators have the events on two screens and are keeping tabs on the movements of the two. One of the fighters is out of sight whilst the other is clearly visible standing in the doorway of the bookies smoking and chatting with males. Once again, however, the police are not informed of this incident because the operator explains, it is all over and sorted out and calling police would be futile. (15 minutes, 2 cameras)

In the following incident the police are eventually notified some ten minutes after the initial offence was first observed:

03.33 – Further people appear outside the all-night store. Four are black females aged in their early 20s and out of the store comes a black Rastafarian. They are surveilled as they talk. As they walk down the street one female in yellow trousers and leather jacket grabs bags of rubbish left out by nearby businesses for early morning collection. In total over the next three minutes the woman picks up eleven black bags, walks the 20 yards or so back to the all-night store and attempts to throw them into the doorway! None hit their target – all fall around the doorway and half of them split open. The other three females can only watch, a couple attempt to remonstrate, but the bag thrower is determined and not until her task is complete does she allow herself a respite and then slowly walks down to the nearby cab office with a self-satisfied look on her face.

At 03.37 people emerge out of the shop now the coast is clear! The bag-lady is tranquil and out step three black males (two with Rasta's locks) and the four black females. One of the latter with one of the former walk to the woman who is standing arms folded leaning against a shop wall and evidently try to calm her down. The operators meanwhile have their own diagnosis 'She must be nuts' and 'There's something wrong with her'. This woman will not be reasoned with, she grabs one of the remaining bags and goes to throw it. Then, putting them down safely she picks up a plastic council rubbish bin, this provokes the other two men to walk towards her and actually physically restrain her from doing whatever she intends to do with it.

One of the men then takes the initiative to get this female out of the way. Seeing a cab parked outside the cab office he speaks to the driver, but to no avail – he drives off! So by 03.45 the situation is that the irate woman is still around (and irate) whilst by now five black males are trying to calm her down via hand expressions and the placing of arms on shoulders. The operators surmise meanwhile 'Too much drugs' and ask 'What are all these people doing here at this time?' Meanwhile the four females return and three of the men depart. This only provokes the bag-lady to grab another rubbish bag and run towards the shop as a black male face appears at the door and wisely chooses to remain inside as she attempts to throw it at him.

The operators then decide what to do (03.47) 'If she continues like this we might have to contact police because she's littering the street'. But they then watch as she collects the bags she has already thrown and throws two more again. So the operator calls the police, but no one answers! He phones again and this time they answer and they are told that a woman is 'littering the street' (not going mad!). By the time the police look at the situation on their screen she is standing alone outside the mini-cab office so the operator moves one camera to show police the trail of litter. However, much of it has been cleared up, obviously by those who were attempting to calm her down.

Within two minutes the woman climbs into a cab and drives out of sight. The police make no attempt to intervene and do not ask for further information. The operators realise their observations are over. (23 minutes, 2 cameras)

The Police Decision to Deploy

As the incident above shows even when the police are notified of activities that constitute an offence, they do not necessarily respond. The reasons for their decision making are not available to us. However, we are certain that such behaviour in County Town or Metro City would have warranted a deployment, not because of its criminal seriousness, although there was a dispute to be investigated as well as the disorder and littering, but because it would have challenged the good image of the city. In the poor and rundown Inner City, street trading, Big Issue sellers, low levels of disorder, bill posting and littering were not seen as threats to the commercial attractiveness of an area already abandoned by large-scale retailers.

As we have outlined in the decision model above, whether police deploy may be determined by their evaluation of what they have seen on the screens or by what the operative states they have seen happening. However even where there is clear-cut evidence of serious assault available to both police and operators deployment did not necessarily result in Inner City.

14.01 – Moving the camera onto the High Street the operator notices a group of 12 young black males standing around a bus stop. One sitting on a seat in the shelter is suddenly struck twice by a youth around the shoulders. Rising to his feet his back now turned to the camera he says something to his assailant before running down the street and turning into another street which is beyond range of the cameras. Moments later he is visible running back towards the bus shelter with a plank of wood in his hands which he uses to lay into his assailant who stands facing him and having received two blows of the wood to no apparent ill effect begins to strike his opponent who then retreats a few yards, but only to posture and show willingness to continue the battle. His adversary remains where he is staring down at the youth, the others around the shelter (4 black girls and 6 black boys – all aged around 16) remain standing around watching proceedings.

Zooming in the operator notices a black woman in her 30s who, walking past this fracas, has realised that the youth who received blows to his shoulder is now sporting a blood-soaked garment around the shoulders. She points this out to him and the operators are alerted. Clearly visible to the cameras the operator now phones the police three minutes after originally discovering this incident. The police take control of the system and the operators are now spectators as they watch both protagonists disappear from view with respective mates. The police do not move the cameras and the operators are resigned to the fact that the police have 'lost' the incident and those involved. Two minutes later as the camera remains stationary up to two dozen young black youths are noticed running from all directions onto a grass area off the High Street. The camera moves slightly to reveal the bloodied black youth who is pointing at someone in the rival gathering and is somewhat bellicose in manner. He then runs into the group only for the fight to move slightly off-screen. The police do not move the camera and all the spectators can see are a few youths watching the resumption of the fight.

Eventually, a minute later the camera moves. Now police have zoomed in on the bloodied combatant who walks down the High Street with a mate. They are followed as they go. The operators realising the police have control only of one camera and not the whole system decide to surveille the youth via another camera, but a minute later he boards a bus and leaves the area. Eight minutes after the incident was first seen the action is over. Still, however, no police are visible in the area and no police call to ask for further details. What has happened quite simply is that the cameras have, by accident, caught a serious wounding taking place, but the police either do not know this (and the operators have not the gumption to tell them) or seeing matters subside have decided not to pursue the issue. (24 minutes, 2 cameras)

The most striking aspect of this incident is the complete lack of system integration. Police appear unable to operate the system, perhaps through lack of experience and training rather than indifference. The operators do not volunteer either help or furnish information, but neither do the police ask for it. What is obviously a major incident of both disorder and assault, at least some of which is available on the police monitor, does not result in a deployment. It may be that the police are actually unaware of the seriousness of the assault. The operator only knew this after he zoomed in with a camera not controlled by the police and this image would not have been displayed on the police monitor. If this was the case they may be treating the incident as minor youthful disorder which could only be inflamed by 'sending in the troops'. Alternatively, by the time they have worked out what is happening, the incident is effectively over and it is decided to let matters lie. Whatever the case they did not deploy and although the cameras have captured a clear picture of both the assailant and the victim on tape which could be used for any post-incident investigation this information is not proffered. This would tend to support our contention that the reluctance of operators in Inner City to alert police is a reaction to the lack of police interest, even when alerted to serious incidents of violence and disorder.

The Police Decision to Arrest

If police are deployed, once they arrive on scene and locate an incident, which they did in forty-three out of the forty-five deployments, they have to determine what the incident is about and whether there is any warrant for formal police action. In many cases there is not. The man crouching down by the side of the car at four in the morning turns out to be a council worker placing no parking cones in preparation for the public procession taking place later in the day, the hooded youth in the car park turns out to own the vehicle he is standing next to, and so on. Where evidence that may justify an arrest is immediately available, this does not mean that police will arrest, individual officers have legally sanctioned discretionary powers to arrest or not as they see fit. Indeed, in those cases where there was taped evidence which was considered sufficient to justify an arrest only 47 per cent actually resulted in one.

The important question in terms of our understanding of CCTV is what role does the system play in shaping police decision-making? Do operators merely monitor the scene passively, do they help to direct resources, are they referenced as a possible source of evidence? In Table 9.1 we set out the way in which operators used the cameras during incidents which resulted in deployments

As Table 9.1 shows the cameras tend to be used to passively monitor, or as an aid to deployment by directing the police to the right location or suspect. Cameras were primarily used in a more active way for either command and control, evidence gathering or searching for suspects in less than one fifth of all deployments.

Table 9.1 All Uses and Primary Uses of the Cameras During a Deployment Incident

Use	All uses during a deployment		Primary use during a deployment	
	no.	%	no.	%
Searching	11	15	5	12
Directing Response	16	23	4	9
Police Command and Control	1	1	1	2
Evidence Gathering	8	11	2	5
Passive Monitoring	35	49	31	72
Total	71	99	43	100

The manner in which the cameras are used is partially dependent on the status of the incident when police arrive. If, on arrival, there is on-going behaviour that would justify an arrest, the cameras may well play no more than a passive role in monitoring the incident rather than having any active part to play in influencing the course of events. For example:

At 20.15 one summer night a man is noticed running through the streets. Immediately the operator latches onto him and follows his motions. Aged in his early 20s and casually dressed he stops after about 45 seconds and turns around. As the camera pulls away from close-up it can be seen that a second man has run to him and the first man is now gesturing to him in an angry manner. The strange thing about the second man is his attire – he has kitchen/chef uniform of white with blue check trousers. As they argue another man appears, also in kitchen whites, the two now argue with the man who seems agitated and repeatedly makes motions as if to be pulling something from the rear pocket of his jeans.

At this point the operator informs the Controller. They immediately deploy mobile officers, as yet another chef appears at the argument. Within a minute four officers in two vehicles have arrived and the pursued young man is, seconds later, held against a wall by one officer as enquiries begin. Three minutes later the man is put into a police car arrested on a charge of Attempted Theft. Apparently seen by the kitchen staff attempting to break into the BMW of the restaurant's owner the staff had pursued him. Noticed by the operator the cameras are credited with an arrest.

In the incident outlined above, the cameras have captured little of evidential value, and the charge, if it is ever made, will be won or lost on the strength of the complainant's statement or the admissions of the accused. The cameras were merely facilitative in drawing the incident to the attention of police, and if they had not noticed the man running it is not known whether this incident would have ever come to police attention. The chef may well have exacted private retribution rather than calling for the police.

In the next incident, however, while there is evidence captured by the cameras that could have been used for the basis of arrest and prosecution, the police controller does not volunteer this and the officers do not ask for it. Nor do they seek to investigative on their own initiative. They treat the incident as one of disorder rather than crime and merely monitor the group and hope that their presence will be enough to deter any future outbreak.

> At 01.10am Saturday morning the two operators are told by the Controller who has received a call about a disturbance to watch a group of revellers leaving a pub on the edge of the city centre. The cameras reveal a six-strong group of three men and their women all in their late 20s with four males of similar age standing nearby looking on at three males involved in a heated altercation in the middle of the road. Seconds later a man is punched to the floor by another which provokes the onlookers to rush in to end proceedings. At this point the Controller deploys a mobile unit, but as the operator awaits the arrival of police the group (now one large party) walks away apparently peaceful with no sign of police.
>
> The police arrive three minutes after being deployed but at the scene where the group were formerly. Whilst visible to the camera a street away the Controller does not inform the mobile but watches as the argument seems to be resurrected. Moments later a male lashes out at another as females intervene to end matters. Police are told where to go by the Controller but when they appear matters are calm once again. The situation whilst obviously drunken and violent is an 'internal' matter between former friends and is permanently on the point of recurring and does so again as this time the two men grapple and fall into the road only to be prised apart by male colleagues. Police are deployed again and this time two vehicles cruise slowly past the once-again tranquil crowd. No one is stopped, no one arrested and the group continue to walk eventually going out of camera range.

Despite the existence of taped evidence for breach of the peace and assault, police do not arrest. This is partly because the controller has not relayed the evidence to the patrol officers which in other circumstances he did freely. One possible interpretation is that as this was occurring in a site not associated with trouble, (i.e. not outside the night clubs, where police seemed keen to stamp out any incipient signs of disorder) there was no symbolic gain to be had from arrest and, given this was an isolated group, the disorder was not likely to spread into a more a more serious brawl.

In other incidents the information garnered from the cameras was actively used to influence patrol officer decision making:

> With dozens leaving the Club and dozens more standing around eating fast food or talking, the Club is its usual revelry. Amidst this scene watched by the operator and two Controllers comes a call which the Controller receives reporting 'trouble' outside the Club. However, there is no trouble that anyone in the control room can witness, but

after 30 seconds they notice an individual who fits the category of 'Trouble'. Probably thrown out of the Club or at least helped on his way by door staff this chap departs very abruptly from the disco's door before turning around to abuse those who assisted his passage. With him is a female of similar age (early 20s). Both are smartly dressed, but as he walks away he is noticeably unsteady, the result of too much alcohol. His companion however seems totally in control.

The pair walk away from the Club through the crowds. They are not talking and, in fact, she is walking a few paces ahead. She looks disgusted and well she might because she has moments earlier dragged him away from the door of the Club thereby ending posturing and his drunken antics but she does not notice as he accidentally bumps into a male of similar age and the pair square up before the female intervenes and literally pulls him away and up the road. All eyes are on him. Furthermore, the Controller seeing a police vehicle near the disco tells them to keep an eye on this pair. By now and via this message the woman has become a suspect even though up to now her behaviour is that of a model citizen. All are agreed in the control room with the operator's evaluation that the man she's with will, sooner or later 'dig someone else out'. But, as he says this the couple walking a few paces behind him disappear up the road into the semi-darkness and out of close vision.

Moments later, the female who has hardly spoken to the male for over a minute stops in a shop doorway and squats. The male stands over her and we can see an animated conversation as he uses his arms to put his point of view over. About a minute later she leaves the doorway and the pair continue up the road. The operator and Controller now watch as two PCs on foot patrol having been warned about him by the Controller approach the pair.

When the woman crouched the Controller presumed she was urinating. This is dubious, she had jeans on and in the dark there was no way of ascertaining if she did or did not. But, to help prove his hunch he asks the operator to get the camera closest to the scene and zoom in to see if there is a trail of urine from doorway to gutter. There is no way the camera can tell. The two PCs who have caught up with them contact the Controller to ask what it is precisely the two have done. Whilst the man is as the Controller states undoubtedly drunk and liable to breach the peace or get into a fight, the Controller then states that the woman has urinated in the doorway – this is his hunch, it is not a fact. Moments later the pair are arrested.

Minutes later in the police station charge bar the arrested woman is furious. She shouts her innocence and is adamant she will not accept that charge. Moments later into the Control Room walks the gaoler laughing with the Controller mimicking her pleas that she had gone to the loo in the disco before leaving. The Controller I suspect is now unsure of his claim. Maybe wary of me he states to the operator that the woman has been abusive to the two beat officers and had to be arrested. Moments later the two officers enter and watch the incident leading up to the apprehension replayed on the Controller's monitor. The Controller tries to convince them that a trail of urine is visible – it is not. They leave uncommitted. The woman is still remonstrating next door insisting on being given the chance to give a urine sample to prove that she is neither drunk nor responsible for incontinence. A police officer enters the Control Room and laughs with the Controller at her claims adding how the man with her can 'stay the night . . . he started givin' it the big he-man'. The end result is two arrests, the male for Breach of Peace, the female for breach and urinating in public. She had in the eyes of the camera done nothing wrong but aroused the suspicion of the Controller. He interpreted and legislated and the camera did not protect her from a very dubious charge.

The above example shows how the patrol officers deferred to the Controller's reading of the evidence from the cameras in making the decision to arrest, even though his interpretation was highly contestable. But it also shows how the images do not produce unequivocal evidence as they are also subject to interpretation. The importance of this is shown clearly in the next incident:

02.53 – The Controller calls to inform the operator of a report he had received about 'trouble outside McDonalds'. Scanning the area the operator notices 30 yards from the premises a man posturing in what seems an aggressive manner outside a fast-food outlet. His stance is unusual, he is crouched, legs quite wide apart and with his arms raised and hands clenched into fists. He is involved in a form of pseudo shadow boxing, albeit he does seem to have someone in mind to hit. Standing near him are two males who look very different to him and do not seem to be offering or willing to fight. The 'aggressor' as the camera sees it is the shadow boxer, a white male in his late 20s who is casually dressed in jeans and T-shirt. The two facing him are also white males, but younger looking and more 'subcultural' in that one has long hair and loose clothing and the other whilst wearing short hair has a jacket and jeans on.

Following 30 seconds of posturing the aggressor throws a punch which connects to the face of the long-haired youth who runs away. The short-haired youth is then approached and would (to the camera observer anyway) seem to be not interested in fighting guessing that his flat palm pushing gestures show a non-aggressive non-participatory intention. The aggressor has none of this and throws a punch which merits a response and this merits the aggressor banging the head of the victim against a lamp post which now stands between them. This provokes a more determined retaliation and punches are exchanged as a dozen passers-by watch. As the two grapple they bounce off a department store window and then, holding each other, fall into an alleyway between two shops. The operator can see nothing, but realises the action continues because two teenage girls passing the alley look down it towards the combatants.

At the first evidence of posturing the operator called the Controller, told him of the disturbance and put the incident onto the police monitor. As the two fall into the alleyway the police have not deployed but seeing that a fight is underway the operator can hear via the scanner that a mobile unit has been sent to the scene. Within 40 seconds of disappearing up the alley the two men reappear with the 'victim' being chased by the 'aggressor'. The chase continues across the market place and behind a row of shops all the while monitored by the operator who has a birds-eye view of events. At one point the victim is hiding behind a waste disposal unit as the aggressor searches for him then finding him the chase begins again – back in the direction they came.

Uniformed police then appear nearby. They have received a sort of commentary of events from their Controller watching his monitor. They appear ahead of the two and heed the pursuer's shouts and apprehend the one being pursued – the 'victim' The 'aggressor' now stands still and points at the 'victim', the former can be seen to have blood running from a head wound, the latter protests his innocence. Meanwhile as more police arrive the two are taken in separate directions whilst the 'truth' is established, but more people arrive on the scene. The two girls who witnessed the fight in the alley arrive as does the long-haired chap who received a punch earlier as do four others – 2 male and 2 female whom it would appear are mates of the 'victim' who appears to be crying. With six police in attendance the long-haired male becomes animated and begins pointing at his colleague and shouting towards them. Whilst mates try to calm him down police approach him. As he continues his message he is promptly arrested and put into a police vehicle!

Over the police radio the operator learns that there is a problem of counter-accusations and one officer is heard to say 'can the tapes help us'. The Controller then phones and repeats the question, the operator replies that in his opinion the protagonist is now the injured party, but he will rewind it anyway to check. Playing the scene again for the benefit of the Controller the police at the incident make a decision independent of the video enquiry – they arrest and handcuff the 'aggressor' (03.05). Meanwhile four officers stand talking to the victim and the two females and moments later two officers search the victim, but find nothing incriminating.

Around half an hour later the arresting officer (of the long-haired male) comes to the Control Room to view the recording of the incident: strangely he was the last officer to arrive at the scene, but the one who arrested the shouter. He explains his actions to the operator in a world-weary way 'they were all stood around not knowing what was going on . . . someone's got to make a decision'. Furthermore the operator learns of the police dilemma re the two males – both have cuts – one to the forehead the other on the rear of the neck. Watching the replay the officer deduces that the former is probably a product of the head being banged against the lamp post the other wound obviously happened in the alleyway. The problem is did the victim produce a blade/Stanley knife whilst in there and cut the neck of the aggressor? Looking carefully at events there is no evidence of any knife and so charges relating to offensive weapons will be impossible. As he takes the tape the officer is asked to sign a new sheet introduced only this week. Unhappy in realising some CCTV footage appears in a widely publicised commercial video on CCTV the scheme's Manager has introduced a 'contract' whereupon police officers who take the tapes have to sign a 'Code of Conduct' which demands that footage never be released for commercial purposes. The officer signed it, but had no idea what it was. Later in the night the operator calls the Controller to ask about the outcome of the incident to be told that both will be charged with fighting and maybe face charges of Assault. (12 minutes, 2 cameras)

In this incident, whilst CCTV brought the incident to the visible attention of police, the incident was not found by CCTV but came to police notice from a call by the public. The end result is three arrests, two for fighting and maybe a wounding and one for shouting. While the police were undoubtably acting within their legal powers to arrest all three, at the point of arrest there was little attempt to utilise the information from the cameras to address the issues of culpability. On the face of it there would appear to be one 'aggressor' and two 'victims' one who seemed to be acting predominately in self defence. But the tapes cannot fully provide answers to questions of culpability. They have not recorded the words that were said by the participants and they were blind as to what occurred in the alley. Although the police do try to utilise the taped evidence to apportion blame, in the end they appear to give up and rely on the 'objective' evidence of fighting and thus both males are treated as offenders and charged. The long-haired male who appeared to protest the unfairness of the arrest of an 'innocent' also found himself subject to arrest. While the cameras do at times provide unequivocal evidence in the complexities of legal discourse, the partial and selective information held on the tapes may provide little help in providing outcomes which are both legal and just.

As the previous incident illustrated, the police can arrest on the available evidence at the scene and then try to utilise the tapes to sort out issues of culpability and charge. This latter point is illustrated in the following incident, where, after an arrest is made for breach of the peace, the camera is used to provide evidence of possession of an offensive weapon.

> The operator notices four males in their mid to late teens casually dressed walking through the town near the central railway station. What provoked him to zoom in on them is the fact that two have bottles in their hands. As they continue their walk the four walk past three males of similar age and appearance walking from the opposite direction. As the two groups pass one of the four turns around and shouts something at the three and seconds later begins striding after them. One of the three stops and the pair stand close and seemingly talk, but, after about 20 seconds, the instigator of the head-to-head tries to head-butt the youth. No contact is made and the intended victim walks away whilst the mates of the instigator walk up to him and pull him away in an attempt to defuse the situation.
>
> For the moment their words work as he continues on his way with them. However, within a minute the same youth walks in a hostile manner towards another passing youth. He does not assault him and once again his mates pull him away. At this point the police who have been made aware of the youth decide to deploy officers in a transit van. The four have continued their walk and when the van appears at their side about 1½ minutes later they, knowing they were in the wrong, all begin to run away.
>
> The main suspect, however, is jumped on by two police. One other officer chases another youth and captures him and his bottle flies in the air as he is caught. The two are placed in the transit van and within a minute the arresting officer of the main suspect radios in to tell of their find of a knife on the main suspect. One other is caught, but he, to the knowledge available to the cameras, was a peacemaker on two occasions.
>
> With two arrests the police make their way back to the station. On the way, maybe three minutes later, the operator notices another of the four youths identifiable by his

white baseball cap standing with two females outside the central station. Telling the Controller, the operator and Comm Room staff watch the male and females as they walk through the streets but as he is not specifically suspected of doing anything police are not deployed to pick him up.

At 23.45 the arresting officer enters the Comm Room wanting to see footage of their arrest. He believed that one of the two (the one calming the incident down) had thrown away a knife as he was pursued by police and only seconds before being apprehended. With the youth arrested they had returned to the location of arrest but found the knife had gone. The question is: did one of the other two mates take it because whilst they have 'a body for a breach they can't put a possession on him' without a knife?

The two arresting officers enter the Comm Room at 00.03. They take the tape away to view the tapes in the privacy of the viewing room. Their inability to get the thing to work means the operator has to go next door to do it for them. In the 25 minutes it takes him to re-wind and find the footage they want the system is unattended (he is the only operator tonight). The officers have got what they wanted – evidence of weapons. One is clearly seen throwing a knife and the other is found to have a knuckle-duster upon him. Because the operator confirms their opinion about the knife the officer has confidence to go ahead and state this in his evidential report. Due to the taped evidence one will face a charge of Possession of Weapons, but added to this will be attempting to pervert the course of justice for trying to get rid of the knife his mate had thrown.

The main suspect is a well-known offender. The Comm Room staff discussing him later agree that he would have mugged or stabbed somebody later in the night. What has the CCTV system provided from this: the evidence of a knife – the operator did not see this; the charges of assault to be applied in the absence of a complainant. (20 minutes, 5 cameras)

Finally, as we have noted even where the cameras have captured evidence of an offence there is no guarantee that this will lead to any formal police action. If there is no evidence available when police arrive at a scene this will depend as to whether police ask the operators what they have seen and recorded or whether this information is volunteered by the operators:

As always at this time of night (02.00am) one camera is fixed on the door of 'The Club' disco. Whilst two operators are working tonight one is on a refreshment break when a disturbance begins outside the door of the club. Involving five men all in their 20s the fracas spills across the road ending on the opposite pavement. The whole event takes 45 seconds by then peace-keeping forces in the shape of other males and females arrive and calm the protagonists down. The operator has shouted over to the Controller who has put out the message 'fight outside The Club' over the air. For some unknown reason police are not stationed outside the disco tonight as they usually are. Thus they arrive at the scene a good two minutes *after* the event had *ended*. Even so the end-result is the arrest of three males all on the minor charge of Breach of the Peace.

The fight cannot be said to be a product of operative vigilance. In the control room at the time were two Controllers (one police, one civilian) and two other police officers, one being the shift Sergeant, the other being a PC on a break. Out of boredom the pair sit with the Controller watching the screen. Thus at the time there were no fewer than five pairs of eyes watching 32 cameras. The fight is seen by accident appearing first on the multiplex sequence, the two police officers who notice it simultaneously shout to the operator who puts the image on real-time as the Controller gives out the message to all mobile units. On hearing this over the radio in the adjacent room other interested parties quickly come to the system; the Duty Inspector, the Turnkey and another PC who happened to be next door. Nothing brings men running like the promise of watching a fight.

There is a fight to watch. Beginning as an animated argument the matter develops into a drunken throwing of punches and wrestling of bodies. Nobody lands a good punch and no one is hurt. The matter ends when the antagonists decide i.e. very quickly. Only two remain verbally hostile. But no one really wants to fight and when others enter as peace keepers we have the two remaining bellicose ones held apart by no fewer than eight males and two females and a general dispersal of the group with no apparent injuries or lost dignity.

When the police arrive in a transit van the event is over. But, over the air the civilian controller informs them which youths were involved and describes the garments of one 'at the centre of it all'. Other police arrive in vehicles – one van, one marked car and one night CID a total of six personnel to supplement the four already there. Various police talk to various parties and meanwhile the operator takes the camera away from the scene to look elsewhere after it had locked on them for three minutes. The various police do not stay too long, most leave the scene after eight minutes and at the moment we are unaware of the outcome. We learn more at 2.45 when a uniformed officer asks the operator if the fracas was on video. The answer is 'yes' and minutes later in walk two CID officers. The three officers sit with the Controller then replay the event watching in silence and leave without saying a word.

An hour later I ask the plain-clothes men what the event produced. The answer is three men charged 'with a Breach' (i.e. Breach of the Peace). Probably reflecting the insignificance afforded the matter two of those charged are not even placed in custody but charged and released immediately. One remains in custody because the Turnkey boasts to the Controller 'he failed the reasonable man act' by remonstrating and express-ing anger at being arrested manifested by 'throwing his shoes at the CID'. Convinced he was not a protagonist but a peacemaker he now faces a charge which he denied and furthermore because of such anger he now finds himself locked up for one night.

As we have shown there is no simple correspondence between the images revealed by the cameras and either deployment or subsequent police action. They are partially conditioned by the level of system integration which facilitates information exchange between the operators and the police. Where integration is low, many incidents which would, on the face of it, seem to warrant deployment, lead to no request being made. Similarly when deployment does result, even when there is taped evidence of an offence, arrest is still not guaranteed. It is dependent on whether, when the police arrive, there is still evidence of an offence, whether the operators volunteer the existence of evidence, or whether the police ask. While the cameras might have been assumed to have reduced the chance that officers will use their discretionary powers to produce informal resolutions, this would not appear to be the case. As we noted, nearly half of all incidents where there was taped evidence of infractions did not produce arrest. This suggests that the CCTV system and taped images become another resource to be selectively utilised by the police in pursuit of their own organisational goals which are not coincidental with the full enforcement of law.

Seeing the images as a selective police 'owned' resource is useful because it reminds us that CCTV is not just a neutral technology merely recording what comes into view. On its own CCTV does nothing, its images have to be decoded as they are filtered through the organisational lens, and their salience will be read in this organisational context. As such, whether a particular incident will lead to deployment or arrest, will depend on a range of contextual features, for instance, how busy a shift is and whether the cells are full. But as a police resource it can, when they choose, become fully mobilised in 'constructing a case for the prosecution'. As we saw in the incident involving the youths fighting outside McDonald's, in the end the police decision to charge both parties was reduced to considering the overt behaviour on the tape. Issues of culpability and the difference between aggressive and defensive violence were eventually swept aside in favour of getting a 'result'. Similarly in the last incident involving the fight outside the disco, the youth who regarded himself as a 'peacemaker' is arrested and held in police custody the longest. The police are acting perfectly within their legal mandate, the youth's use of force for the purpose of pacification is as much a breach of the peace as if it were used offensively. Finally, in the incident where the woman was arrested for 'urinating in public', the taped evidence should, if anything have led to her being released, but it did not.

The importance of these three cases is that in a quarter of the incidents involving arrest the evidence on tape becomes subsidiary to police concerns with producing legal and organisational closure rather than establishing the 'truth' of the matter. This has some very significant implications.

Social order in urban spaces is not primarily generated by policing, but by the routine and natural surveillance and interventions of citizens (Jacobs 1961). In two of the three incidents by the time police arrived on scene the disorder had been quelled by citizens − friends and acquaintances of the protagonists − and there was no continuing need for police intervention. But, in all three, the very forces of natural social control become subject to criminalisation. In this way, cameras and the subsequent police actions may be undermining the very processes which naturally promote social order.

In the long term, if citizens learn that acting to quell disorder will lead to censure and sanction, they may well become more hesitant to intervene. Then, the natural forces which constrain violence and disorder from becoming serious may be eroded and public space will be more disorderly and more reliant on coercive policing to keep the peace. This erosion of natural control mechanisms may also result from a more generalised effect of CCTV which allows citizens to defer their interventions on the grounds that it is being monitored by those whose job it is to respond, and therefore personal intervention becomes unnecessary.

The standard response to critics of CCTV from police and political supporters has been 'if you have got nothing to hide you've got nothing to fear'. As David McClean a junior Home Office Minister declared of CCTV, 'This is a friendly eye in the sky. There is nothing sinister about it and the innocent have nothing to fear. It will put criminals on the run and the evidence will be clear to see' (cited in Groombridge and Murji 1994). This misses the point: you may indeed have nothing to hide, but the chances that your good intentions will be misinterpreted, because the evidence is not clear to see, may well give you something to fear. And the cameras which promoted the intervention that led to your arrest may well become a tool for the police to promote closure through the production of a legally sustainable charge, based on behaviour rather than intention, regardless of any concern for natural justice.

Selective Visibility: CCTV and the Police

In our discussion of targeting and deployment practice we have shown how both suspicion and intervention are socially constructed and we have noted that not only does this determine who and what gets watched but which incidents result in deployment and authoritative intervention. There is, however, one group who although not intentional targets of the system, inadvertently find themselves routinely filmed by the cameras: the police themselves. In Skinns' study of the impact and effectiveness of CCTV in Doncaster he found that nearly a quarter (24.3 per cent) of police officers interviewed saw one of the key disadvantages of the CCTV system was that it watched them (Skinns 1997: 46). Such ambivalence is perhaps not surprising as numerous studies of the occupational culture of policing have shown, patrol work has traditionally been an area of low visibility to the supervisory gaze, and street-level officers have jealously guarded their independence (Chatterton 1979; Holdaway 1983). Moreover, in the absence of an independent record, patrol officers' accounts of events on the street have been accorded a high status by both the police organisation and the criminal justice system (Norris 1989). But the relationship between such accounts and the realities of street policing is problematic. The paperwork gloss provided is a construction which serves to portray police actions in a favourable light and provide the justification for any subsequent police action. As has been documented by a number of studies at times this moves beyond matters of presentational style to officers knowingly falsifying accounts in the knowledge that there is little chance of their account being successfully contested (Holdaway 1983; Norris 1989).

The presence of CCTV cameras radically alters this position. Firstly it can be used as a general managerial tool to monitor officer performance and activity. Therefore the practice of street policing, which traditionally enjoyed low visibility from managerial scrutiny is now potentially subject to a far more intrusive supervisory gaze. Secondly, it can provide an independent record which can challenge the police version of events and, finally, it can capture police as well as citizen deviance.

One police commander, for instance, told us that he thought CCTV had significantly improved the quality of policing in the area by forcing the local city centre patrol 'to clean up its act' and he went on to note that the number of complaints against the police had declined in the months after the cameras were installed. However, as Ericson and Haggerty have argued in the context of Canadian policing, the introduction of video cameras in police patrol vehicles led to the development of strategies to protect officers from the cameras' gaze. As they noted:

> Patrol officers maintain technical control over every aspect of taping. They can turn the tape recorder and microphone on and off as they choose. The tape recorder is kept in the trunk and the only key fastened to the car's key-chain. Although tampering can be detected, officers can simply remove a troublesome tape, reinsert it, and six hours later the entire tape has been erased. (Ericson and Haggerty 1997: 139)

Moreover systems can be redesigned specifically so as not to record police activity.

> During our fieldwork a supervisor expressed a concern that the video system he was about to have installed would display the speed of the police vehicle as well as the speed of the vehicle being pursued. He worried that police vehicles would regularly be shown to be travelling at excessive speeds, even during routine patrols . . . The installer agreed to remove the speed display for the police vehicle, so that only the speed of the oncoming vehicle would be registered. (ibid.)

Our evidence suggests similar processes at work enabling patrol officers to escape the disciplinary gaze. This was achieved either through control of the cameras or informal accommodations with the camera operators, so that video footage of questionable policing tactics is not recorded.

On two occasions whilst the operators were cruising the cameras their attention focused on the sight of four uniformed officers standing in a group in a city centre street talking. On each occasion the operator was given a signal to move the cameras away (one officer would raise an arm and waive a hand suggesting the camera be moved elsewhere). When this was also spotted by the Controller the message both silently from those surveilled and verbally from behind him was move the camera

– which the operator did. The Controller went onto explain that the Divisional Commander had his monitor on and if he saw four patrol officers standing in a group would 'go mad'.

In one site two operators reported that when struggles ensued with suspects the Controller had shouted 'move the camera to the trees'. This way the full nature of the arrest was not recorded. In another site, an operator explained in all innocence a procedure he probably did not realise the true implication of: 'the police ask us for the cameras and then move it onto a wall. All we can see is the blue light flashing nearby reflecting onto the camera. We don't know what it's all about and we don't ask.'

One way patrol officers can mitigate against the adverse inferences that could be drawn by senior management or others viewing or reviewing their action is to ensure that such instances are not recorded. Even if they are recorded it is unclear what procedures operators should follow. For instance, the manager of one site explained how they had filmed an incident where a police office was caught on camera 'punching a young man in the back of a police van'. While this evidence would have undoubtably allowed the youth to press charges for assault against the officer had he known of the recording, there was no mechanism for the operatives or the manager to alert the youth or his defence solicitor about the existence of the evidence. Moreover, in the absence of a formal request from a defence solicitor they were under no obligation to disclose its existence at all. In the event, the system manager, himself a former police officer, gave copies of the tape some time after the event to the duty inspector 'not for disciplinary purposes, we did not want that. But for training purposes'.

Similarly another operative described how:

One Thursday night a large-scale public order situation was a product of a local officer leaving a night-club and picking a fight with three black youths. The latter sitting in a car outside a snooker club were approached by him and were not impressed by his suggestion that drug dealers like them should 'fuck off to where they came from'; in the ensuing fight the CCTV system located the PC, shirt off brawling as more black youths spilled out of the snooker club. The end product was the deployment of 20 uniformed officers to the scene and the spiriting away in the rear of a police vehicle of the offending officer. Two black youths were arrested. According to the CCTV operator the tape was never released to either the police or any other agency and the officer was never disciplined for his actions.

The confusion surrounding operators' roles and responsibilities when confronted with what they believe to be evidence of police misconduct is highlighted in the incident below.

The first Saturday night in November produced a scenario which I had hypothesised with the two operators only two nights before. Discussing the scheme's line management I had asked of the operators what they would do if they witnessed police misconduct on camera and felt the victim had a right of redress. The question stumped the operators, they had never considered the system to be anything but benevolent to all people and had never been told by Management that such scenarios could arise. When pushed to answer the presumed one-in-a-million drama they had no idea as to whom they would turn to. Eventually the older and more politically aware of the two, said he might consider contracting a female Labour Councillor who sat on the Police Committee. His reasons? 'she's a right anti-police Leftie'. His younger colleague concurred, he had heard of this councillor's reputation, but he did not specify he would contact her. Even so their response was significant: the operators realised that neither their security company, nor police, nor Council could be relied upon to support them in a controversy. Their only hope was a perceived left-wing malcontent whom neither had ever met.

Two nights later whilst cruising the cameras the two operators came across a scene which police had not brought to the attention of the system. At 23.07 by a taxi rank standing shoulder to shoulder were two well-built white males casually dressed and in their late 20s. Backs to a low wall the two were facing four uniformed officers, one of whom was a WPC. One of the male officers had a long baton drawn and from the silent image it is unclear for the operators what is unfolding. Within a minute the operators have deduced that one of the two men is 'wanted', i.e. about to be arrested, by police but his mate is not permitting police to take him away. The latter stands between the wanted man and the police who, only feet away, have made some attempt to pull their wanted man away but without success. In this stand-off one police officer has drawn his newly-issued long baton.

The baton-wielder is dressed differently to the other police around him. Wearing a black boiler suit he is identifiable to the operators as a police dog-handler. However whilst the dog van is parked nearby there is no dog in evidence, without his animal he has seemingly taken the lead role in this affair and it is he conversing with the male who is making gestures with his hands towards surrounding police that implies he wishes matters to calm down. Additionally he turns out his trouser pockets to prove to police that he is not carrying anything that can be construed as a weapon. Finally, as if to alleviate all suspicion, he even lifts up his shirt to reveal a bare midriff. The police like the watching operators should have got the message – he has no implements to endanger them and he does not want to fight them. However he will not do as he is instructed by police.

There are now no fewer than eight uniformed officers in a semi-circle around the two men. Passers-by waiting for a taxi have been cleared away and the man is not visible due to police standing around him. The eight officers watch and wait as the baton-wielder shouts at the man whilst pointing towards the ground. This has no effect, the male continues to shield his mate and continues to talk to the baton-wielder. A female by-stander in her 20s intervenes, she speaks to the man and the police, but her words have no effect and the impasse continues as police move her away. It is now 23.09 and two uniformed officers move towards the two suspects and try to separate them as they link arms. Neither offer violence just stubborn muscular resistance which seems to work as the two officers then walk back to their colleagues.

Tiring of this at 23.10 the dog-handler puts his baton to use and lands the first blow on the upper thigh of the protecting male. This seems to have little effect – the male continues to talk towards his beater. This provokes more strokes, in fact over the next 90 seconds the male receives a further 17 strikes, mainly across his legs, then, when he squats and puts out his arms to protect his lower body, the strokes hit his forearms. All the time seven other officers stand watching, feet away. Eventually, by his own choice it would seem (but no doubt encouraged by his assailant) the male slumps to his knees and when a uniformed officer moves towards him he lies face down, prostrate and he and his mate who has perhaps seen the folly of resistance are handcuffed. At 23.12 both are taken away by two uniformed officers to two separate police vehicles and are driven away.

The dog-man's night is not yet over. Across the town centre a disturbance has begun which has provoked officers on the scene to request assistance. This request is relayed over the dedicated phone-line to the operators from the Police controller. At 23.19 outside a fast-food outlet a confrontation has polarised along racial lines. Two youths, one black one white, have exchanged words and squared up and whilst a fight has been avoided there are protagonists and peacemakers on both sides, but the situation is tense. Standing in this melee are five uniformed police officers who have arrived in a van parked nearby. Due to the time (pub kicking-out) and the location (a popular late food outlet) a crowd of over 100 male and female black and white are gathered in this street within two minutes. The doves amongst the black males have done an effective job in calming down two of their main men willing to fight, one is more or less physically restrained by a large black male who drags him down the street, the other whilst animated is behind the barrier of three other black males who walk him against the direction he shouts towards.

The situation whilst very busy would seem to the operators to be under control. The officers present are talking to some of the black youths and assisting in walking the group away from the white lads. More police arrive at 23.21, seven in total climb out of a van and spread out along the street. By now only one black youth seems to want to persist in fighting and he now has the added restraint of a young white female (aged around 18–20). Things would appear to be over until at 23.23 things are spoiled when the dog-man arrives. This time he has his dog on a chain wildly lunging towards, and barking at, anyone nearby. He indiscriminately scatters groups of youth – male and female – standing around in this street and eventually goes towards the black youths at the bottom of the street. What was basically calm thanks to his actions now becomes animated. He agitates non-combatants by commanding them to get on their way and to achieve this unleashes the lead allowing the dog to jump towards them. The mood now turns nasty as bystanders turn against him.

Some of the former peace-makers now turn taunters towards the dog-man. They, for their trouble, receive more police attention as those officers on foot walk towards and pull and push them away. Eventually one black youth is chased by the dog and falls as the dog begins to bite his lower leg. As he lays there two officers jump on him and a scuffle ensues as the youth makes a frantic attempt to break free which escalates the situation as more officers run over to assist their arresting colleagues. Amidst all this a white youth runs close to the scene, picks something up from the floor and runs off into the crowd. In hindsight the operator found out it was a gold chain belonging to the arrested black youth, whether the white youth was retrieving it or stealing it they never found out!

By now a crowd of 100 has gathered shouting at police, three of whom are sitting on the black youth as they attempt to handcuff him, whilst another six stand feet away ensuring no one can come to his assistance. By 23.28 the argument and shouting are somewhat futile. The black youth is carried by police into the back of a van and the dog-man continues to chase watching people away. His job, however, is somewhat frustrated when a white youth holding a tray of fast food continually throws chips and Kebab meat towards the dog. The dog it would seem has a dilemma – can food overcome the enjoyment of provoking fear? However seconds later the police are told to disperse and leave the area. By 23.30 the drama is over, the 17 officers departing via vehicles, the camera operator is left spanning the surrounding areas as the various onlookers make their way home.

The events mentioned above as captured on video can be presented to an audience as *fact*. What the cameras do not show is what led up to the incidents nor what words were exchanged nor in the former incident how dangerous the two men were by repute or by on-the-spot assessment or whether the latter situation could only be redeemed by the indiscriminate unleashing of a dog. Also absent is the verbal exchange between operators and police as the incident unfolded and the subsequent procedures police indulged in to get hold of the tape. By describing what happened a reader might gain some idea of how, when a crisis occurs, the operators felt they had no line management to turn to and had to improvise a script no one who implemented the scheme thought was needed.

The operators' problems began as the initial drama unfolded. Realising that the police Control Room monitors had this exact scenario in front of them and possibly had it recording on their facility, the Police controller contacted the system as the first of the 19 blows were landing asking the operator to 'pull out' the camera. This was done, the camera's vision was widened to show the surrounding 20 yards and the detail of the event was no longer so close-up. However, unknown to the Controller the operators using their other monitor recorded the event close-up using another camera.

When the incident ended the issue of who controls the copy of the video's record and in a sense in whose interests the cameras were for became a subject of controversy. The elder operator immediately made a copy of the events and hid the tape in the Control Room. This 'cute copy' was, he told me, for his and his colleagues' benefit should 'anything go wrong'. As if by cue as he finished his own recording the phone rang and the police controller requested the incident be replayed from the Control Room onto the police monitor for the benefit of the Duty Inspector. To police amazement the elder operator refused to do so explaining that the Council were sensitive about permitting such a facility because they (the police) could, on their system, make an unauthorised copy without the knowledge of the scheme. The Controller was not impressed stressing that the Duty Inspector wanted to see it there and then. In reply the operator posited that if the police waited until the tape finished its recording then an officer could call in person and take the tape tomorrow having signed for it. He further explained that both he and his colleague were about to finish work, but both were prepared to come in tomorrow (their day off) to process the recording and do the paperwork as per procedures and do the necessary statement that a handing-over of a tape required. The Controller only repeated his comment that the police wanted it now and that the Inspector would overrule his stance. In reply the operator suggested the Inspector get a Magistrate to adjudicate and with that the Controller ominously threatened to pass such advice on to the Inspector.

The night operator beginning the midnight-8.00am shift inherited this impasse and was told by the departing operator not to let police have the tape without going through the procedures and meanwhile not to show it to them on their monitor. Half an hour into his shift the Controller called requesting a viewing only this time stating that two Inspectors wanted to see the tape and were not prepared to wait. Whilst he politely informed the Controller that he was under instructions not to show the event without proper procedures being adhered to the Controller politely told him that if they considered he was obstructing the course of justice they would enter the Control Room and seize the tape. Promising to make enquiries as to what could be done the operator had only one option – he phoned the Senior Operator at home at 01.00am on his day off. Having explained his dilemma the supervisor told him to let police have the tape. Thus at 01.20am a police officer called to the Control Room and took the tape which included both the beating and the events later involving white and black youths.

Between 01.30 and 03.30am that same night there were various police visitors to the Control Room. The first to arrive were two dog-handlers – including the one who had provided so much drama in the town hours earlier. He watched a replay of his actions and narrated his version of events to his colleague justifying how he had to beat the man. Later two patrol officers called for 'a coffee and chat' and requested to see what everyone at the station was talking about. On Monday morning the city-centre police sergeant called in to watch the events (he was not on duty Saturday night) and seemingly considered the event funny. Later on Monday another officer called asking the operator (the same one who recorded the incident Saturday night) if there were any spare copies of the events because the police copy had 'corrupted'. The operator knew the police had the one and only signed for copy and kept quiet about the 'cute copy' and suggested the officer sign for another copy as per procedure. The officer was not willing to do so and left. A further six officers entered over the next 24 hours to watch the event and three weeks later two dog-handlers from another town in the county called in to view. None of the viewers ever entered their names in the visitors' book.

The day following the dilemma (Sunday) the two operators on duty at the time and their supervisor met at the Control Room to discuss the issues. Their main dilemma was their status and job – the two operators working at the time of the drama felt they could be dismissed because they had recorded misconduct and furthermore had refused police demands to preserve what they considered the integrity of the system. For this reason they decided to present their case to as many people as possible. The Area Manager of their security company was initially informed because the operators wanted someone with a higher status than them to know of proceedings. He was a former police officer with the local force and he, in turn, offered no advice. Early Monday morning the assistant car parks manager called in from his next door office for the routine daily five minute chat and was shown the recording. Being a Special Constable he explained that with the new long batons police were trained to demand of suspects they fall to their knees on the floor and to strike them around the legs until they did. As far as he was concerned a correct procedure was adopted and deployed. Hours later, the car park manager came in for a viewing. As a former Inspector in the local police he might be forgiven for seeing matters only from a police perspective. Opining that what the officer did was 'over the top' he merely added that he disagreed with the new batons and left the matter at that. The operators had thus no advice from Management regarding their status and none had suggested whether the victim had any right to see what was on the tape.

A few days later I discussed the incident with the operators' supervisor, the one who had authorised the tape being given to police on the night. He held no sympathy for the beaten or bitten youths stating his approval for the police 'going in hard'. Furthermore, he pointed out, I did not know the 'scumbags' like the police and operators did and what trouble they had been in the past. Thus, in his opinion, the police doing what they did had prevented an escalation of trouble. A week later when I brought the subject up the same man revealed he had no idea who the people were on the receiving end of police batons and dogs! Precisely what happened to those involved in the events the operators never got to know fully. Two weeks later they were told by police calling in for a coffee that an Inspector from Complaints and Discipline was studying the tape regarding the actions of the dog-man. After the same time period they were told that all those arrested had been cautioned not charged. The tape had not been given to any defence solicitor but the 'cute copy' remained hidden in the room. This copy was taken away when the operator who recorded it was dismissed, for an unconnected matter, a month later.

There are a number of important issues to highlight that emerge from this incident. First, the codes of practice provided little assistance for the operators in deciding what they should do and their various managers were reluctant to offer procedural, as opposed to moral advice. The CCTV operator was clearly concerned to protect the integrity of the system. As the codes of conduct state 'in all cases the reviewing of the tapes and the use of video recording must be carried out under the supervision of the duty controllers'. By refusing the request to replay the incident on the police monitor, the operator was exercising this supervisory power, and since he was concerned that an unaccountable copy would be made, felt justified in refusing. When the police demanded that the tape be handed over the operator was faced with two further issues. Given that the tape was still running in the video recorder, normal procedures suggested that it would not be removed until it had come to the end. Then, if the police wanted to view it they could come and do so in the CCTV control room under the supervision of the operative. If they wanted to review the tape away from the control room, they could have a working copy made by the CCTV operators. The 'master copy' could also be handed over but only after it had been signed and sealed so that in court a 'chain of custody' could be vouched for ensuring that any allegation of tampering with the tape could be rebutted. By demanding that the 'master' tape be handed over immediately for the purposes of review, without a working copy being made the police were clearly suggesting a course of action which could jeopardise the integrity of the tape as evidence. This would be in clear breach of the codes of practice and undoubtably raised the suspicion of the operator that they might indulge in a cover-up. The codes of practice were also breached time and time again as visitors who flocked to see the recording did not sign the visitors' book. Neither were the visits cleared with the police control room in line with the explicit guidance in the codes which states, when 'police officers arrive unexpectedly, the purpose of the visit should be established and confirmed with . . . (the) . . . Police Control Room'. Finally, the codes did little to protect the system from unauthorised recording by the operators and the subsequent removal (theft?) of the tape.

The moral of this tale is that as the operators had received no support or guidelines from their management, they had made their decisions alone. Faced with threats from police they succumbed to their demands and were given no advice at a later date. The system, it might be said, had worked to the benefit of the arrested men in that police had dropped criminal proceedings possibly because video evidence would not present them in a good light, but the victim of a beating at the hands of police did not have video footage made available to him. It is here that the asymmetry of power between the surveilled citizenry and those responsible for monitoring and responding to the images becomes starkly apparent. The informal practices mean that the cameras are unlikely to record police deviance and, if it is recorded, the codes of practice provide no procedures for dealing with the situation. But perhaps most of all it signals the weakness of the codes of practice in regulating CCTV, not only because the codes were routinely broken, but because it is precisely in situations which are conflictual, ambiguous and raise moral dilemmas that codes should provide clear guidance to the operators as to their duty. Only then will they be protected from the consequences of acting against the interests of those who are more powerful, and ensure that when power is abused it is brought to account.

Summary and Discussion

In the absence of any concrete information as to who they should monitor, CCTV operators selectively target those social groups they believe most likely to be deviant. This leads to the over-representation of men, particularly if they are young or black. Nine out of ten target surveillances were on men, and four out of ten on teenagers. Black people were between one-and-a-half to two-and-a-half times more likely to be surveilled than one would expect from their presence in the population.

Three out of ten people were surveilled for crime-related matters, two out of ten for forms of disorderly conduct, but the largest category, nearly four out of ten were surveilled for 'no obvious reason'. This was echoed when we examined the basis of suspicion, with only one quarter of people subject to targeted surveillance because of their behaviour. In a further third of cases, operators' suspicion was alerted from outside the system, but the most significant was categorical suspicion where people were surveilled merely on the basis of belonging to a particular social or subcultural group.

The reason for the surveillance and the suspicion on which it was based were also found to be socially differentiated. The young, the male and the black were systematically and disproportionately targeted, not because of their involvement in crime or disorder, but for 'no obvious reason' and on the basis of categorical suspicion alone. When older people and women did become targets it was far more likely to be for crime or order-related offences and because of their overt behaviour.

In order to explain how CCTV systems produced this particular configuration we argue that it was necessary to examine the working rules operators developed in response to their key occupational concerns. For operators the most pressing problem faced was how, in the absence of prior knowledge as to a person's intentions, could they maximise the chance they would select those with deviant or criminal intent? Eight working rules were identified, the first three rules showing how suspicion was predicated on stereotypical assumptions as to the distribution of criminality, behavioural displays which operators associated with trouble, and prior knowledge as to a person's criminal record.

The first of these was seen to be most important, with suspicion being generated by operator's negative attitudes towards male youth in general and black male youth in particular. Visual clues as to a person's moral character were also read off from a person's clothing and posture. Thus, if a youth was categorised as a 'scrote' they were subject to prolonged and intensive surveillance. Unsurprisingly, overt displays of disorderly conduct led to targeting, but more significantly so did running and loitering, even though these rarely led to the identification of any criminal activity. Personalised knowledge was found to be used rarely by operators as the basis for targeted surveillance, but was an important component in transmitted suspicions, especially from store detectives.

These three primary working rules, were accompanied by four other working rules which classified people and their behaviour in relation to their location in time and space and operators' normative conceptions of place. These rules were especially important in determining which particular young men, out of all those potentially available, were subjected to prolonged surveillance because they were deemed to be 'out of time and out of place'. The temporal and spatial classification served to compound categorical suspicion but was also based on a normative ecology of place which singled out certain people and behaviours as inappropriate. This was found to be less influenced by strictly crime-related concerns than the commercial image of city centre streets which saw certain people being defined as 'other'. Thus drunks, beggars, the homeless, street traders were all subject to intensive targeted surveillance.

Operators' attention was also drawn to those whose orientation to the locality suggested unfamiliarity or showed signs of unease. People who appeared lost or confused were targeted as were those who suddenly changed direction or back-tracked as such behaviour was seen as indicative of criminal intent.

Finally, anyone who directly challenged, by gesture or by deed, the right of the cameras to monitor them was especially subject to targeting. Operators became particularly sensitised to the possibility that people may be trying to conceal their identity and intentions and thus deceive them as to their true purpose or deny them the opportunity to identify them at a later time.

Although these working rules produced nearly 900 targeted surveillances, they only led to forty-five deployments, predominately for crime and order related incidents. The deployments produced an arrest of one or more persons in twelve incidents. The majority of arrests (seven) were related to fighting and involved charges for breach of the peace or assault and three related to theft. Moreover, there was significant variation in deployment and arrest frequency between the three sites. Inner City produced only three deployments and no arrests. In County Town there were ten deployments and three arrests and in Metro City thirty-two deployments and nine arrests.

The low level of deployment was accounted for by two factors: that CCTV operators could not themselves intervene nor could they demand intervention by the police. This was compounded by the fact that suspicion rarely had a concrete, objective basis which made it difficult to justify to a third party such as a police officer why intervention was warranted.

The stark variation in deployment and arrests between the sites was found to be related to how integrated the CCTV system was with the police deployment system. This was dependent on the formal and informal organisational features which facilitated information sharing. In practice this meant it was not possible to under-stand operator or subsequent police behaviour merely on the basis of the evidence displayed on the monitors. Where there was low system integration, as in Inner City, even where there was clear evidence of offences, operators were hesitant to call the police and, when they did, the police often failed to respond. System integration, rather than evidence from the cameras, was shown to be more important in determining operational deployment practice.

Only twelve incidents where police were deployed resulted in arrest, even though in twenty-one cases there was evidence held on the tape which would have probably been sufficient to justify an arrest. Police discretion to resolve incidents informally was not undermined by the existence of CCTV systems. However the cameras were not irrelevant to police decision-making. The influence the CCTV system exercised over the outcome was shaped by the complex interaction between the CCTV operatives, police dispatcher and police patrol officer, and were also dependent on system integration. Officers at times chose to ignore the existence of the cameras and made their decisions on the basis of what was immediately apparent; sometimes they asked whether the operators had any information or evidence which might influence their decisions, at other times operators or dispatchers proffered this without being asked; and finally officers occasionally used the system after they had arrested someone, often on a low-level charge, such as breach of the peace, to see if a more serious charge could be sustained.

As we argued in our introduction, the Panopticon's primary strength lies in assuring the 'automatic functioning of power'. We stressed, however, that, because of the differences between surveillance in bounded institutional spaces and surveillance in city centre streets, direct physical intervention would be more significant to generating conformity than in the prison or asylum. But deployment turned out to be a relatively rare event, particularly in Inner City and County Town, and the key panoptic element, the certainty of a disciplinary response to deviancy, is absent.

However, while street populations are generally characterised as being composed of strangers, they are also at certain times and in certain places frequented by networks of acquaintances, linked together through overlapping personal relationships; the 'club scene' in Metro City or the 'three o'clock club' outside Santana's in Inner City would be cases in point. The extent to which CCTV will induce automatic conformity will depend on whether these loose-knit collectives come to see themselves as targets of both surveillance and, more importantly, intervention. In Metro City, which had the most deployments, there were on average one and a half deployments per shift, and while this cannot be considered high, over the course of a year it would be the equivalent of over fifteen hundred interventions. This, of course, represents only a tiny and insignificant fraction of the hundreds of thousands of people who use the streets on a daily basis. Deployment is, however, heavily skewed towards the late-night revellers and it is possible that this loose-knit group, through personal experience, 'war stories' told by friends, and media reports will come to see themselves as part of the panoptic machine and become the authors of their own conformity. It is in this partial, localised and diffuse way that disciplinary affects of the Panopticon may be said to be infiltrating city centre streets, rather than through omnipresence and omniscience implied by a simple translation of panoptic principles.

Yet, as we noted, the same processes which could produce anticipatory conformity may, ironically, actually undermine the informal processes of social control which are predicated on citizen intervention to quell disorder. If those acting as 'peacemakers' learn that they may also become subject to criminalisation will they also become less likely to intervene?

Another key difference between the Panopticon and the city centre CCTV systems was seen to be the virtual absence of any dossiers which would allow the identification and classification of those using the street. Unlike their institutional counterparts, street populations are largely anonymous. One consequence of this is, as we have shown, the development of an informal set of working rules which classifies people and behaviours as worthy of attention.

The two central features of the Panopticon, an inevitable and rapid response to deviance and the compilation of individualised records, were seen to be largely absent from our systems. However, as we have noted, the potential that CCTV offers is only starting to be realised and there are various moral and technological entrepreneurs who are seeking to develop system capacities to exploit its full potential. But we should not fall into the trap of technological determinacy. As we have seen, CCTV in its operation and its effects is contingent on a host of social processes which shape how the technology is actually used. We simply cannot know in advance what CCTV is, means and does, since it is dependent upon its organisational implementation. Similarly, whether and how the new technologies will actually be used is an empirical question which necessarily should become the subject of detailed future study.

As we argued in our introduction, it is not just as a variant of the Panopticon that CCTV should be analysed but also in its potential for exclusionary and net widening forms of social control. In our three sites its exclusionary potential was not particularly marked in practice, primarily because deployment was such a rare feature in at least two of the sites. In part this was because, without a specific legal mandate, police are understandably reluctant to intervene. Where exclusion was evidenced it was against the legal and economically marginal entrepreneurs such as street traders, although this varied from site to site. Known shoplifters, especially in County Town, although subject to intensive surveillance, were not, in the main, subject to court orders forbidding their presence in the town centre or from particular shops (although this is a feature of other systems we are aware of) and, without the legal basis for intervention, CCTV was merely used to track rather than mobilise deployment. However, in one of our sites, after the research had ended, a new bye-law was passed making drinking in certain public areas of the city an offence. We do not know how this has affected the use of the cameras, but this now gives police the direct power to arrest and criminalise the scores of homeless and vagrant who congregate to talk and drink. The cameras, if the police choose to exercise this new power, will certainly provide a powerful exclusionary tool which, in the long term, we would guess, will simply shift the 'offenders' to areas outside the cameras' gaze. This, of course, will not solve the problem but will serve the purpose of sanitising certain areas of the city, reclaiming it for what some would see as more appropriate pursuits, and simultaneously contributing to enhancing the image of the city as desirable space whose main rationale has become the promotion of acceptable consumerism (Fyfe and Bannister 1996; Reeve 1998).

It is in this context that the net-widening potential for CCTV is particularly marked as more towns pass bye-laws to regulate anti-social behaviour (Reeve 1998: 80). In the absence of a permanent patrol presence, such ordinances may well be symbolic rather than consequential. However, coupled with CCTV and an active policy of enforcement by the police, they may lead to powerful exclusionary and net-widening effects as more and more behaviour, of less and less seriousness, becomes subject to official and authoritative intervention. We have documented how this is already happening in relation to fights, with incidents which would have been previously unnoticed being captured by the cameras and triggering deployment. Further, the cameras at times make arrest a more viable option, even if, when the police arrive the fight is over and order restored.

This net-widening potential is even more important when it is seen in the context of the socially differentiated nature of targeting, and discretionary nature of deployment. The gaze of the cameras does not fall equally on all users of the street but on those who are stereotypically predefined as potentially deviant, or through appearance and demeanour are singled out by operators as unrespectable. In this way youth, particularly those already socially and economically marginal, may be subject to even greater levels of authoritative intervention and official stigmatisation, and rather than contributing to social justice through the reduction of victimisation, CCTV may become a tool of injustice through the amplification of differential and discriminatory policing.

An awareness of these issues takes on an added significance when we realise that as yet CCTV systems are still very much in their infancy, with system managers only just starting to understand their potential and trying to find ways to exploit it. This is limited by technological difficulties in exploiting the potential for the systematic identification, recording and classification of people in public space. Various software companies, such as Memex and Dectel, are already supplying police forces with sophisticated image-handling software. Central Scotland Police, for example, are currently installing a new force intelligence system based on Memex's computerised database handling software. This software not only enables the integration of all existing force, or even external databases, but can hold visual and audio data too. As was made clear by the Chief Constable, the purpose of this new system is to facilitate a massive expansion of the intelligence capacity of the force: 'What do we class as intelligence in my new system in the force? Everything: the whole vast range of information that comes into the possession of a police force during a twenty four hour period will go on to my corporate database. Everything that every person, vehicle is associated with . . .' ('SciFiles', BBC2, March 1996). The potential to hold visual as well as textual information on computerised databases brings with it one mechanism whereby CCTV systems may increase disciplinary power, as they may facilitate the specific identification of those subject to surveillance. And it is the consideration of this future prospect that is the subject of the next chapter.

Part III
Seeing the Future

–10–

Towards the Maximum Surveillance Society

Although our own research and that of others suggest that the use of CCTV cameras offers no simple panacea to the problem of crime and raises serious issues about justice, equality and fairness, we do not think that in Britain this will lead to a slowing down of their introduction. As we have already noted, the rise of CCTV surveillance has to be seen in the context of underlying social, political and economic pressures which have led to the intensification of surveillance across a whole range of spheres and by a host of new technologies. Moreover, in the case of CCTV there are a number of specific reasons which suggest current trends are set to continue.

First, negative findings are crowded out by the industry and practitioner-led claims of 'success' which dominate the newspapers and trade magazines. Moreover, when they are discussed they are dismissed. The *London Evening Standard* argued in an editorial on the negative results of the Sutton evaluation that, since the findings did not accord with that 'older discipline called common sense' and 'crime professionals consider . . . (cameras) . . . critically important in identifying and deterring criminals', the authors must be wrong. Indeed, the headline declared in defiance of the study – 'Why cameras deter crime' (*Evening Standard*, 3 January 1996). This approach was echoed by a spokesman for the Association of Chief Police Officers (ACPO) who argued 'it is impossible to prove one way or another whether the cameras work' but it was 'common sense' and 'patently obvious that if someone is going to put a brick through a window they won't do it in front of the cameras' (*Independent*, 2 January 1996).

Second, as the evidence of displacement firms up, areas without CCTV will fall under increasing pressure to introduce systems as well. This has already happened in Sussex where the Hove Traders Association stated in a leaflet to drum up private funding for a system: 'During the last year CCTV has been installed in Brighton . . . it has been noticeable that the more unsavoury elements of our society have moved into Hove. Aggressive beggars and street drug traders to name but two' (cited in Squires and Measor 1996). Furthermore, when a particularly serious crime does occur in an area not under camera surveillance, the absence of cameras can be seen as partially responsible. For example, the *Guardian* story on the murder of a Woolworths' shop assistant ran under the headline 'Killer raided stores without security cameras' and quoted a Detective Superintendent describing Woolworths as 'easy pickings' as they had no security cameras in their stores (*Guardian*, 5 November 1994). Similar calls were made after the fatal stabbing of head teacher Philip Lawrence outside his school in North London when he intervened to stop youths fighting (*Scotland on Sunday*, 10 December 1995).

Third, for many towns and cities, there is an element of 'keeping up with the Joneses' or, more accurately, 'keeping up with the Aidries', but this is not just a matter of unjustified civic rivalry. As cities are increasingly competing to attract and keep inward investment from ever more mobile multinational corporations, CCTV is seen as part of a package of measures to attract and keep business and, therefore, jobs, in the town. (McCahill 1998a).

Fourth, regardless of its effects on the overall crime rate, CCTV can be a very useful tool in investigating statistically rare but serious criminal offences such as acts of terrorism, murder and rape. If all the video footage from public and private systems are painstakingly examined, a task that can take a team of detectives weeks to complete, evidence of suspects or their vehicles may be revealed.

Finally, even when CCTV is shown to have a limited impact on crime, it provides a very useful tool for the police to manage the problem of informational uncertainty and for allocating resources to incidents. The ability to see whether a 'disturbance' is actually still in progress and involves two youths engaged in horseplay rather than a violent confrontation between rival gangs, is a powerful factor in its appeal as a management tool.

For these reasons Graham may well be right when he suggests that CCTV is set to become the 'fifth utility' as he notes:

> The most striking thing about the wiring up of Britain with CCTV is how similar the process is to the initial development in 19th century cities of the networked utilities that we now all take for granted – gas, electricity, water and telecommunications . . . . In the 19th century, water, waste, energy and telegraph utilities first emerged as small, special-ised networks, geared towards a myriad of uses, utilising wide ranges of technologies, and covering only small parts of cities . . . These networks, of course, have long since merged and extended to become technologically standardised, multi-purpose, nationally-regulated utilities, with virtually universal coverage. I would argue, that CCTV looks set to follow a similar pattern of development over the next twenty years, to become a kind of fifth utility. (1998: 107–8)

As we discuss below, this process is already beginning as systems expand and forge technological and operational links enabling not only the integration of CCTV in diverse sites and under independent operational control, but also integration with other elements of the local security nexus, both public and private.

System Integration – Totalising the Panoptic Gaze

> The future is made up of interfacing each system; you can have individual systems in the car park, the football grounds, the railway station but at any one time you can link the whole system together under one command. (Manager of a City centre CCTV system)

System integration was certainly seen by many site managers as the way forward. Not only does it bring a considerable economy of scale, as the monitoring costs of different systems can be centralised, but it also has the potential to bring all the cameras in a locale under one centralised command and control system facilitating the coordination of a host of different camera systems: both public and private. This quantitatively increases the size and scope of systems and qualitatively impacts on the ability to target and track individuals as they move through a much larger area.

System integration is not, however, a simple matter. It requires inter-organisational cooperation as well as technical compatibility which, because of the piecemeal development of CCTV and the lack of any agreed industry standards, is far from guaranteed. Even so, some police forces have started to take the lead in developing integrated systems. Here it is instructive to look at the City of London police's Camerawatch scheme which represents one possible and, in our view likely, scenario of the shape of things to come. The following account is taken from an interview with one of the police officers responsible for the development and operation of the City of London scheme and clearly illustrates a strategic plan and vision of an integrated system:

> We have around 100 cameras, all run by the police in total. In terms of the public ones, the ones that are in Camerawatch are in excess of 1,250, but that's not an accurate reflection of cameras, it's a reflection of how many people have decided to join our 'Camerawatch' scheme . . . Camerawatch was set up after the Bishopsgate bomb, and basically it's a service, which our Crime Prevention officers supply to businesses who are looking to upgrade their current camera system or are looking to install a new one . . . They will give them advice on cameras, what lighting is required, the quality of the cameras and therefore the quality of the final image if they're recording onto tape, and also give them advice on what the planners, the local authority, will and will not accept . . . It's a free service, but what we get in return is them joining Camerawatch and getting a remit that their tape recordings are available to the police should they ask for them. So we're trying to get a standard of video recordings and also trying to encourage to put into place evidential procedures which will enable us to use the recordings in a court of law and then making sure all tapes are available to the City of London police.

We can see here how the first phase of system integration is the gradual and piecemeal standardisation of the system in an area and the police coordinating standardisation. The second phase, involves linking systems both technically and operationally, as he continued:

> a group of businesses in a small area are got together and talk to each other. One with 24 hour security on their premises will tell the others, who maybe can't afford that amount and only has 8–10 hours security. And we will tell those businesses that if you linked all your CCTV systems by fibre optic cable to the one company with 24 hour security system and shared that cost, then outside the normal security times for the majority of them, all the cameras can be fed to one control room and you've got 24 hour security for all the premises, at a substantially reduced cost because it is now being shared. Rather than everybody putting in a CCTV system and everybody putting in a control room, then everybody supplying 24 hour security staff, you've got one business doing it, and half a dozen sharing that cost. So these are the concepts behind Camerawatch that have evolved over a period of 2 or 3 years.

For the City of London the final stage is to link all the systems to their own command and control system to enable them to view all the 1,250 cameras. As he went on to explain:

> How we want to develop 'Camerawatch' is to look at ways of linking those images to our force communication centre and that's a project that is being currently undertaken; to look at the feasibility of doing that and financing it from the private sector, albeit we would finance the bit that looks into this end of the scheme and the main cost will be the transmission medium between their cameras and our monitors . . . There are things we are looking at in terms of 'Camerawatch' scheme, that would not end up with us monitoring their cameras for them. It would be very much an additional security for them, in which their staff could phone up . . . and we would be viewing the same picture as their security officers in their premises and pool the resources in a better way than which we're doing at the moment. So that is something we see as a gradual development with Camerawatch which may or may not link all or some of the 1,250 cameras that are currently in the scheme.

The technological integration of different camera systems so that they can relay pictures between sites is one element in the move toward total panopticanisation. However, as we have illustrated, a key difference between the Panoptican and the city centre CCTV systems was seen to be the virtual absence of any dossiers which would allow the identification and classification of those using the street. Unlike their institutional counterparts, street populations are largely anonymous. One consequence of this is, as we have shown, the development of an informal set of working rules which classifies people and behaviours as worthy of attention. However, this is a poor substitute for the ability to record, store, and recall data about known individuals. We did note one exception, and this was in relation to 'known shoplifters' whose presence was brought to the attention of CCTV operators by store detectives. In other sites we visited, systems managers revealed the increasing operational integration of police, private security and CCTV systems aimed at the specific targeting of known offenders:

> The prime source of information are the idiots that are arrested. We follow the '5 W's' which are when, where, what, who and why and if you get that in to your mind you start to become a lot more proactive. The police gave a lot of info about the types of crime, basically all of those W's – what crimes, where in Northtown, who is committing them, when are they doing it and to some degree why. The view in this town is that shoplifting is drugs-driven. They steal to order. But we get them on a breach of bail if they're going into Boots to get methadone. Bail conditions often mean that they come into town to get methadone between 11 am – 12 midday and if they're seen at 10.30 am, the police lift them for breach of bail.

This sharing of intelligence is facilitated in Northtown by the existence of what is termed locally as their 'Crime Net' management system. The system involves collaboration between the local police and the council-run CCTV system so that 'known' offenders are tracked. For example, at a weekly liaison meeting the police provide the CCTV control room with the names, accompanied by photographs of 'top ten' suspects who may be associated with shoplifting, car crime, vandalism or are on bail and have, as part of their bail conditions, been barred from entering the town centre or certain high street stores. This enables the operators to alert police if someone is in the town centre in breach of bail or to intensively surveille those 'known' to be most actively involved in crime. In another system, the manager described how the integration of the CCTV operations room with the retail radio network enabled personalised tracking across the whole town centre:

> Shops each have a portfolio of 50 top criminals . . . They know those faces and how they network around the city. For example John Smith is walking down City Mall now, and Smiths come on and say 'yes, he's just passing our shop now' and then Boots come on and say 'yes, he's just come into Boots' and then he goes out by the North End and the store detectives contact the CCTV operators and tell them that he's dressed in such and such. The cameras track him across Neptune Street and contact BHS and tell them that he's coming into their store.

The integration of discrete systems is leading to what McCahill has termed the development of a 'Surveillance Web' linking a variety of public and private systems as he writes of one northern city:

> This shopping based coalition provides the highest level of inter-connectedness between the individual systems. But other systems, such as the council's residential concierge systems, the car park, university and hospital systems also form part of the web sustained

by telephone contact, formal membership of the City Centre Security Group, and informal contact between the security guards and camera operatives many of whom have worked on a number of different sites throughout the city. (McCahill 1998b)

The technological and organisational integration of systems is, then, already beginning to occur and, driven by concerns of cost-effectiveness and operational efficiency is likely to continue. We can also see a blurring of the distinctions between public and private policing, with CCTV providing the interface between the two spheres. And it may be that this marks an intensification of the trend noted by Ericson of the police increasingly operating not so much as law enforcement agents in their own right, but as knowledge brokers who collect, process and share information for a whole range of non-state agencies engaged in the provision of security and private protection (Ericson 1994).

Towards Automated Algorithmic Surveillance

In the three systems that we studied, the citizenry remained largely anonymous in the face of the surveillance gaze, and, therefore, in the main, the operators rarely knew the identity of those they were tracking. However in a number of other sites we visited, the creation of a pictorial database containing 'mugshots' of known suspects coupled with biographical information from police intelligence reports is enabling the full disciplinary potential of the surveillance gaze to be felt. But this is still very partial and is limited to the select few identified as 'the most wanted'. The true panoptic potential is only fully realised when the mass of the citizenry is not only subject to being watched by the cameras, but when the information derived from surveillance can be documented and dossiered. Then an individualised file can be built up on each person's movements and habits and this can be cross-referenced with the panoply of other files held by police and government. While CCTV systems remain dependent on human monitoring, the prospect of such a scenario would appear to be confined to the dystopic imaginations of science fiction writers. However, with the advances in digital computing technologies, algorithmic processing techniques based on statistical comparison of images are rapidly being applied to CCTV systems to enable automatic monitoring and identification, fiction and reality are fast converging and this is being fuelled by a recognition of both the limitations and costs associated with human monitoring.

The Limitation of Human Monitoring

The exponential increase in visual surveillance creates a massive and costly problem of information processing and handling. If we imagine a typical town centre CCTV system, consisting of twenty cameras filming twenty-four hours each day, this produces the equivalent of 480 hours of video footage. To be fully effective, many schemes have recognised the necessity of providing 24-hour monitoring of the screens; this, however, is a very expensive resource. To adequately monitor any large-scale system twenty-four hours a day requires a minimum of ten full-time personnel. This allows for two operatives to be on duty on each shift, three shifts per day, one shift on rest days and two people to cover for sickness and holidays. Even at the low rates of pay found in the security industry (Jones and Newburn 1996) it is unlikely that the total cost of employing an operative is less than £8,000 a year, and thus the minimum cost to properly monitor a system is £80,000 per annum, in staff costs alone. As a result, some systems are not monitored at all, and many only part-time.

From our own database of 150 sites, we have details of the running costs of forty-five of them. The average annual costs for these sites is £72,000; the highest, £250,000 and the lowest, £2,000. We would estimate that about 80 per cent of any budget is for staff costs associated with monitoring the system, so the average cost of monitoring a scheme is £58,000. With some 500 schemes in operation throughout the country this equates to about £26 million per year. If one adds to these systems those found in the retail, commercial and transport sectors it is probable that the annual cost of monitoring CCTV systems is in excess of £100 million in the UK.

But it is not only the cost implication that is driving moves towards automation: human monitoring is limited by the sheer volume of information that is relayed from even a medium-sized system. It is not possible for one or even two operatives to continuously monitor the output of a twenty-camera system and, of course, as soon as they selectively focus on one incident, other screens are going unmonitored. This is exacerbated by the inherent boredom of watching dozens of screens and the inattentiveness that results. But even the most attentive of operators are swamped by the volume of information. For instance, consider how much incoming information there is in a medium-sized 24-hour city centre system with twenty cameras.

The answer, as we can see from Table 10.1, is a quite staggering 43 million 'pictures' per day. Foucault reminds us that knowledge is power but if the mass of images is to be transformed into knowledge somehow they must be made amenable to automated processing, and this can now be achieved through the computer manipulation of digital images. The importance of digitalised images is that they facilitate, with the use of computer-based storage and analysis software, the identification of people and vehicles en masse, as they move through public space. There are three related technological developments which are promoting this possibility.

First, the introduction of high speed/high volume digital transmission systems such as fibre optic cables. British Telecom, for example, envisage, and are working towards, a completely wired city, where the flow of digitalised images through fibre optic cables will be as routine as the transmission of telephone conversations (BT 1995).

Table 10.1 Incoming Information as Measured by Individual Frames of Video Footage in a 20-camera, 24-hour, City Centre System

Cameras and frames	Total number of frames		
1 camera	frames per second	=	25
x 20 cameras in system	total number of frames entering		
	the system per second	=	500
x 60 frames per minute	total number of frames entering		
	the system per minute	=	30,000
x 60 frames per hour	total number of frames entering		
	the system per hour	=	1,800,000
x 24 frames per day	total number of frames entering		
	the system per day	=	43,200,000

Second, the development of a new generation of sophisticated database products which can link all existing databases, regardless of the platform on which they were created. These are increasingly being linked to state-of-the-art Geographical Information Systems, which can map events in space and time (Graham 1998b).

Third, the rapid development of image manipulation and pattern recognition software has found receptive markets in the security and law enforcement sectors in three major areas: intelligent scene monitoring; licence plate recognition and facial recognition systems.

Intelligent Scene Monitoring

For some time cameras have been coupled to a variety of remote sensors, such as motion detectors, as may be found in a burglar alarm, so that when the sensor is triggered the camera starts recording and may even signal an alarm to alert a security guard of potential trouble. However, while such sensors enhance the power of CCTV systems to monitor continuously over larger areas, they are still relatively primitive, because the cameras and the images they capture are predominately being used as a recording device. One of the main advantages that comes with the use of digitalised images is the images themselves and all the information contained in them can be subjected to automated processing by computer-based pattern recognition software. The effect of this is to dramatically increase the scope and intensity of the surveillance gaze and to simultaneously reduce monitoring costs. The Sentinel system, developed by EDS, is one of the leading products in the field and its development and capabilities were explained to us by a company spokesman:

> The Sentinel System is an application of neural networks to look at pixel patterns in video signals . . . Now Sentinel came about because we did some work about 4 or 5

years ago for the government to see what the capabilities of technology were for image processing. I think it was for the police, the Police Scientific Development Branch. What they wanted to do was to see if it was possible to identify a vehicle when looking at a scene and to see if it stopped in a certain area, and then also to track a person who got out of that vehicle and to provide information to another pan, tilt, zoom camera to follow them. Basically they said, 'can technology do this?' and we said yes.

The way in which we did that was to take some of the clever boxes of tricks from other systems and applying it to analysing pixels and video signalling, and out of that we got Sentinel . . . Until that point, people had been able to produce motion detection systems which basically looked at pixels and said 'something's changed', and that's a slightly limited solution if you've got a real world problem. It's fine if you've got an indoor scene, in a corridor in a prison where the lighting level is fairly constant and there isn't much happening anyway, so anything that does happen, you'd be happy to know about. If you're looking at an outside wall of a prison, when the prison is in a town centre you can't really do much with that. What we wanted to do was to build a system that was two sides of the same coin, which was tolerant of potential sources of false alarms, so it could understand what it was looking for, but also understand something it wasn't looking for.

So what we did was to build a system with two levels of neural networks. The first level is like a couple of filters, with basic pixel valves going into a neural network. What this does is to convert the binary statistics to a pattern. It tries to describe what it is seeing in statistical terms. You also have a cleverer neural network which is effectively a short term memory which says, 'this is what I can see now' and 'this is what I can see now' and it does that by sampling around ten times a second. This second neural network says, 'yes, I recognise that. It's what I saw a minute ago'. What that allows us to do is, for example, tolerate changes in lighting levels where the basic structure of the picture is the same. It knows that if the clouds part and the picture gets brighter that it is essentially the same scene.

It also allows you to do things like say 'most of this is the same, but it has changed and it's this big.' It has a memory facility in which you can remember from the previous frame where the change was, how big it was and in the next frame work out where it has gone to. That's important because it means we can start to track things. It's a very simple structure of two levels of neural network and some software which can do things like tracking and to check whether a certain set of alarm parameters have been satisfied. In a scene with cars and trees, you will see little dots of excitement as Sentinel is tracking. The software is saying 'I can see you, I know how big you are, and have you done this yet.' The way we define this, the thing of interest is to paint onto the backdrop of a scene information about where an object has to come from, how long it has to take and we give a definition of perspective. We set up a lot of alarm parameters which say 'it has to come through this gate we've painted on, come around this way and do it in 8 seconds and it is this big.' So we can get away from simple things like a person walking this way as opposed to one walking that. Or even a cat jumping on a car. Basically we provide filtering mechanisms which define an alarm event, and eradicate potential sources of false alarms.

This system has found markets in prisons, conference centres, freight yards and military security. In Dollands Moor, the Channel Tunnel rail freight marshalling yard, it currently monitors inputs from 150 cameras and, as the promotional material for the system states:

> Through the use of algorithms to interpret the images, a system can react to motion or non motion; to object size, speed and direction; to duration in an area; and direction of exit and entry. What this means in practice is that systems can automatically monitor complex scenes and trigger alarms and other security mechanisms when unsanctioned events occur. For instance, a stationary vehicle can trigger an alarm, as can a person heading in the 'wrong' direction. (EDS 1995)

The revolutionary aspect of this system is that nobody watches the cameras. As the company spokesman explained:

> In the Channel Tunnel installation, they took a big decision and said 'that does not work' (operator monitoring) and it's expensive, you've got lots of monitors and complex wiring and its got to have lots of people to watch it. You need to bring in a new shift every 4 hours. So they decided to have no monitors and accepted the fact that looking at those was as good as looking at nothing, and they put all their faith in Sentinel. So you have one blank monitor and the only time it shows anything is when Sentinel shows the world that something has happened.

Automatic Licence Plate Identification

In Britain all motorised vehicles used on public roads must, by law, display a standardised number plate which enables the vehicle, through the unique combination of letters and numbers, to be linked to a registered owner. This register is held in computerised form by the Driver and Vehicle Licensing Agency and the information is shared with the police via the Police National Computer. The police have been utilising this resource for many years, with patrol officers routinely asking control room operators over their radios to carry out PNC checks on suspicious vehicles and to obtain information on the vehicle's 'registered keeper'. However, for the purposes of mass surveillance the sheer volume of traffic and the relative scarcity of patrol officers makes the process extremely limited and only a fraction of vehicles are logged in any one day. If it is possible to automatically read a licence plate, in real time, extract the characters so they can be read into a database and compared to a register of owners then the movements of all vehicles within a locale can be tracked, linked to a named individual and the information stored for use at any future time. True, this is not foolproof method on individual identification, because the person driving the car may not be the registered owner, but in that case traditional policing methods can normally ascertain who was driving the vehicle at the time. It is precisely this technology which was first deployed in the City of London in the wake of the Bishopsgate Bombing in 1993, as part of the so-called 'Ring of Steel'.

The system consists of over ninety CCTV cameras recording the movement of all traffic in and out of the square mile of the city. Twenty-eight of these security cameras have been installed at the eight official entry points to the Square Mile. The camera lenses are capable of preventing wide-screen glare and reflection, and clearly identify the occupants of the car and the vehicle registration plate (*Guardian*, 24 November 1993). In May 1996, the capacity of the system was significantly enhanced with the addition of automated licence plate recognition. The system creates a database of the licence plates of all cars entering and exiting the area. Any vehicle which does not exit the system after a specified time automatically triggers an alarm and alerts the operators to the presence of a suspect vehicle. A City of London spokesman explained:

> Licence plate recognition is the next stage in this integrated system we've got and all that does is utilise what we've been doing on the entry points recording the number plates of vehicles and all we're doing is using the images from cameras to look at number plates and storing into a system, a number plate record. So we are still bringing in the images from that camera of the vehicles coming through, it's still being pushed down fibre optic network and being recorded, but linked into that is a number plate reader, which grabs the image and reads it, and it goes through a matching process simultaneously with three databases, the Police National Computer database, our own vehicle database from our local force intelligence bureau and what we set up locally, a vehicle 'hot-list' database, purely for local issues and any operation we might be looking at. So simultaneously, the information is snatched, read and matched and then the information on that vehicle is read within four seconds by an operator in our control room or by an operator in our force intelligence bureau. If for instance it was a stolen vehicle, it would go straight to the control room, the operator would be alerted by an alarm system and a dedicated monitor would record information about that vehicle and that would happen within 4 seconds of the vehicle entering a specific zone. The time is 4 seconds from entry to being a match with the information in front of the operator.

Now this technology has been perfected it is rapidly being introduced by other public sector agencies. It was announced in July 1997 that the Metropolitan Police are also planning to introduce automatic licence plate recognition throughout the capital (*Independent*, 22 July 1997). Customs are installing the technology to log the licence plates of every vehicle entering the UK and the DVLA is planning to invest in a nationwide system of cameras to identify untaxed cars being driven on the roads and data from the cameras will also be shared with the police (*Sunday Telegraph*, 15 September 1996: 9). The private sector is also keen to exploit the potential of this technology. Trafficmaster, who currently have 100,000 customers nationally, have been active in developing markets for information about traffic flows, which can be sold commercially to individuals and companies so they can minimise journey times. They have installed 4,264 infra-red cameras on over 7,500 miles of motorways and trunk roads. The cameras film the number plates of all passing vehicles, relay this to a computer where the licence plate details are extracted and stored. Every few minutes the system is updated and thus the time it has taken a vehicle to move between two points can be monitored to provide a constant flow of accurate journey times. This information can then be aggregated and relayed back to the end users via an on-board computer or even a mobile phone. While the primary use of this system is to provide general information about average traffic flows so that drivers can make informed choices to avoid congested areas, it rests on the ability to store, process and retrieve data on individual vehicles. Once such a system is in place there are a whole variety of other applications that can be developed, for instance, the 'real-time' identification and location of a stolen vehicle or the tracking of any individual vehicle for whatever reason. Moreover, if the data is downloaded and stored, a complete historical record of vehicle movements on the major road network is created. And as John Burrow, the Chief Constable of Essex police has made clear he would expect police to have access to such systems for the purposes of crime prevention and detection (Burrow 1998: 118 para 382).

Digital Facial Recognition Systems

Most commentators agree that the prospect of being able to automatically identify people moving through city centre streets, rather than their vehicles, through facial recognition systems is still some way off (Norris et al. 1998; Bruce 1998; Haig 1998). The reasons for this are both technical and operational. Although humans have a remarkable ability to remember and recognise faces, the manner in which they do so is still poorly understood and therefore development is hindered by a lack of an adequate model to mimic the process automatically (Haig 1998). Even so, under experimental conditions comparing pictures of pre-defined faces, researchers have had quite high levels of success, using a variety of different statistical techniques for comparison and matching (see Norris et al. 1998 for a review). However, in footage from security cameras, faces are not dismembered from bodies or isolated from the backgrounds in which they occur, and merely trying to identify which part of the picture comprises the face is an extremely difficult task. Burel and Carel (1994: 963) stress that these difficulties are compounded because in the real world the distance between the camera and the face is often unknown; the lighting conditions are only partly controlled; facial orientation and rotation are not held constant and neither are backgrounds or shadows; faces may be partially occluded, for example by a hand or a piece of clothing.

In the light of these problems a number of companies and defence establishments are trying to develop more sophisticated systems to crack the problem. In particular, both the Ministry of Defence and Software & Systems International (SSI) are exploiting the formidable capacity of the new neural network technologies for pattern matching to develop more reliable systems (Haig 1998: 172; SSI 1997). SSI's Mandrake system is described by the company as a fully automated facial recognition system based on neural network software and which can scan the faces of the crowd in 'real' time and compare the faces with images of known 'trouble-makers' held on a digital database. The company claims that the initial trials have been successful and the system was expected to become fully operational at the end of 1997. (*Computer Weekly*, 24 July 1997).

It would appear that the prospect of automated, real-time, facial matching from public and privately held CCTV is advancing rapidly and the technical problems are likely to be overcome, certainly within the next decade and probably much sooner. However, the ability to match faces requires not only the technical ability to do so but a register or database of faces with which to compare the target image. While all vehicle registrations are held by the DVLA and link licence plates to named individuals, there is no national archive of faces. This means at present systems such as Mandrake can only be used to locate already known, photographed offenders within a crowd, but could not be utilised to identify an, as yet, unknown suspect. But this is set to change as two extensive digital databases of faces are being developed.

The new photo Driver's Licence is almost certainly going to be held in digital form (Davies 1996, 196); and second, the Passport Agency has announced that they are moving to a digital system to store applicants' photographs (*Computer Weekly*, 3 July 1997) and expect to process 4 million digital-imaged passport applications each year (Home Office 1998). However law enforcement agencies are already compiling their own digital photo albums of prisoners, witnesses, suspects and demonstrators and deploying digital cameras so that pictures may be relayed instantaneously over radio and telephone lines. For instance the National Criminal Intelligence Service's 'hooligan' database holds details and pictures of 6,000 suspected football hooligans which in the run-up to the 1996 European Football Championship was made available to all the participating football grounds through the use of 'photo-phones' enabling digitalised photographs to be transmitted from one central location to a remote terminal in each stadium (*Guardian*, 10 February 1996).

Similarly, the Metropolitan Police's Public Order Unit is now deploying Kodak digital cameras at demonstrations used to digitally photograph protesters, and immediately relay the image to operational units so as to identify and detain troublemakers as they leave the area (Hook 1994: 11). According to the Home Office this type of usage is 'set to increase rapidly' (Home Office 1998: 126). The

Sussex police have also been reported to be digitally photographing peaceful demonstrators and, in an effort to establish protester identities, have demanded that once photographed an individual gives them their name. According to one report, when demonstrators have refused, they have been searched and under the pretext of looking for an offensive weapon (a razor blade) had their wallets examined, whereupon details from credit cards, etc. were written down by the officers (personal communication from David Turner, 29 November 1998).

In Scotland the creation of the Scottish Digital Prisoners' Database is being coordinated by the Scottish Criminal Records Office and it currently holds 50,000 stored images. According to the Association of Chief Police Officers in Scotland 'Over the next few years the number of stored images is expected to rise to approximately 400,000. Additionally, three forces either use or are introducing the use of digital cameras as part of their custody processing systems' (ACPOS 1998: 153). In short this means that around one in twelve of the population of Scotland will have their photographs lodged on a digital database.

As we have already seen with the Greater Manchester Police's Football Intelligence System these digitalised photographic databases are increasingly finding operational uses. But this system is entirely manual and has no automated features, however a commercial company called Dectel have launched a semi-automated facial matching system called Crime Net. At present the system is being used to compare digitalised photographs of unidentified building society robbers against a database of known offenders. Crime Net is as yet only semi-automatic. Each face is coded manually according to the distinctive spatial relationships between key points (such as the corner of the mouth and the bridge of the nose). This gives each face a unique identifying code. As new faces are added to the database for identification, they are measured and automatically compared with the other images. The system has been piloted by the Metropolitan Police's Flying Squad, and Dectel aims to market the system for use by retailers to identify shoplifters and in town centre surveillance systems.

With these piecemeal and incremental developments it is difficult to predict the scope of their impact. However, the speed at which automatic licence plate recognition has moved from the drawing board to implementation has been very rapid. According to Nelson the promise of commercial applications only became apparent in 1989, by 1993 it was available in the commercial market and by 1997 there were at least twenty-four companies selling 'off-the-shelf' automated systems. (*Traffic Technology International*, June/July 1997: 105–10). The majority of the systems have been for road tolling systems but, as we have seen, the law enforcement and security applications are rapidly emerging. In the case of CCTV one of the leading industry commentators, John Comfort recently stressed 'the future is in digital CCTV working on a digital super-highway' (*CCTV Today*, May 1996).

While predicting the future is always a risky business, current developments suggest that trends Norris et al. identified in 1996 have continued and are gathering an increasing momentum. In 1996 we wrote:

> for law enforcement purposes, advances will be piecemeal and incremental. Applications will first be developed which exploit the storage and retrieval capacities of digitised databases. As the technology advances, these databases will be subject to limited automatic matching. Rather than producing a definitive single match, the system will identify, for example, the four most likely faces and the human operative will make the final judgment. Increasingly, as the technology advances, in more or less controlled conditions, reliable automatic recognition systems will be introduced. (Norris et al. 1996)

The Data Subject in the Age of the Smart Machine

What is crucial to understand is that the move from a mass surveillance society towards a maximum surveillance society is only partially dependent on the spread of the cameras. Cameras, or other sensing devices are a necessary, but not a sufficient, condition in the move towards panopticanisation. It is the ability to store, sort, classify, retrieve and match which is all important. In the nineteenth century the use of photographs for the purposes of criminal identification was hindered until statistical classification procedures had been developed which, when ordered and classified within the filing cabinet, enabled accurate and speedy identification. In the late twentieth century, the same problems have faced those wanting to utilise CCTV systems for law enforcement purposes, but on a massively increased scale as the potential archive includes every face captured on every frame of videotape. Ironically, the solution is identical, only this time aided by the use of computers, which enable the statistical process of classification to be performed at incredibly high speeds and the filing cabinet to be replaced by the computerised database. And it is in the database that the true power of the panoptican lies, for it enables what Gandy (1996) calls the Panoptic Sort.

Although Gandy was writing about mass consumer surveillance, facilitated by advances in cybernetic intelligence and driven by the concerns of business to engage in more and more sophisticated niche marketing and making finer and finer judgments as to creditworthiness, the process is remarkably similar to that faced by CCTV systems; for the key to the panoptic sort is the process of 'identification, classification, and assessment' (Gandy 1996: 135). Firstly, there is a need to identify individuals so that their current behaviour or actions can be seen in the light of their biographical profile and that any current behaviour can be linked to them so they may be held to account for it. Once identified people can be assigned to various categories, 'suspected terrorist', 'known shoplifter' etc., which can be used to determine future actions. However, unlike in the marketing applications, classification may also occur in the absence of establishing a person's identification and may be based solely on behavioural clues, thus, with 'intelligent scene monitoring', a vehicle travelling the wrong way along a street or one that is stationary for 'too long' in an area is identified and classified as potentially troublesome. Once individuals or incidents have been identified and classified, they need to be assessed to determine, on the basis of their classificatory status, what action should follow. In the context of marketing Gandy writes:

> Once identification has determined that consumers are who they say they are, and classification has guided decisions about what kinds of people they are, it is the process of assessment that determines whether they should be included in or excluded from the stream of promotional information. (Gandy 1996: 136)

In terms of law enforcement we might talk about 'citizens' rather than consumers and the exclusion from certain spaces rather than from targeted advertising, but the assessment process is similar. While consumer assessments can be automatically performed based on a pre-programmed decision model, the judgments needed to understand complex visual scenes are more likely to require some human judgment. However the power of automated surveillance systems is that they can automatically perform a range of initial identification and classification tasks. Only if a person or incident is classified as 'troublesome', for example by being listed on the database as 'of police interest' or a vehicle travelling the wrong way along a road, are system operators alerted to make a final assessment and evaluation. Indeed these issues of cost-effectiveness, identification, classification and assessment are at the heart of the City of London's 'Ring of Steel' as one interviewee explained:

> We found fairly rapidly that they ['no entry' and 'one way' signs] were being ignored; people actually ignored the entry point system for one reason or another. Because it's so labour intensive putting officers on the entry points, the option of putting more officers on the 13 exit points, was really not an option because resources wouldn't allow it. So we looked at a technological response to the exit problem and came up with a camera, a single fixed mounted camera at those 13 exit points looking specifically at the junction in question and being linked to a motion detection system. That motion detection system is specifically geared up to only look at vehicles coming in a specific direction, whilst ignoring vehicles travelling in the legal direction and out the zone. We don't want to know about that, but we do want to know about vehicles who come in against the one-way street and go through the no-entry signs. So the system is geared up to monitor the junctions, ready to seize a vehicle travelling the wrong way. It grabs a frame of that image, 24 frames of that image – it's a digital system and it sends the image down fibre optic lines to our control room where a dedicated monitor and an alarm operate. By that time, the operator's attention is brought to that monitor and they see the 24 frames of the vehicle actually coming through the wrong way. They then manipulate the 24 frames and get the best recognition of the number plate and circulate them to patrolling officers,

who locate it, stop it and speak to the driver, who make an assessment of whether to prosecute or issue a fixed penalty.

In the example above, automated identification and classification are based on the capacity of the computer software to 'understand' the scene that it is monitoring, and trigger human intervention and it is the officers on the street who, in a face-to-face encounter must make an assessment of the response to the errant driver. Increasingly, however, this assessment is prefigured by, not only the automated classification of the ongoing activity, but by reference to the 'digital persona' contained in the database. To the database the person:

> is the sum of the information in the fields of the record that applies to that name. So the person . . . now has a new form of presence, a new subject position that defines him for all those agencies and individuals who have access to the data base. The representation in the discourse of the data base constitutes the subject . . . in highly caricatured yet immediately available form. (Poster 1996: 118).

The coupling of databases with cameras and automated identification systems, (already a reality in the case of vehicles and an increasingly likely prospect in the case of individuals based on facial recognition) represents a profound transformation in the surveillance capacity. Not only is it possible to create a log of the movements of individuals as they move through space, but it is also possible to automate assessment of all peoples' moral worthiness as they enter a locale based on information contained in the database. In this scenario, the working rules of operators which determine who and what is surveilled under conditions of anonymity can be replaced by rules based on individualised classifications contained in the database. The shift from mass to maximum surveillance means it is not just the individual known offender who is subject to being dossiered. Everyone is a dossiered 'data subject' with a 'digital persona'. As soon as a person enters a surveilled domain their 'status' can be determined from the database, and the database automatically updated as to their movements. But, as Poster has argued, this 'digital persona' leads a life of its own beyond the control and, at times, even the knowledge of the real self. (Poster, 1990: 97–8). And these personae have more than just an electronic existence: they have concrete material effects.

This was revealed starkly in the case of two Welsh football fans when they were erroneously entered onto the National Football Intelligence Unit's database of suspected hooligans. As a result, when the two were travelling to an overseas match in Belgium, they were identified by the Belgium police, arrested and deported. In effect, the two were no longer free to travel anywhere in Europe to support their team despite having done nothing wrong because their electronic classification had more import and authority than their real selves. After a six-year campaign, the brothers found that their identities had been logged on various other European and national databases and managed to have their names removed from the Belgian records, although it is unclear on which other databases their details might still be recorded (Statewatch, March/April 1993; July/August 1996).

The coupling of cameras, computers and databases heralds what Poster has termed the 'superpanopticon':

> Unlike the panopticon, then, the superpanopticon effects its working almost without effort. What Foucault notices as the 'capillary' extension of power throughout the space of disciplinary society is much more perfected today. The phone cables and electric circuitry that minutely crisscross and envelop our world are the extremities of the superpanopticon, transforming our acts into an extensive discourse of surveillance, our private behaviours into public announcements, our individual deeds into collective language. (Poster 1996: 184)

Like Gandy, Poster is primarily concerned with the power of commercial databases aimed at niche marketing and credit assessment, and the irony of consumers' collusion with their own surveillance through the use of credit and loyalty cards, which allow the minutia of an individual's spending habits to be archived and analysed. In the case of databases constructed from identifying a person's movements through public space, there is little collusion. As consumers, individuals may refuse to use credit cards and opt out of loyalty card schemes. As citizens it is much harder to refuse to drive for example, and, if facial recognition becomes a reality, citizens will have to avoid their town centres and high streets to prevent themselves being entered into the files.

Increasingly, citizens will be acted on not as autonomous corporeal subjects – not by their physical flesh and blood presence – but through their electronic dopplegangers residing ghostlike in the machine. As Poster alerts us:

> Now through the database alone, the subject has been multiplied and decentred, capable of being acted upon by computers at many social locations without the least awareness by the individual concerned yet just as surely as if the individual were present somehow inside the computer. (Poster 1996: 185)

For Laudon, the proliferation of multiple electronic selfs decentres, destabilises and ultimately diminishes our concept of self:

> My electronic image in the machine may be more real than I am. It is rounded; it is completed; it is retrievable; it is predicable in statistical terms . . . I am in a mess; and I don't know what to do. The machine knows better – in statistical terms. Thus is my reality less real than my image in the store. That fact diminishes me. (Laudon cited in Lyon 1994: 194)

And as Lyon has observed, the very concept of personhood is threatened as individuals no longer have control over, or even knowledge of, the situations in which information about them is communicated.

> The society of strangers is now abstracted into machine systems within which no face-to-face human relations are possible. The data are collected, transmitted, sifted, sorted and shared promiscuously so that voluntary communication, and even consent, is seldom considered. (Lyon 1994: 195)

The import of this proliferation of multiple electronic selves is their relationship to the 'corporeal' self. It is the intersection of the two selves, mediated by agents of social control that most concerns us. For it is here that the full political effect of databases as an instrument of what Foucault terms 'governmentality' can be seen. This type of governmental power, which has become increasingly important during the twentieth century, is based on the collection of vast amounts of information on individuals and populations which is then used to manage the activities of the state in both its welfare and control functions. As Poster argues:

> Governmentality, or the form of power of the welfare states of the advanced industrial societies of the late twentieth century, is inconceivable without databases . . . An important political effect of databases, as they have been disseminated in our societies, is to promote the 'governmental' form of power, to make knowledge of the population available to coercive institutions at every level. (Poster 1996: 189)

The marriage of cameras, computers and databases enables the expansion of state and corporate surveillance capacities to an unparalleled degree. For instance, the Police and Criminal Evidence Act limits the police power of stop and search to situations where they have reasonable suspicion that the person was involved in an offence. Even when they do exercise this power they have no additional power to demand a person's name, address or date of birth (English and Card 1991: 40). However, whilst English law has sought to protect citizens from arbitrary police surveillance and intelligence gathering there is little protection in the face of automated recognition systems coupled with database technology.

Widening the Net and Thinning the Mesh

The growth of automated surveillance systems simultaneously increases the size, scope and intensity of the formal control system. To use Cohen's analogy, the size and reach of the social control nets are widened and the mesh strengthened and thinned (Cohen 1985). In practice, this widening and thinning will mean that more and more people will be drawn into the net of the formal system and, as we have argued elsewhere, the implications for public order policing are dramatic, since:

In public order policing, the priority has traditionally been the preservation of public tranquillity rather than the detection and prosecution of offenders. However, the potential of the new technologies is increasingly being exploited with the use of surveillance and intelligence-gathering squads and footage from CCTV systems being retrospectively examined and analysed to provide evidence for prosecution. Not only, therefore, is the net widened, but the potential for deviancy amplification in public order situations is increased. And as previously marginal demonstrators are caught up in the mêlée and subsequently identified, arrested and prosecuted, their fledgling deviant identities may well become entrenched. (Norris et al. 1998: 268–9)

Moreover, there is what Lustgarten and Leigh refer to as the 'chilling effect' of surveillance which can negatively constrain the operation of democratic political actions. The chilling effect:

> Can be seen most clearly in relation to participation in demonstrations, signing petitions, or any other form of political activity which enables the participants to be identified individually. Knowledge that some official body is keeping lists of those who sign petitions supporting some policy disapproved of by government is guaranteed to intimidate potential signatories. It is not even necessary that such a practice be calculated to achieve that result; regardless of motive, the effect is significant. (1994: 48)

However, such dystopic visions need to be considered in tandem with socially desirable outcomes that result from an increasing in the scope and intensity of surveillance. In traffic policing, the 'thinning of the mesh and widening the nets' that is facilitated by algorithmic surveillance brings with it the prospect of significantly reducing road traffic congestion, accidents, and fatalities (Dempsey 1997). As Bagot has argued, as well as enforcing speeding restrictions and red light violations:

> This new technology has the potential to open up a whole new area of traffic regulations that may have existed before but, in practice were unenforceable. Lorry bans through towns, dangerous or careless driving, illegal right turns and more – all transgressions that require more manpower than is currently available – could be captured automatically on hard disk. (Bagot 1998: 93)

Digital and semi-digital enforcement systems have now been installed in Victoria, New South Wales and Queensland in Australia and British Columbia in Canada. And all have seen dramatic results in reducing speeding and therefore accidents, injuries and fatalities (ATS 1996). In the Australian state of Victoria, the number of speeding vehicles fell from 15 per cent of all vehicles to under 3 per cent. As a consequence, there has been a massive fall in the number and seriousness of collisions, leading to a fall in injuries from over 40,000 per annum to 15,000 and fatalities from 1,000 to under 250. And the benefits do not just relate to a reduction in personal misery and pain suffered by accident victims and their families. Insurance costs have also fallen, bringing economic benefits to the entire community.

The End of Discretion?

As we have shown, the human targeting conducted by CCTV operatives is also inherently discretionary and the result is discriminatory target selection based on crude indices of race, age, appearance and demeanour. In this context the development of algorithmic surveillance systems, blind to a person's social characteristics, may be seen as a positive social good. As Marx has noted, one argument used to support automated enforcement systems is that:

> Fixed physical responses that eliminate discretion also eliminate the potential for corruption and discrimination. The video surveillance camera and heat sensing devices do not differentiate between social classes. Data are gathered democratically from all within their purview. Accountability is thus increased and the prior ability of those with power to shield their behaviour is lessened by electronic trails and tails. (Marx, 1995: 238)

Whether the effect of algorithmic enforcement systems will lead to equalisation of enforcement is open to question, as is the assumption that this may be experienced as advantageous. This is for a number of reasons.

First, the discriminatory nature of discretion lies less in the fact that certain social groups are over-policed, but that others are under-policed (Lustgarten 1986). This means that the equalisation of, for instance, stop and search, arrest and prosecution, will see those social groups who have enjoyed the privilege of under-enforcement suddenly finding themselves subject to the full weight and majesty of the law. And those who already feel themselves over-policed will notice little difference. This may have some profound implications for public perceptions of police legitimacy. In a review of the literature on public attitudes towards the police Reiner found: 'It became clear from the majority of studies that even at the level of generalised opinions, views of the police were less favourable among the young, males, Afro-caribbeans, inner city dwellers and the unemployed or economically marginal' (Reiner 1992b: 472).

The reason for this negative evaluation is because it is these groups who are disproportionately involved in adversarial police-initiated encounters (ibid: 474). If other, traditionally more privileged and powerful social groups, find themselves increasingly targeted and subject to adversarial policing we may expect to see a general decline in public support for the police. This is not to argue against the desirability of the equalisation of the impact of policing across all social groups, but to caution against the assumption that it would lead either to a reduction in over-policing or the belief that policing is being carried out more fairly and legitimately. And equalisation may indeed have the positive benefit of encouraging a more critical engagement from the middle classes about the nature, extent and exercise of police powers.

Second, unless such technologies are deployed evenly across communities, some areas will experience the full impact of maximised enforcement while others will not. There may be equity within a locale but considerable inequity between different locales. It is not difficult to imagine that the primary candidates for the most extensive forms of surveillance will be the socially and economically disadvantaged residents of inner city areas or 'problem' housing estates, rather than the well-heeled residents of the suburbs.

Third, the same algorithmic technology that facilitates full enforcement also allows for far more discriminatory target selection. If individuals and their vehicles can be identified, systems may be used far more proactively to 'target the criminal not the crime'. For instance, in line with the Audit Commission's recommendations (1993) many police forces are establishing a local 'most wanted' list of 'known' criminals to become the focus of intensive surveillance and intelligence gathering. But, as Sherman has argued, unless the initial choice of who is to become a target is carried out by objective and/or random methods of selection it has the potential to lead to 'systematic discrimination against certain ethnic or political groups' (Sherman 1992: 173).

Finally, just as human operatives were found to discriminate in their target selection on the basis of age, gender and race, there are no technical reasons why algorithms cannot do the same. While heat and light sensors are indeed blind to differences in race or gender, the algorithmic processing of digital images can distinguish between black and white and, if current developments continue, may be able to differentiate between young and old, male and female. There is nothing inherent in the technology which makes it a force either for egalitarian or discriminatory enforcement practices. And as yet there are no laws to prevent the use of discriminatory algorithms.

While automated enforcement systems have the ability to equalise detection and enforcement rates through the ending of certain forms of discretionary judgment, they can also magnify the consequences of other discretionary decisions and therefore intensify already existing inequalities. As Marx has rightly argued, it is necessary to avoid falling into the trap of technological determinism either of the utopians: that the new electronic technologies will prove the 'silver bullet' of crime control, leading to fairer and fuller enforcement with the prospect of the eradication of crime; or the dystopians: that the new technologies mark the move towards an Orwellian future of totalitarian control. Neither are inevitable. As he argues, it is necessary to take a 'realistic view' that 'either position could in principle be correct' but that the current reality is both 'messy and contradictory' and above all dependent on the social and political contexts in which it is deployed (Marx 1992: 238).

The social and political context was brought out starkly in an interview with a representative of a company engaged in selling advanced algorithmic surveillance systems:

> The next step you have to decide is at what point do you give a security guard advice – they are generally of low intellect – and you could just have automation, which raises a whole raft of other queries. We are putting the system into a prison in Malaysia and it may end up controlling a machine gun. So if you're found between the two fences, then tough.

When pressed on the ethical issue of providing a product that will automatically kill people he responded:

> We are about providing technology that will solve a problem for somebody, now in terms of ethics it becomes very difficult. We provide systems for military equipment – if that goes out to Indonesia is it less ethical than being used in Bosnia? At the end of the day most companies take the view that the ethics lie with the people who buy the products. If you take the view that we can't use this product because it will do this then we would all be living in caves.

Given this frank assessment of corporate ethics, it is clear that the use of this technology urgently needs to be brought under legal control: in this case to prevent its sale and export to dictatorial regimes, but equally importantly to regulate its deployment and use in democratic states. For while, it is unlikely that Western democracies will allow automated surveillance systems to act as judge, jury and executioner, there are more subtle, albeit less permanent forms of exclusionary ends to which they can be put. For instance as Norris et al. have suggested:

> Not unreasonably, high street stores faced with high losses from shoplifting and fraud seek to exclude those who are responsible. Once a person is convicted of an offence, automated systems can be deployed to monitor all those entering a store and alert for the presence of known shoplifters. Security personnel can then be swiftly deployed to remove them from the premises. This exclusionary policy can be extended within a high street chain, and, as systems become widespread, can encompass all city centre stores. It will then not be possible to simply be a 'customer buying groceries' on certain days in some venues, and to become a 'shoplifter intent on stealing' on other days and in other stores. The status of 'shoplifter' is likely to prevail, and the designation 'once a shoplifter always a shoplifter' will predominate. The digitalised persona of 'data subjects' (Lyon, 1994) thus has the potential to become a truly powerful 'master status' through which exclusionary social control can be achieved. (1998: 271)

But it is not just within the commercial realm where the consequences will be felt. The developments in traffic surveillance mean the ability to log and record the movements of vehicles across large tracts of the road network is now possible. In an effort to identify those who may be working while claiming state unemployment benefit, it would be possible create a list of those who, while simultaneously in receipt of benefits had vehicles registered to them which had travelled more than, say, 250 miles in the preceding month. Those identified would become the targets for more extensive investigation. Given that the prevention of welfare fraud is not an unreasonable measure for governments to undertake, it is difficult to think of on what grounds such a practice could or even should be challenged. But if we are all to become 'data subjects' for the purposes of law enforcement we need mechanisms that ensure that systems are used fairly and equitably and in accordance with democratic principles.

Accountability and Control

At present the regulatory system in the United Kingdom is both weak and ineffective. Indeed, at present there is no general statutory control over the use of CCTV systems and, for most intents and purposes, their operation remains outside of the law (France 1998; Maguire 1998). However, the Data Protection Act does provide some regulation when data is processed automatically by reference to the data subject – for instance as in the City of London system. In these circumstances data processors are required to: register with the Data Protection Registrar; describe the kinds of information they hold; state the purposes for which it will be used; limit the collection of information to that which is necessary for the purpose; name those to whom the information might be disclosed; ensure that the information is accurate and up to date; and grant access to data subjects to their files. While this might appear to provide a tough regulatory environment, Maguire has argued:

> the potential effectiveness of the legislation is greatly diluted in a number of ways. The drafters of the Act did not regard privacy as a fundamental right, but as one that had always to be balanced against other interests. Many exemptions are allowed, and there are numerous ambiguities and loopholes in the wording which can be exploited by companies or agencies wishing to avoid the controls (Campbell & Connor 1986). The practicalities of enforcement are also highly problematic. There are no published Codes of Practice with the force of law, as recommended by the Lindop Committee, and compliance is generally sought through persuasion, with sanctions seen very much as a last resort. The investigation of possible breaches of the Act depends principally upon individual citizens making complaints. However, not only do most people not know what data is kept about them by whom, but few are aware of their rights or know how to exercise them. (1998: 232)

As was clear from the Deputy Data Protection Registrar's evidence to the House of Lords Select Committee on Digital Images as Evidence, current data protection law was not drafted to deal with the prospect of mass, automated surveillance (Aldhouse 1998) and is therefore of limited applicability. Moreover given the general exemptions in the Act for the purposes of the 'prevention and detection of crime', it is unclear whether many of the uses we have described fall under the provisions anyway. Indeed, as Justice starkly pointed out in relation to automated recognitions systems, 'Present data protection law is not designed to cover such activities' (Justice 1998: 26).

In the absence of effective democratic oversight and accountability we are in effect hostages to our faith that those operating and running such systems will do so in an enlightened way. Unfortunately the history of the twentieth century is replete with examples of how, in the absence of proper accountability and control, the surveillance capacity of the liberal state has been used for profoundly undemocratic ends: the anti-communist witch-hunts of Senator McCarthy and James Edgar Hoover in the USA and the targeting of activists from the Campaign for Nuclear Disarmament by the security services in Britain, to name but two. But the most disturbing episode could be seen to be the use of American Census data by the US military in the wake of the Japanese bombing of Pearl Harbour (Diffie and Landau 1998: 137–8). American Census data was gathered from its citizenry under the strict understanding that it was confidential, that unauthorised disclosure was illegal, and that no one other than sworn employees of the Census Bureau could examine individual files. Indeed in 1980 the Bureau boasted that even during World War II, when there had been questions as to the loyalty of Japanese-Americans to the Stars and Stripes, the Bureau had never breached its solemn duty to protect the principle of confidentiality and had not given out information about individuals. The Census Bureau was lying. A United States Department of War Document dated 1943 unambiguosly states:

> The most important single source of information prior to the evacuations was the 1940 Census of Population. Fortunately, the bureau of the census had reproduced a duplicate set of punched cards for all Japanese in the United States shortly after the outbreak of war and had produced certain tabulations for the use of war agencies. These special tabulations, when analysed became the basis for the general evacuation and relocation plan. (Cited in Diffie and Landau 1998: 138)

This 'evacuation and relocation plan' was in fact nothing more than a euphemism for the rounding up of more than 100,000 Japanese-Americans and forcibly interning them in concentration camps in the desert (Brogan 1985: 586). As a consequence, they lost their property, livelihoods, and their constitutional rights.

If constitutional and basic rights are so easily disregarded in liberal states, what of states with no such pretensions? The history of the twentieth century should also remind us that democratic institutions are not assured, they can and have been captured by totalitarian regimes of both the left and the right. We should not be seduced by the myth of benevolent government for, while it may only be a cynic who questions the benign intent of their current rulers, it would surely be a fool who believed that such benevolence is assured in the future.

This suggests that there is an urgent need to consider how the new technologies of mass surveillance can be harnessed to encourage participation rather than exclusion, strengthen personhood rather than diminish it, and be used for benevolent rather than malign purposes (Lyon 1994). It is our belief that the first step along this road is to establish proper systems of democratic accountability, control and oversight over the implementation and use of these technologies. For, as Wright has argued, the only criterion which distinguishes a modern traffic control system from the apparatus of political control is democratic accountability (1998: 16–17).

Bibliography

ACPOS – Association of Chief Police Officers in Scotland (1998), Written Evidence given to the House of Lords Select Committee on Science and Technology sub Committee II: Digital Images as Evidence. Published in House of Lords Select Committee on Science and Technology, *Digital Images as Evidence*: Evidence, HL Paper 64-I, London: The Stationary Office.

Agre, P.E. (1994), 'The Digital Individual', *The Information Society*, vol. 10, no. 2, April–June, Special Issue, pp. 73–138.

Aldhouse, F. (1998), 'CCTV systems and the Data Protection Act', Memorandum to the House of Lords Select Committee on Science and Technology sub Committee II: Digital Images as Evidence. Published in House of Lords Select Committee on Science and Technology, *Digital Images as Evidence*: Evidence, HL Paper 64-I, London: The Stationary Office.

Armstrong, G. and Giulianotti, R. (1998), 'From Another Angle: Police Surveillance and Football Supporters' in C. Norris, J. Moran and G. Armstrong (eds), *Surveillance, Closed Circuit Television and Social Control*, Aldershot: Ashgate.

ATS – American Traffic Systems (1996), 'Speed Cameras for Advanced Traffic Management', in I. Nuttall (ed.), *Traffic Technology International* 1996, Surrey: UK and International Press.

Aubrey, C. (1981), *Who's Watching You?* Harmondsworth: Penguin.

Audit Commission (1993), *Helping with Enquiries: Tackling Crime Effectively*, London: HMSO.

Augarde, T. (ed.), (1991), *The Oxford Dictionary of Modern Quotations*, Oxford: Oxford University Press

Bagot, N. (1998), 'In the Name of The Law', *Traffic Technology International*, Feb/Mar, pp. 91–7.

Bailey, S. H., Harris, D. and Jones, B. (1991), *Civil Liberties: Cases and Materials*, London: Butterworths.

Bannister, J., Fyfe, N. and Kearns, A. (1998), 'Closed Circuit Television and the City', in C. Norris, J. Moran and G. Armstrong (eds), *Surveillance, Closed Circuit Television and Social Control*, Aldershot: Ashgate.

Baxter, J.D. (1990), *Protecting Privacy: State Security, Privacy and Information*, Brighton: Harvester Wheatsheaf.

Beats, N. (1995), 'Neural Network Licence Plate Recognition', *Traffic Technology International*, Summer, pp. 72–4.

Beck, A. and Willis, A. (1995), *Crime and Security: Managing the Risk to Safe Shopping*, Leicester: Perpetuity Press.

Beck, U. (1992), *Risk Society: Towards a New Modernity*, Sage: London.

Bennett, T. and Gelsthorpe, L. (1996), 'Public Attitudes Towards CCTV in Public Places', *Studies on Crime and Crime Prevention*, vol. 5, no. 1, pp. 72–90.

Blumenthal, H.J. (1988), 'CCTV: The Big Picture', *Security Management*, vol. 32, Iss. 11, November, pp. 7–10.

Bogaert, M. (1996), 'Video-based Solutions for Data Collection and Incident Detection' in *Traffic Technology International '96*, Dorking, Surrey: Traffic Technology International, UK and International Press.

Bowden, T. (1978), *Beyond the Limits of Law*, London: Quartet Books.

Bowling, B., Graham, J. and Ross, A. (1994), 'Self-Reported Offending Among Young People in England and Wales', in J. Junger-Tas, G. Terlouw, and M. Klein (eds), *Delinquent Behaviour Among Young People in the Western World*, Amsterdam: Kugler.

Brahams, D. (1993), 'Video Surveillance and Child Abuse', *The Lancet*, vol. 342, no. 8877, p. 994, October.

British Telecom (1995), CCTV *Transmission Guide, Remote Video Applications*, London: British Telecommunictions

Brock, R. (1987), 'The Guard in the Year 2000', in *Security in the Year 2000 and Beyond*, L. Tyska, and L. Fennelly (eds), California: ETC Publications.

Brogan, H. (1985), *The Pelican History of the United States of America*, Harmondsworth: Penguin.

Brogden, M., Jefferson, T. and Walklate, S. (1988), *Introducing Policework*, London: Unwin Hyman.

Brown, B. (1995), *Closed Circuit Television in Town Centres: Three Case Studies*, Crime Prevention and Detection Series Paper 73, Home Office: London.

Brown, S. (1998), 'What's the Problem Girls? CCTV and the Gendering of Public Safety' in C. Norris, J. Moran and G. Armstrong (eds), *Surveillance, Closed Circuit Television and Social Control*, Aldershot: Ashgate.

Bruce, V. (1998), 'Letter from Professor Vicki Bruce' to the House of Lords Select Committee on Science and Technology sub Committee II: Digital Images as Evidence. Published in House of Lords Select Committee on Science and Technology, *Digital Images as Evidence*: Evidence, HL Paper 64-I, London: The Stationary Office.

BSSRS – British Society for Social Responsibility in Science, Technology of Policital Control Group (1985), *TechnoCop: New Police Technologies*, London: Fress Association Books.

Bulos, M., Chaker, W., Farish, M., Mahalingham, V. and Sarno, C. (1995), *Towards a Safer Sutton? Impact of Closed Circuit Television on Sutton Town Centre*, London: London Borough of Sutton.

Bulos, M. and Grant, D. (eds) (1996), *Towards a Safer Sutton? CCTV One Year On*, London: London Borough of Sutton.

Bulos, M. and Sarno, C. (1994), *Closed Circuit Television and Local Authority Initiatives: the First National Survey*, London: South Bank University, School of Land Management.

Bulos, M. and Sarno, C. (1996), *Codes of Practice and Public Closed Circuit Televison Systems*, London: Local Government Information Unit.

Bundred, S. (1982), 'Accountability and the Metropolitan Police: A Suitable Case for Treatment', in D. Cowell, T. Jones and J. Young, *Policing the Riots*, London: Junction Books.

Bunyan, T. (1977), *The Political Police in Britain*, Harmondsworth: Penguin Books.

Burel, G. and Carel, D. (1994), 'Detection and Localisation of Faces on Digital Images', *Pattern Recognition Letters*, vol. 15, pp. 963–7.

Burrow, J. (1998), Oral Evidence given to the House of Lords Select Committee on Science and Technology sub Committee II: Digital Images as Evidence, 11 December 1997. Published in House of Lords Select Committed on Science and Technology, *Digital Images as Evidence*: Evidence, HL Paper 64-I, London: The Stationary Office.

Burrows, J. (1979), 'The Impact of Closed Circuit Television on Crime in the London Underground' in P. Mayhew, R. Clarke, J. Burrows, M. Hough and S. Winchester, *Crime in Public View*, Home Office Research Study, no. 49, London: HMSO.

Cahill, M. (1994), *The New Social Policy*, Oxford: Blackwell.

Campbell, D. and Connor, S. (1986), *On the Record: Surveillance, Computers and Privacy*, London: Michael Joseph.

Cartwright, C. (1865), *Criminal Management*, London: National Association for the Promotion of Social Science.

Chatterton, M. (1979), 'The Supervision of Patrol-work Under the Fixed point System' in Holdaway (ed.), *The British Police*, London: Edward Arnold.

Chibnall, S. (1981), 'The Production of Knowledge by Crime Reporters', in S. Cohen and J. Young (eds), *The Manufacture of News*, London: Constable.

Cohen, S. (1985), *Visions of Social Control*, Polity Press: Cambridge.

Coleman, C. and Moynihan, J. (1996), *Understanding Crime Data*, Milton Keynes: Open University Press.

Coleman, R. and Sim, J. (1998), 'From the Dockyards to the Disney Store: Surveillance, Risk and Security in Liverpool City Centre', *International Review of Law Computers and Technology*, vol. 12, no. 1, pp. 27–45.

Constant, M. and Turnbull, P. (1994), *The Principles and Practice of CCTV*, Hertfordshire: Paramount Publishing.

Coulter, J., Miller, S. and Walker M. (1985), *State of Seige*, London: Canary Press.

Crampton, R.J. (1994), *Eastern Europe in the Twentieth Century*, London: Routledge.

Critchley, T.A. (1978), *A History of Police in England and Wales*, London: Constable.

Bibliography

Crofton, W. (1863), *A Few Observations on a Pamphlet Recently Published by The Rev, John Burt on the Irish Convict System*, Bristol: Arrowsmith.

Crofton, W. (1868), *The criminal classes and their control*, London: Victoria Press.

Dandeker, C. (1990), *Surveillance, Power and Modernity*, Cambridge: Polity

Darwin, L. (1914), *The Habitual Criminal*, Presidential Address to the Eugenics Education Society, London: Eugenics Education Society.

Davies, S. (1996), 'The Case Against: CCTV Should Not be Introduced', *International Journal of Risk, Security and Crime Prevention*, vol. 1, no. 4, pp. 327–31.

Davies, S. (1996), *Big Brother: Britain's Web of Surveillance and the New Technological Order*, London: Pan Books.

Davis, M. (1990), *City Of Quartz: Excavating The Future In Los Angeles*, London: Verso.

Davis, M. (1992), 'Beyond Blade Runner: Urban control. The Ecology of Fear', *Open Magazine*, Pamphlet number 23.

Dawson, T. (1994), 'Framing the Villains', *New Statesman and Society*, 23 January, pp. 12–13.

De Lia, R. (1993), 'Seeing in to the World of Fibre Optics for Security', *Security Management*, vol. 37, no. 3, March, pp. 7–11.

Dempsey, P. (1997), 'A New Focus for Enforcement Cameras', *Traffic Technology International*, June/July pp. 96–102.

Didi-Huberman (1987), 'Photography – Scientific and Pseudo-scientific', in J. Lemagny and A. Rouillé (eds), *A History of Photography: Social and Cultural Perspectives*, Cambridge: Cambridge University Press.

Diffie, W. and Landau, S. (1998), *Privacy on the Line: The Politics of Wire-taping and Encryption*, Cambridge, Mass: MIT Press.

Ditton, J. (1998), 'Public Support for Town Centre CCTV Schemes: Myth or Reality', in C. Norris, J. Moran and G. Armstrong (eds), *Surveillance, Closed Circuit Television and Social Control*, Aldershot: Ashgate.

Ditton, J. and Short, E. (1998), 'Evaluating Scotland's First Town Centre CCTV Scheme.' in C. Norris, J. Moran and G. Armstrong (eds), *Surveillance, Closed Circuit Television and Social Control*, Aldershot: Ashgate.

Dixon, D., Bottomley, A.K., Coleman, C., Gill, M. and Wall, D. (1989), 'Reality and Rules in the Construction and Regulation of Police Suspicion', *International Journal of the Sociology of Law*, 17.

DOE – Department of the Environment (1988) *A Better Reception: The Development of Concierge Schemes*, London: Department of the Environment.

Downes, D. (1997), 'What the Next Government Should Do About Crime', *The Howard Journal of Criminal Justice*, vol. 36, no. 1, Feb 97.

Dunnighan, C. and Norris, C. (1999), 'The Detective, The Snout, and the Audit Commission: The Real Costs in Using Informants', *The Howard Journal*, vol. 38, no. 1, Feb.

Durham, P. (1995), 'Villains in the Frame', *Police Review*, 20 January, pp. 20–1.

EDS (1995), *Sentinel: Intelligent Scene Monitoring*, (product information), Surrey: EDS Defence Group.

Edwards, S. (1989), *Policing 'Domestic' Violence*, London: Sage.

English, J. and Card, R. (1991), *Butterworths Police Law*, London: Butterworths.

Ericson, R. (1994), 'The Division of Expert Knowledge in Policing and Security', *British Journal of Sociology*, 45: 149–75.

Ericson, R.V. and Haggerty, D. (1997), *Policing the Risk Society*, Oxford: Clarendon Press.

Evans, G. (1998), 'Searching for Growth', *CCTV Today*, January, vol. 5, no. 1, pp. 20–1.

Feeley, M. and Simon, J. (1994), 'Acturarial Justice, the Emerging New Criminal Law', in D. Nelken (ed.), *The Futures of Criminology*, London: Sage.

Feldman, D. (1993), *The Scope Of Legal Privacy: Civil Liberties and Human Rights In England and Wales*, Oxford: Clarendon Press.

Flaherty, D.H. (1988), 'The Emergence of Surveillance Societies in the Western World: Toward the Year 2000', *Government Information Quarterly*, vol. 5, no. 4, pp. 377–87.

Flusty, S. (1994), *Building Paranoia: The Proliferation of Interdictory Space and the Erosion of Spatial Justice Los Angles*, Los Angeles: Forum for Architecture and Urban Design.

Foucault, M. (1977), *Discipline and Punish: The Birth of the Prison*, New York: Vintage.

France, E. (1998), Oral Evidence given to the House of Lords Select Committee on Science and Technology sub Committee II: Digital Images as Evidence. Published in House of Lords Select Committee on Science and Technology, *Digital Images as Evidence*: Evidence, HL Paper 64-I, London: The Stationary Office.

Fulbrook, M. (1995), *Anatomy of a Dictatorship: Inside the GDR 1949–1989*, Oxford: Oxford University Press.

Fyfe, N.R and Bannister, J. (1994), 'The Eyes On The Street: Closed Circuit Television Surveillance in Public Spaces', presented at the *Association of American Geographers Conference*, Chicago, March, pp. 1–13.

Fyfe, N.R. and Bannister, J. (1996), 'City Watching: Closed Circuit Television Surveillance in Public Spaces', *Area*, vol. 28, no. 1, pp. 37–46.

Gandy, O. (1989), 'The Surveillance Society: Information Technology and Bureaucratic Social Control', *Journal of Communication*, vol. 39, no. 3, Summer, pp. 61–76.

Gandy, O. (1996), 'Coming to Terms with the Panoptic Sort', in D. Lyon and E. Zureik (eds), *Computers, Surveillance and Privacy*, Minneapolis: University of Minnesota Press.

Gardner, J. (1854), *Photography as an Aid to the Adminstration of Criminal Justice*, held in the Pamphlet Collection of the London School of Economics Library.

Garland, D. (1994), 'Of Crime and Criminals: The Development of Criminology in Britain', in M. Maguire, R. Morgan and R. Reiner (eds), *The Oxford Handbook Of Criminology*, first edition, Oxford: Clarendon Press.

Gibson, T. (1995), 'Recognition for the Law', *Traffic Technology International*, Summer, pp. 28–31.

Giddens, A. (1985), *The Nation State and Violence: Volume Two of a Contemporary Critique of Historical Materialism*, Cambridge: Polity Press.

Gilliom, J. (1994), *Surveillance, Privacy and the Law: Employee Drug Testing and the Politics of Social Control*, Michigan: University of Michigan Press.

Goffman, E. (1971), *Relations in Public: Microstudies of the Public Order*, Harmondsworth: Pelican.

Goodwin, M., Johnstone, C. and Williams, K. (1998), 'New Spaces of Law Enforcement: Closed Circuit Television, Public Behaviour and the Policing of Public Space', unpublished paper, Aberystwyth: Institute of Geography and Earth Sciences, University of Wales.

Gotlieb, C. (1996), 'Privacy: A Concept Whose Time Has Come and Gone', in D. Lyon and E. Zureik (eds), *Computers, Surveillance and Privacy*, Minneapolis: University of Minnesota Press.

Graham, S. (1998), 'Towards the Fifth Utility? On the Extension and Normalisation of Public CCTV' in C. Norris, J. Moran and G. Armstrong (eds), *Surveillance, Closed Circuit Television and Social Control*, Aldershot: Ashgate.

Graham, S. (1998b), 'Spaces of Surveillant Simulation: New Technologies, Digital Representations, and Material Geographies', *Environment and Planning D: Society and Space*, vol. 6, pp. 483–504.

Graham, S., Brooks, J. and Heery, D. (1996), 'Towns on the Television: Closed Circuit TV in British Towns and Cities', *Local Government Studies*, vol. 22, no. 3, pp. 3–27.

Graham, S. and Marvin, S. (1996), *Telecommunications and the City: Electronic Spaces, Urban Places*, Routledge: London.

Graham, V. (1995), 'Caught on Film', *Police Review*, 31 March, pp. 18-19.

Groombridge, N. and Murji, K. (1994), 'As Easy as AB and CCTV', *Policing*, vol. 10, no. 4. Winter 1994.

Haig, N. (1998), 'Memorandum on Automatic Face Recognition', sent to the House of Lords Select Committee on Science and Technology sub Committee II: Digital Images as Evidence. Published in House of Lords Select Committee on Science and Technology, *Digital Images as Evidence*: Evidence, HL Paper 64-I, London: The Stationary Office.

Hain, P. (ed.), (1979), *Policing the Police*, 2 vols., London: John Calder.

Bibliography

Hall, S., Critcher, C., Jefferson, T., Clarke, J. and Roberts, B. (1981), 'The Social Production of News: Mugging and the Media', in S. Cohen and J. Young (eds), *The Manufacture of News*, London: Constable.

Hancox, P. and Morgan, J. (1975), 'The Use of CCTV for Police Control at Football Matches' in *Police Research Bulletin*, vol. 25, pp. 41–4.

Harris, J. and Sands, M. (1995), 'Life-saving Speed Camera Technology', *Traffic Technology International*, Spring, pp. 63–4.

Hastings, G.W (1875), 'Address on the Repression of Crime', delivered as Chairman of the Repression of Crime Section of the Social Science Congress, Glasgow, October 1874, London: Spottiswoode and Co.

Hearnden, K. (1996), 'Small Businesses' Approach to Managing CCTV to Combat Crime', *International Journal of Risk, Security and Crime Prevention*. vol. 1, no. 1 pp. 19–31.

Hobsbawm, E. (1995), *Age of Extremes: The Short Twentieth Century*, London: Abacus.

Holdaway, S. (1983), *Inside the British Police*, Oxford: Basil Blackwell.

Home Office (1982), *Efficiency and Effectiveness in the Civil Service*, Cmnd. 8616, London: HMSO.

Home Office (1990), *Digest of CCTV Schemes*, London: Home Office.

Home Office (1994), *CCTV: Looking Out For You*, London: Home Office.

Home Office (1996), *Criminal Statistics, England and Wales 1995*, London: HMSO.

Home Office (1996), *Closed Circuit Television Challenge Competition 1996/7 Successful Bids*, Home Office: London.

Home Office (1998), Written Evidence given to the House of Lords Select Committee on Science and Technology sub Committee II: Digital Images as Evidence. Published in House of Lords Select Committee on Science and Technology, *Digital Images as Evidence*: Evidence, HL Paper 64-I, London: The Stationary Office.

Honess, T. and Charman, E. (1992), *Closed Circuit Television in Public Places, Its Acceptability and Perceived Effectiveness*, Home Office, Police Research Group, Crime Prevention Unit series, Paper 35, London: Home Office.

Hook, P. (1994), 'Faces in the Crowd', *Police Review*, 22 July, pp. 22–3.

Hook, P. (1995), 'Speed Cameras to Target M25 Snarl-ups', *Police Review*, 20 January, p. 11.

Hooke, A., Knox, J. and Portas, D. (1996), *Cost benefit analysis of traffic speed cameras*, Police Research Series paper 20, Police Research Group, London: Home Office.

Horne, C. (1996), 'The Case For: CCTV Should be Introduced', *International Journal of Risk, Security and Crime Prevention*, vol. 1, no. 4, pp. 317–26.

Hutchinson (1994), *The Huchinson Dictionary of Ideas*. Oxford: Helicon.

Huxley, A. (1932), *Brave New World*, Harmondsworth: Penguin.

Jacobs, J. (1962), *The Death and Life of Great American Cities*, London: Jonathan Cape.

Jefferson, T. (1992), 'Discrimination, disadvantage and police work', in *Out of Order, Policing and Black People*, edited by E. Cashmore and E. McLaughlin London: Routledge.

Jenkins, J. (1992), 'Eye Can See You', *New Statesman and Society*, 21 February, pp. 14–15.

Jones, T. and Newburn, T. (1995), 'How Big is the Private Security Sector', *Policing and Society*, vol. 5, pp. 221–32.

Jones, T. and Newburn, T. (1996), 'The Regulation and Control of the Private Security Industry' in W. Saulsbury, J. Mott and T. Newburn. (eds), *Themes in Contemporary Policing*, London: Policy Studies Institute.

Justice (1997), *Digital Images as Evidence* – Submission to the House of Lords Select Committee on Science and Technology, September 1997, London: Justice. Also published in House of Lords Select Committee on Science and Technology (1998), *Digital Images as Evidence*: Evidence, HL Paper 64-I, London: The Stationary Office.

Kamel, M.S. and Shen, H.C. (1994), 'Face Recognition using Perspective Invariant Features', *Pattern Recognition Letters*, vol. 15, pp. 877–83.

Kidd-Hewitt, D. (1995), 'Crime and the Media: A Criminological Perspective', in D. Kidd-Hewitt and R. Osborne (eds), *Crime and the Media: The Post-modern Spectacle*, London: Pluto Press.

Krass, A. and Smith, D. (1982), 'Nuclear strategy and technology', in M. Kaldor and D. Smith, *Disarming Europe*, London: The Merlin Press.

Lash, S. and Urry, J. (1994), *Economies of Signs and Space*, London: Sage.

Laudon, K. (1986), *The Dossier Society: Value Choices in the Design of National Information Systems*, New York: Columbia University Press.

Law Reform Commmision – New South Wales (1997), *Surveillance: Issue Paper no. 12*, Sydney: Law Reform Commission.

Lemarie, F. (1994), *Video and Image Processing for Traffic Data Analysis and Automatic Incident Detection*, Belgium: Traficon Company Product Information.

LGIU – Local Government Information Unit (1994), *Candid Cameras: A Report On Closed Circuit Television*, June, London: LGIU.

LGIU – Local Government Information Unit (1997), *Digital Images as Evidence* – Submission of the Local Government Information Unit to the House of Lords Select Committee on Science and Technology, September 1997, London: LGIU. Also published in House of Lords Select Committee on Science and Technology (1998), *Digital Images as Evidence*: Evidence, HL Paper 64-I, London: The Stationary Office.

Liberty (1997), *Digital Images as Evidence* – Submission of Liberty to the House of Lords Select Committee on Science and Technology, September 1997,

London: Liberty. Also published in House of Lords Select Committee on Science and Technology, (1998) *Digital Images as Evidence*: Evidence, HL Paper 64-I, London: The Stationary Office.

Lilly, J.R. and Knepper, P. (1992), 'An International Perspective on the Privatisation of Corrections', *The Howard Journal*, vol. 31, no. 3.

Lofland, L.H. (1973), *A World of Strangers: Order and Action in Urban Public Space*, New York: Basic Books.

Lombroso, C. (1876), *L'Uomo Delinquente*, Turin: Fratelli Bocca.

Lustgarten, L. (1986), *The Governance of Police*, London: Sweet and Maxwell.

Lustgarten, L. and Leigh, I. (1994), *In from the Cold: National Security and Parliamentary Democracy*, Oxford: Carendon Press.

Lyon, D. (1993), 'An Electronic Panoptican? A sociological critique of surveillance theory', *Sociological Review*, 1993, vol. 41, no. 4, pp. 653–78.

Lyon, D. (1994), *The Electronic Eye: The Rise of Surveillance Society*, Cambridge: Polity Press.

Lyon, D. and Zureik E. (1996), *Surveillance, Privacy and the New Technology*, in D. Lyon and E. Zureik (eds), (1996), *Computers, Surveillance and Privacy*, Minneapolis: University of Minnesota Press.

Lyon, D. and Zureik E. (eds), (1996), *Computers, Surveillance and Privacy*, Minneapolis: University of Minnesota Press.

Maguire, M. (1998), Restraining Big Brother? The Regulation of Surveillance in England and Wales, in C. Norris, J. Moran, and G. Armstrong (eds), *CCTV, Surveillance and Social Control*, Aldershot: Ashgate.

Maguire, M. (1998), 'Restraining Big Brother: The regulation of surveillance in England and Wales', in C. Norris, J. Moran and G. Armstrong (eds), *Surveillance, closed circuit television and social control*, Aldershot: Ashgate.

Mahalingham, V. (1996), 'Sutton Town Centre Public Perception Survey', in M. Bulos and D. Grant (eds), *Towards a Safer Sutton? CCTV: One Year On*, London: London Borough of Sutton.

Manwaring-White, S. (1983), *The Policing Revolution: Police Technology, Democracy and Liberty in Britain*, Brighton: Harvester.

Markusen, A. and Yudken, J. (1992), *Dismantling the Cold War Economy*, London: Basic Books.

Marx, G. (1988), *Undercover: Police Surveillance in America*, Berkeley: University of California Press.

Marx, G. (1992), 'The Engineering of Social Control: The Search for the Silver Bullet' in J. Hagan and R. Peterson (eds), *Crime and Inequality*, Calif.: Stanford University Press.

Marx, G. (1995), 'Electric Eye in the Sky: Some Reflections of the New Surveillance and Popular Culture', in J. Ferrell and R. Sanders, *Cultural Criminology*, Boston Mass.: North Eastern University Press.

Mayhew, P., Aye Maung, N. and Mirrles-Black C. (1993), The 1992 British Crime Survey, Home Office Research Study no. 132, London: HMSO.

McCahill, M. and Norris, C. (1999), 'Watching the Workers: Crime, CCTV and the Workplace' in P. Davis, V. Jupp and P. Francis (eds), *Invisible Crimes*, London: MacMillan.

McCahill, M. (1998a), 'Beyond Foucault: Towards a Contemporary Theory of Surveillance', in C. Norris, J. Moran and G. Armstrong (eds), *Surveillance, Closed Circuit Television and Social Control*, Hampshire: Ashgate.

McCahill, M. (1998b), 'The Surveillance Web' paper presented at *Surveillance: an Interdisciplinary Conference*, 5–6 June 1998, Liverpool: John Moores University.

McCahill, M. (1999) 'CCTV in a northern town', unpublished manuscript, Univeristy of Hull: Centre for Criminology and Criminal Justice

McConville, M., Sanders, A., and Leng, R. (1991), *The Case for the Prosecution*, London: Routledge.

Memex (1996), *Inside Information* (product information), Memex, 2 Redword Court , Peel Park, East Kilbride G74 5PF.

Mirlees-Black, C., Mayhew, P. and Percy, A. (1996), *The 1996 British Crime Survey: England and Wales*, Home Office Statistical Bulletin Issue 19/96, London: HMSO.

Monaco, J., Pallot, J. and Baseline (1993), *The Second Virgin Film Guide*, London: Virgin Publishing.

Morris, T. (1994), 'Crime and Penal Policy', in D. Kavanagh, and A. Seldon, *The Major Effect*, London: MacMillan.

Musheno, M., Levine, J. and Palumbo, D. (1978), 'Television Surveillance and Crime Prevention: Evaluation of an Attempt to Create Defensible Space in Public Housing', *Social Science Quarterly*, vol. 58, no. 4, pp. 647–56.

Nock, S. (1993), *The Costs of Privacy*, New York: Aldine De Gruyter.

Norris, C. (1989), 'Avoiding Trouble: The Patrol Officer's Perception of the Public', in M. Weatheritt, (ed.), *Police Research: Some Future Prospects*, Hampshire: Avebury, Gower.

Norris, C. (1995), 'Algorithmic Surveillance', *Criminal Justice Matters*, no. 20, Summer, pp. 7–8.

Norris, C., Kemp, C., Fielding, N. and Fielding, J. (1992), 'Black and Blue: an analysis of the effect of race on police stops', *British Journal of Sociology*, vol. 43, Issue no. 2, June.

Norris, C. and Armstrong, G. (1998), 'Power and Vision', in C. Norris, J. Moran and G. Armstrong (eds), *Surveillance, Closed Circuit Television and Social Control*, Aldershot: Ashgate.

Norris, C., Moran, J. and Armstrong G. (1996), 'Algorithmic Surveillance', paper presented at *CCTV and Social Control*: a one-day conference organised by the

Centre for Criminology and Criminal Justice, University of Hull, 9 July 1996.

Norris, C., Moran, J. and Armstrong, G. (1998), 'Algorithmic Surveillance: The Future of Automated Visual Surveillance in C. Norris, J. Moran and G. Armstrong (eds), *Surveillance, Closed Circuit Televisiony and Social Control*, Aldershot: Ashgate.

Norris, C., Moran, J. and Armstrong, G. (eds), (1998), Surveillance, Closed Circuit Television and Social Control, Aldershot: Ashgate.

Orwell, G. (1949) *Nineteen Eighty-Four*, London: Martine Secker and Warburg.

Pawson, R. and Tilley, N. (1994), 'What Works in Evaluation Research?', *British Journal of Criminology*, vol. 34, no. 3, pp. 291–306.

Piepe, A., Crouch, S. and Emerson, M. (1978) *Mass Media and Cultural Relationships*, Westmead: Saxon House.

Poster, M. (1990), *The Mode of Information*, Cambridge: Polity Press.

Poster, M. (1996), 'Database as Discourse; or, Electronic Interpellations', in D. Lyon and E. Zureik (eds), (1996), *Computers, Surveillance and Privacy*, Minneapolis: University of Minnesota Press.

Poyner, B. (1988), 'Video Cameras and Bus Vandalism', *Journal of Security and Administration*, no. 11, pp. 44–51.

Poyner, B. (1992), 'Situational Crime Prevention in Two Parking Facilities', in R. Clarke, (ed.), *Situational Crime Prevention: Successful Case Studies*, New York: Harrow and Heston.

Reeve, A. (1996), 'The Private Realm of the Managed Town Centre', draft manuscript, Oxford: Joint Centre for Urban Design, Oxford Brookes University. A revised version also published in *Urban Design International*, vol. 1, no. 1, pp. 61–80.

Reeve, A. (1998), 'The Panopticisation of Shopping: CCTV and Leisure Consumption', in C. Norris, J. Moran and G. Armstrong (eds), *Surveillance, Closed Circuit Television and Social Control*, Aldershot: Ashgate.

Reiner, R. (1992), *The Politics of the Police*, London: Harvester Wheatsheaf.

Reiner, R. (1992b), 'Police Research in the United Kingdom: A Critical Review', in M. Tonry and N. Morris (eds), *Modern Policing*, Chicago: University of Chicago Press.

Ross, N. and Cook, S. (1987), *Crimewatch UK*, London: Hodder and Stoughton.

Rouillé, A. (1987), 'The Rise of Photography (1851–70)', in J. Lemagny and A. Rouillé (eds), *A History of Photography: Social and Cultural Perspectives*, Cambridge: Cambridge University Press.

Rule, J. (1973), *Private Lives, Public Surveillance*, London: Allen-Lane.

Sacks, H. (1978), 'Notes on Police Assessment of Moral Character', in J. van Maanen and P. Manning, (eds), *Policing: a View From the Street*, New York: Random House.

Sarno, C. (1996), 'The Impact of Closed Circuit Television on Crime in Sutton

Town Centre', in M. Bulos and D. Grant, (eds), *Towards a Safer Sutton? CCTV One Year On*, London: London Borough of Sutton.

Schlesinger, P. and Tumber, H. (1994), *Reporting Crime*, Oxford; Clarendon Press.

Scraton, P. (1982), *The State of the Police*, London: Pluto Press.

Sekula, A. (1992), 'The Body and the Archive' in R. Bolton (ed.) *The Contest of Meaning: Critical Histories of Photography*, Cambridge, Mass: MIT Press.

Seldon, A. (1994), 'The Conservative Party', in D. Kavanagh and A. Seldon, *The Major Effect*, London: MacMillan.

Seldon, A. (1997), *Major: A Political Life*, London: Phoenix.

Sewell, G. and Wilkinson, B. (1992), 'Someone to Watch Over Me: Surveillance, Discipline, and the Just-In-Time Labour Process', *Sociology*, vol. 26, May, pp. 271–89.

Sharpe, S. (1989), *Electronically Recorded Evidence: A Guide to the Use of Tape and Video Recordings In Criminal Proceedings*, London: Fourmat Publishing.

Sherman, L. (1992), 'Attacking Crime: Policing and Crime Control', in M. Tonry and N. Morris (eds), *Modern Policing*, Chicago: University of Chicago Press.

Short, E. and Ditton, J. (1995), 'Does CCTV Affect Crime?', *CCTV Today*, vol. 2, no. 2, pp. 10–12.

Short, E. and Ditton, J. (1996), *Does Closed Circuit Television Prevent Crime? An Evaluation of the Use of CCTV Surveillance Cameras in Airdrie Town Centre*, Edinburgh: The Scottish Office Central Research Unit.

Sibley, D. (1995), *Geographies of Exclusion: Society and Difference in the West*, London: Routledge.

Simey, M. (1982), 'Police Authorities and Accountability: the Merseyside Experience', in D. Cowell, T Jones and J. Young, *Policing the Riots*, London: Junction Books.

Simmel, G. (1971), 'The Metropolis and Mental Life' in K. Wolff (ed.), *The Sociology of Georg Simmel*, Glencoe: Free Press.

Skidmore, P. (1995), 'Telling Tales: Media Power, Ideology and the Reporting of Child Sex Abuse in Britain', in D. Kidd-Hewitt, and R. Osborne (eds), *Crime and the Media: The Post-modern Spectacle*, London: Pluto Press.

Skinns, D. (1997), *Annual Report of the Safety in Doncaster Evaluation*, October 1995 – September 1996, Doncaster: Safety in Doncaster.

Skinns, D. (1998), 'Crime Reduction, diffusion and displacement: evaluating the Effectiveness of CCTV in C. Norris, J. Moran, and G. Armstrong (eds), *Surveillance, Closed Circuit Television and Social Control*, Aldershot: Ashgate.

Smart, B. (1985), *Michel Foucault*, London: Tavistock.

Smith, D. (1995), *The Sleep of Reason: The James Bulger Case*, London: Arrow Books.

Smith, S. (1984), 'Crime in the News', *British Journal of Criminology*, vol. 24, no. 3, pp. 289–95.

Sparks, R. (1992), *Television and the Drama of Crime: Moral tales and the place of crime in public life*, Buckingham: Open University Press.

Sparks, R. (1995), 'Entertaining the Crisis: Television and Moral Enterprise' in D. Kidd-Hewitt and R. Osborne (eds), *Crime and the Media: The Post-modern Spectacle*, London: Pluto Press.

Squires, P. and Measor, L. (1996), *Closed Circuit TV Surveillance and Crime Prevention in Brighton: Half Yearly Report*, Brighton: Health and Social Policy Research Centre, University of Brighton.

Squires, P. and Measor, L. (1997), *CCTV Surveillance and Crime Prevention in Brighton: Follow-up Analysis*, Brighton: Health and Social Policy Research Centre, University of Brighton.

SSI (1997), *Mandrake: Face-Recognition. The Ultimate in non-invasive, user friendly security*, Product Information Software and Systems International, 3 Bristol Way, Slough SL1 3QE.

Stanko, E. (1985), *Intimate Intrusions: Women's Experience of Male Violence*, London: Routledge and Kegan Paul.

Stenson, K. and Cowell, D. (1986), *The Politics of Crime Control*, London: Sage.

Thomas, T. (1994), 'Covert Video Surveillance', *New Law Journal*, 15 July, pp. 966–7.

Tilley, N. (1993), *Understanding Car Parks, Crime and CCTV*, Crime Prevention Unit Series paper 42, London: Home Office.

Tilley, N. (1998), 'Evaluating the Effectiveness of CCTV Schemes' in C. Norris, J. Moran and G. Armstrong (eds), *Surveillance, Closed Circuit Television and Social Control*, Aldershot: Ashgate.

van Dijk, T. A. (1998), 'Opinions and Ideologies in the Press', in A. Bell and P. Garrett (eds), *Approaches to Media Discourse*, Oxford: Blackwell.

Virilio, P. (1994), *The Vision Machine*, Indiana: Indiana University Press.

Webb, B. and Laycock, G. (1992), *Reducing Crime on the London Underground: An Evaluation of Three Pilot Projects*, Crime Prevention Unit Paper no. 32, London: Home Office.

Wilcox, R. (1996), *Facial Feature Database. Standardised Input Information*, London: Home Office.

Wilkins, G. and Addicot C. (1998), *Motoring Offences: England and Wales*, London: Home Office.

Wright, S. (1998), *An Appraisal of Technologies of Political Control*, European Parliament, Scientific and Technological Options Assessments working document (consultation version), Luxembourg: European Parliament, Director General for Research, Direcorate B, the STOA Programme.

Young, J. (1991), 'Left Realism and the Priorities of Crime Control', in K. Stenson and D. Cowell, *The Politics of Crime Control*, London: Sage.

Index

Index

Index